THE
GOLDEN AGE
OF BOSTON
TELEVISION

THE
GOLDEN AGE
OF BOSTON
TELEVISION

TERRY ANN
KNOPF

UNIVERSITY PRESS

OF NEW ENGLAND

HANOVER AND

LONDON

University Press of New England
www.upne.com
© 2017 University Press of New England
All rights reserved
Manufactured in the United States of America
Designed by Richard Hendel
Typeset in Utopia and Transat
by Tseng Information Systems, Inc.

For permission to reproduce any of the
material in this book, contact Permissions,
University Press of New England,
One Court Street, Suite 250, Lebanon NH 03766;
or visit www.upne.com

Library of Congress Cataloging-in-Publication Data
available upon request

5 4 3 2 1

To SARAH-ANN SHAW
who gave so much and paved the way
for so many others

In 1978, I threw my television set out a
second-story window. When I went to retrieve it,
it sported a third-degree crack across the screen—
but it still worked. That was when I knew:
Television is forever, or at least televisions are.
— Linda Ellerbee

CONTENTS

ACKNOWLEDGMENTS

One of the joys of writing this book involved reconnecting with many of those who participated in Boston's Golden Age of local television—former players whom I had the privilege and pleasure of covering as a TV critic. Even after all these years, they gave generously of their time to reminisce, fill in the blanks, and provide perspective on a little-known but eventful time in Boston's history. Sadly, Bob Bennett, Channel 5's former general manager and a broadcast visionary, died in November of 2016 at the age of eighty-nine. But as fate would have it, I had the good fortune to interview him some months earlier by phone. He and his wife Marjie had just returned from Mexico after a monthlong sailing trip on their yacht. Indeed, he seemed in fine form as we exchanged stories about the good old days. At one point, he confirmed an industry rumor that ABC executives had prevailed on him to drop the name of *Good Morning!*, his popular local talk show, as they prepared to introduce a new show to compete with NBC's *Today*—which is how Boston's *Good Morning!* came to be renamed *Good Day!*, and how ABC in 1975 launched a new show called *Good Morning America*.

Martha Raddatz (then Martha Bradlee) went from Channel 5's chief correspondent in the 1980s to Pentagon correspondent at National Public Radio from 1993 to 1998, then joined ABC News in 1999 as a State Department correspondent. Since that time, she has enjoyed a meteoric rise at the network—most recently appointed Chief Global Affairs Correspondent and cohost with George Stephanopoulos on *This Week*. Somehow, she managed to find the time to trade emails with me about her earlier days in Boston. It was a measure of the market's ambitions that she (and other reporters as well) traveled abroad, covering events in such places as Geneva (for the first Reagan-Gorbachev Summit), Ethiopia, the Philippines, and Lebanon. "I think everything I did in local TV helped me be a better reporter for the network," she said.

Similarly, I had several delightful conversations with Tom Ellis, Boston's first superstar anchor. Now in his eighties and living a comfortable retirement with his wife Arlene on Cape Cod, he seemed genuinely happy to revisit the past, despite having been the target of merciless press criticism. Asked why he was willing to speak to one of his critics after so many years, he replied cheerfully: "My mother told me always to be a gentleman." Texas Tom had the good sense to ignore us all, and laugh all the way to the bank.

I also made a nostalgic trip to visit Sonya Hamlin at her vacation home in the Berkshires. A formidable presence on the Boston TV scene for nearly twenty years, she was best known as a cultural reporter for Channel 4's *Eyewitness News*—the first in the country—and later the host of a cutting-edge talk show. There were so many facets to her astonishing career—Martha Graham dancer, chairman of Radcliffe and Harvard's dance department, talk-show host, business and communications consultant, lecturer, blogger, author of five books— even acting with Tina Packer's Shakespeare & Company.

Still, she had an unhappy memory of the time in the 1970s when the *Sonya Hamlin Show* was abruptly canceled. At the time, her station played it "cute," announcing to the press that the decision was her own. Beneath a *Boston Globe* headline that read "Sonya Hamlin Quitting Her TV Talk Show," her general manager, Sy Yanoff, said: "She has made her mark in Boston television and her departure will be felt deeply." Even Sonya played along, saying she had come to "a standing still place" in her life and it was "time for me to move on."[1]

The reality was quite different, she explained forty years later, and brutal in the way only the television industry can be. Coming on the eve of the fifth anniversary of her talk show, she recalled "a five-minute meeting" with Yanoff on a Monday, who told her she was to be out the door that Friday. Despite her best efforts, the tears flowed on camera during her final show. "I still have the tape," she said wistfully.[2]

So many others to thank as well: Caryl Rivers, my dear friend and Boston University journalism colleague who functioned as an informal editor and invaluable sounding board; Emily Rooney, with whom I jousted so many times when she was a Channel 5 news director, but who could not have been more helpful to me in researching this book; former Channel 4 program executive Francine Achbar, who provided invaluable assistance in tracking down people who had disappeared from the Boston market (by the way, in those days we jousted a lot as well); Jim Byrne, who worked at four Boston stations, sharing his knowledge of the independent stations, and who constantly inspires me with his decency in a tough business; and longtime Boston friends Marianne Perlak and Diana Morse, who provided useful feedback on different chapters.

I am also indebted to the dedicated and good-natured reference librarians at the Washington Street branch of the Brookline Public Library and the Thomas Crane Public Library in Quincy, Massachusetts (especially Theresa Tangney), who put up with my incessant, picky, and annoying questions. Also, let me not forget Sophie, my beloved Maine Coon—surely the world's most adorable cat—who charmed and calmed me with her sweetness during moments of writer's block. I especially wish to thank Phyllis Deutsch, the editor in chief of the University Press of New England and her superb editorial and production staff. Phyllis had the vision to see that this book was not only an untold story about a fascinating period in television but also a sociocultural and political history of Boston told through the prism of local television. Besides, she turned me on to *The Americans*, one of her favorite television shows, to which I am now addicted. (Once an addict . . .)

Finally, I remain eternally grateful to Philip Meyer, professor emeritus in journalism at the University of North Carolina, a pioneer in communications technology, polling, and citizen journalism as an executive with Knight Ridder—and the person most responsible for my getting my first job as a TV critic at the *Miami Herald*.

INTRODUCTION

Since the early days of television, when Howdy Doody, Ozzie and Harriet, Uncle Miltie, and Perry Mason had become household names, much has been written about the wondrous, complex, much-maligned, and often misunderstood medium of television—its history, its power, its stars, its alleged evils versus its many benefits, and its impact on our culture. By comparison, however, little attention has been given to the importance of local television, especially when it comes to how people get their news. In March 2015, the Pew Research Study Center, in association with the John S. and James L. Knight Foundation, published a lengthy report called "Local News in the Digital Age," which contained some startling findings. Analyzing the news environments in three disparate cities—Denver, Colorado; Sioux City, Iowa; and Macon, Georgia—the researchers found that:

> Whether in a tech-savvy metropolis or a city where the town square is still the hub, local news matters deeply to the lives of residents . . . nearly nine-in-ten residents follow local news closely—and about half do so very closely [and residents in all three cities turned to local TV] at higher rates than any other news source.[1]

And, in an updated survey in June 2016, Pew reported that despite the gradual decline in local television viewership and the uncertainty of local TV's future in a digital era, "U.S. adults continue to report turning to local TV in greater numbers than many other news sectors such as radio, print newspapers and network news, even for national news such as the 2016 presidential election."[2]

But local television is not only important per se; it also contributes to a given area's unique history, politics, and culture. It doesn't simply passively record the events of a city; it can intervene and even change the trajectory of its history. Take, for example, a couple of examples from Boston's own history. Within hours after the assassination of Dr. Martin Luther King Jr. on April 4, 1968, scores of American cities, including Boston, erupted into racial violence, in what became the greatest wave of social unrest in the United States since the Civil War. But the next night, Boston was nearly alone among major cities spared of rioting after Mayor Kevin White, in a bold but risky move, decided not to cancel a previously scheduled James Brown concert at the Boston Garden. Instead, he arranged for Boston's public station, Channel 2, WGBH-TV, to televise the event live. In this way, many Bostonians stayed at home in front of their TV sets rather than being out on the streets.

More recently, when John Silber, Boston University's combative president, was running as a Democrat for Governor of Massachusetts in 1990, his candidacy was derailed by a petulant outburst directed at Channel 5's Natalie Jacobson, a beloved local anchor, during an "at home" television interview—the last and most serious in a series of "Silber Shockers" that helped cost him the election. A Silber administration would have been very different from that of the eventual Republican winner, Bill Weld. Boston television, as was true elsewhere, had become an important player in the workings of democracy.

The Golden Age of Boston Television deals with a significant chapter in this town's past, when local television played an important part not only in *Boston's* history but also in *television's* history. It is a unique, never-been-told-before story, which explains how this magical era arose and why it eventually fell. It is about a twenty-year period— from the early 1970s to the early 1990s—when Boston was the site of the country's Golden Age of local television. To be sure, Boston was an unlikely candidate for distinction in television's highly competitive marketplace. Though considered a major market, Boston was only ranked sixth compared with other cities, well behind such heavyweights as New York (#1), the center of the world's finance, art, and fashion; Los Angeles (#2), with its glitz and glamour, the heart of the country's entertainment industry; and Chicago (#3), the country's third most populous city.

And yet, the Boston market not only became the nation's leader in locally produced news, programming, and public affairs, but it also became a model for the country's other local stations. It was a time of award-winning local newscasts, lively talk shows, thought-provoking specials and documentaries, ambitious public service campaigns, and even originally produced TV films featuring Hollywood stars.

The Boston market also drew the attention of the major networks, while its stations additionally syndicated their programming to hundreds of the country's other local stations. When ABC launched *Good Morning America* in 1975, it borrowed heavily from the format and even the name of a popular local talk show originally called *Good Morning!* on Channel 5 (WCVB-TV), an ABC-affiliated station. When Channel 4 (WBZ-TV) produced an original, locally produced television drama called *Jenny's Song*, about a teenager's grief over her father's death, it was additionally sold to more than 100 TV stations around the country. And, in one especially remarkable instance, Channel 5 produced *Summer Solstice*, a poignant drama starring Henry Fonda and Myrna Loy, about an elderly couple assessing their marriage. ABC later purchased the TV movie and aired it nationally. This innovation did not go unnoticed. After working on air for nearly twenty years at three different Boston television stations—WGBH, WBZ, and WCVB— Sonya Hamlin recently recalled her shock when she moved to New York City in the 1980s and surveyed the local television scene. "I was horrified at what I saw," she said. "It (the market) was twenty years behind the times. It was so corny, so predictable. There was no innovation, no creativity. I thought, 'This is New York?'"[3]

Already well known for its politics, culture, and sports-crazed fans, Boston itself is an important part of this story, for in the 1980s, the city had an especially high profile nationally. Indeed, this book represents a sociocultural and political history of Boston through the lens of local television. "Everyone's eyes were on Boston in the 1980s," recalls Jim Byrne, who worked at several Boston TV stations at the time. "In 1980, Boston had a year-long celebration of its 350th anniversary, complete with John Williams leading the Boston Pops playing his own composition, 'Jubilee 350 Fanfare.' [Boston mayor] Kevin White and [Senator] Teddy Kennedy had become national figures and 'Tip' O'Neill was the House Speaker. And, don't forget the 'Massachusetts Miracle.'"[4] (In 1987, the House Speaker even had a starring role in a Miller Lite beer TV commercial.) All this and Democratic Governor Mike Dukakis, too, who ran for the presidency in 1988 (though he eventually lost to his Republican opponent George H. W. Bush). It is probably more than a coincidence that no less than four network television shows were set in Boston during this time:

Cheers (1982–1993), NBC's smash hit sitcom, set in a Boston bar
modeled after the Bull and Finch Pub on Beacon Street;

St. Elsewhere (1982–1988), NBC's gritty, often hilarious medical
drama took place in a fictitious rundown hospital in Boston's
South End;

Goodnight, Beantown (1983–1984), a short-lived CBS sitcom,
about an anchor—a Boston University graduate—who is
joined by a female co-anchor in an effort to improve the
station's news ratings; and

Spenser: For Hire (1985–1988), an ABC series centering on a
private eye and based on the novels of Boston author Robert
Parker. Most of the show was actually filmed in Boston.

My own interest in this subject of Boston television grew out of two
of my great loves, one of which dates back to my early childhood. In
1947, when television was in its infancy and my twin brother Kenny
and I were little kids, our father, a physician who adored gadgets,
surprised us one day with a clunky black-and-white DuMont TV.
Whether or not we were the first family in Jackson Heights, Queens,
to have a television set, as Dad liked to boast, is open to question.
Still, I well remember hordes of neighborhood kids knocking on our
front door, asking if they could come watch some television, while I
went on to become one of the world's littlest addicts. I was—and remain—entangled in this lifelong obsession. Even now, the first thing
I do upon waking up, even before brushing my teeth, is to click on my
46-inch flat screen TV.

My other passion is Boston, a place that I got to know when I came
up from New York to attend Harvard's Graduate School of Education, and decided to settle here permanently. Every city is unique, but
some cities are arguably more unique than others. With its celebrated
history, quirky character, rich culture, and excellent medical schools,
colleges, and universities, Boston remains a very special place, a
pretty small town (as the song goes, "where everybody knows your
name"), with a big-city feel—from historic Faneuil Hall where colo-
nials such as Sam Adams and James Otis plotted their independence;
to First Night, the annual New Year's cultural celebration, with its

spectacular ice sculptures and waterfront fireworks; to Fenway Park, home of our beloved Red Sox. All this, and its very own cream pie!

Not that the town is perfect. Boston can be self-important, narrow-minded, hopelessly neurotic, and parochial, and is arguably among the cities with the worst weather in the country. And, like the weather, one thing Boston is not is predictable. But for a brief stint as a TV critic for the *Miami Herald*, I have spent much of my adult life in the Boston area, working *in* or writing *about* television. An important stop along the way came when, from 1967 to 1973, I was a research associate at a now-defunct think tank at Brandeis University called the Lemberg Center for the Study of Violence. With many of our cities in flames, particularly in the aftermath of the assassination of the Rev. Dr. Martin Luther King Jr., our mission was to study racial disorders and devise an "early warning system" to help prevent impending violence. I was in charge of a small research operation that, through a newspaper clipping service, helped us track thousands of incidents, while providing us with an extraordinary overview of the press coverage. One recurring theme, reflected in various articles and a book I authored called *Rumors, Race and Riots*, was that all too often the media, particularly the press, were guilty of inaccurate, biased, distorted, and sensationalized coverage. By this time, however, my professional interests became more focused on television, so that when the Lemberg Center closed, I set my sights on working in television.

From 1973 to 1975, I was an associate producer on Channel 5's new talk show called *Good Morning!*, followed by a one-year stint as the host/producer of a modest weekly public affairs show at WJAR-TV, the NBC affiliate in Providence, Rhode Island. I did everything there, from booking and transporting the guests to making them coffee. One time I snared the British actor Brian Bedford, then appearing in Boston in Peter Shaffer's brilliant play *Equus*. When I indicated I would be pleased to send "a car" for him, he quickly accepted my offer. Unfortunately, the "car" turned out not to be a limousine, but rather my battered old Toyota Corolla, with me as the driver. During the drive to Providence, the esteemed actor didn't utter a single word, nor did he on the way back to Boston.

From 1978 to 1982, I was a *Boston Globe* correspondent, specializing in the arts and television; and later, from 1982 to 1991 I was the TV critic for the *Patriot Ledger*, a suburban South Shore paper. I additionally spent six of those years (1986–1991) as a contributing writer to *Boston Magazine*, and later was a correspondent for *Electronic Media* (1990–1993), a trade weekly that covered the television industry. In my later years, I freelanced and spent more than a dozen years as a lecturer in Boston University's journalism department, teaching courses in arts criticism and media criticism.

The material for this book has been drawn from a variety of sources: my personal experiences working in local television; recent interviews with many of the principals featured in the book; columns and articles from the aforementioned publications; freelance pieces for publications such as the *New York Times*, *Boston Globe Magazine*, and *Columbia Journalism Review*; and numerous secondary sources—newspapers (some dating as far back as the 1940s), magazines, journals, and books.

The book is divided into two distinct but related parts:

Part I: "The Transformation of the Boston TV Market." This section examines the forces and prevailing conditions that set the stage for a Golden Age, including a station-by-station analysis of the important events and developments; an examination of some of Boston television's major players and personalities who shaped the market; and a look at the ferocious news "war" among the stations that resulted in chaos, but paradoxically, also ushered in a period of further creativity and growth.

Part II: "Local Television and Boston's Culture." This section is an analysis of Boston's sociocultural and political history through the lens of local television. It also includes a look at the life of a TV critic during the Golden Age and examines television criticism in a time of proliferating celebrity; the effects of Boston's puritanism and parochialism on the local television scene, particularly when it involved censorship; the powerful presence of Boston's Roman Catholic Church, including its effects on the media, with reference to the infamous clerical sex abuse scandal; the explosive issues of race, gender, and sexual orientation; and how Boston's TV stations went national in 1988 when Massachusetts Governor Mike Dukakis ran for the presidency.

David Carr, the late *New York Times* media columnist, was fond of repeating Steve Jobs's advice to him: "Change happens slowly, and then it happens all at once." It turned out both were right. *The Golden Age of Boston Television* is very much a labor of love—for without knowing it at the time, I had the good fortune to be present during a historic era, as both a participant and a chronicler of that time. It didn't get much better than that.

: PART ONE :
THE TRANSFORMATION
OF THE BOSTON
TV MARKET

MARKET FORCES SET THE STAGE

       It is often said that things just happen—but do they? At any given time, events may seem to take place randomly, occurring as they may. But with the passage of time comes greater perspective, along with the realization that certain seemingly disparate events were actually connected and provide meaning to the past.

       Throughout the years of commercial television, there have been between 200 and 210 local television markets across the country, according to Nielsen, the marketing company that also measures television ratings. But only one out of the 200-plus markets became the site of the Golden Age of local television—Boston. The question is, why? Boston's Golden Age of local television didn't just happen overnight or occur willy-nilly. Rather, it grew out of a confluence of factors and forces: the basic broadcast television structure in the United States; the rare occurrence when not one, but two Boston TV stations underwent license changes, each becoming locally owned—Channel 5 in 1972 and Channel 7 in 1982; an economic boom in Massachusetts during the 1980s when companies, including the local TV stations had money—lots of it—to spend; and finally, television trends at the national level, such as cable, that would affect the Boston market.

       To understand the television structure, we begin with a few basics. When television was first introduced to Americans in the late 1940s, few people realized how popular the medium would become, and no doubt even fewer had any inkling of the powerful effect it would exert on American culture. By 1955, half of all the homes in America had a TV set; today, of course, nearly every household has one or more. As television took hold in the country, three commercial broadcast networks came to dominate the landscape—NBC, CBS, and ABC. These networks formed relationships with local stations around the country. The federal government permitted the networks to own some of the local stations (called owned-and-operated, or O&Os); others were simply affiliated with the networks (called "network affiliates"). With the exception of the Public Broadcasting Service (PBS), it was a decentralized, market-oriented television system.

The "Big Three," as the networks were called, provided a significant amount of programs to local stations. Licensed by the Federal Communications Commission (FCC), created by the 1934 Federal Communications Act to regulate local TV stations, the locals carried network newscasts and primetime, daytime, and sports programming. For airing those programs, the locals received money in return—officially called "compensation." Periods of time during the day were also reserved for the affiliates for local programming in news, talk shows, and syndicated programs, where they were allotted time to sell local commercials. Though highly profitable for both parties, the arrangement could be (and still is) a volatile one, especially when it came to how much compensation a local station received. There was also the issue of "preemptions," i.e., when a local station elected to produce its own shows or carry syndicated programming that could typically generate even greater profits.

As a check on the powerful Big Three networks, the FCC initially limited the number of local stations (O&Os) each could own. At first it was three; then five; then seven; and by 1985, twelve. During the years of the Reagan Administration, which was strongly committed to government deregulation, the FCC continued to relax its media ownership rules.[1] For obvious reasons, each of the networks selected O&Os in the country's most heavily populated (hence more lucrative) markets—New York (#1), followed by Los Angeles (#2), and Chicago (#3). Rarely able to deviate from the parent company's wishes, the O&Os were forced to take much of the network programming, basically functioning as cash cows. By contrast, while Boston was considered a major market (ranked #6), its VHS stations (1–13) were simply *affiliated* with the networks. Thus, by not being O&Os, the Boston stations had considerably more freedom to preempt the networks and offer many more locally produced shows. And it was during the Golden Age that the locals could more easily thumb their noses at the networks and go their own merry way, often much to the networks' chagrin.

The FCC also had the power to award, renew, and revoke station licenses. The Federal Communications Act of 1934 states that the FCC should assess the "character . . . of the applicant to operate the station," and ensure that the "public interest . . . would be served by the granting" of a license. Indeed, the possibility that broadcasters could lose their licenses, worth millions of dollars, was one that certainly caught their attention:

> "Revocation" is perhaps the deadliest word to a television or radio station.
>
> Applied to a station's license, it sounds the cataclysmic death knell of a broadcast operation that can render a multimillion-dollar investment worthless.[2]

However, the FCC's penalty of revocation—its ultimate weapon—has rarely been imposed.

In their book *The Reluctant Regulators*, Barry Cole and Mal Oettinger, both experts on the FCC, wrote: "Renewal tends to be automatic, provided the applicants' papers are in order." In fiscal year 1976 alone, they reported that of the 2,972 processed (not counting radio) applications, less than one-quarter of 1 percent (0.0027) of the applicants were denied a license.[3] This is what makes the situation in the Boston market so unusual. For over the course of a single decade, not one, but two Boston TV stations would each lose its license: WHDH-TV (Channel 5), owned by the Boston Herald Traveler Corporation, in 1972, followed by WNAC-TV (Channel 7), owned by General Tire, in 1982. Both cases were extremely complicated, with numerous twists and turns; both took years to settle; and, most significantly, both stations would wind up locally owned. And while the two license changes do not appear directly connected, but simply stand as an interesting anomaly, each would profoundly unsettle and invigorate the market, though in different ways. And in combination, both decisions would become important factors in ushering in Boston's Golden Age of local television.

5

CHANNEL 5 LICENSE CHANGE (1972)

In what seemed like routine fashion, WHDH-TV (Channel 5), owned by the Boston Herald Traveler Corporation, along with WHDH 850 AM radio and its FM sister 94.5, went on the air November 26, 1957, having been granted a license from the FCC. In what was considered a pro forma move, the losing applicants appealed the FCC decision to the District of Columbia, U.S. Circuit Court of Appeals. But in the meantime, during hearings being held by the House Committee on Legislative Oversight in 1958, almost by happenstance, it was disclosed that in the winter of 1954 and spring of 1956 then-FCC chairman George C. McConnaughey had lunch at the request of Robert Choate, the CEO of the Boston Herald Traveler Corporation, at a time when WHDH, Inc., and several other applicants were under consideration to operate the Boston station. This raised the issue of "ex parte," a legal term that also describes a judge—in this instance, the FCC chairman—who communicates with one party to a lawsuit to the exclusion of the other party or parties. In a decision that shocked many observers, the Court of Appeals remanded the case back to the FCC for reconsideration. The revelation was doubly upsetting to the FCC, which was already embarrassed over *The $64,000 Question* and *Twenty One* TV quiz show scandals, as well as the "payola" scandals involving record companies and radio stations in violation of FCC rules.

And so began a bitter, bruising, confusing, and hugely expensive legal battle between the Boston Herald Traveler Corporation and several other parties that would go on for another fifteen, years until 1972, making it the longest regulatory case in the country's history.[4] Over the years, this famous case would involve hundreds of petitions, briefs, filings, and appearances at the FCC and the U.S. Court of Appeals, while involving three presidential administrations—Eisenhower, Kennedy, and Nixon. Three times the case would go before the U.S Supreme Court, and each time it would be turned down.

The stakes were high. At the time, WHDH, worth an estimated $50 million, was vitally important because profits from the TV station helped keep the *Herald Traveler*, Boston's only Republican newspaper, in business. Shortly after WHDH lost its license, the paper would fold. But the case had larger implications as well. The FCC had never before taken away the license of a TV station in a major market; many broadcasters in the industry were now concerned that they, too, could lose their licenses. And with public complaints surfacing about the overconcentration of media properties in so few hands, the 155 publishers who also owned some 260 television stations around the United States were also very jittery.

With WHDH on the air, but remaining under a cloud, a new group called Boston Broadcasters, Incorporated (BBI), entered the fray in 1963, filing an application for ownership with the FCC. BBI quickly emerged as an intriguing, if not formidable challenger among the three groups vying for the license. Besides the usual complement of businesspeople, this group featured a glittering array of civic leaders and distinguished academics, including Leo Beranek, a former MIT professor and a prominent acoustics expert who had written a classic textbook in this field; Oscar Handlin, the Pulitzer Prize–winning American historian from Harvard; John Knowles, general director of the Massachusetts General Hospital; Robert Gardner, an anthropologist, filmmaker, and Harvard professor (his grandmother was Isabella Stewart Gardner); and Henry Jaffe, an Emmy Award–winning TV producer and entertainment attorney. The group was also notable for its unusually ambitious plans set forth in its application, among other things promising to air more local programming than any other station in the country.

With the case entangled in the courts until the very end, each side came to despise and demonize the other, hurling about claims of dirty tricks and illegal activities. Harold Clancy, a relentless, tough-talking Irishman who headed the Boston Herald Traveler Corporation, was convinced that BBI had placed a spy in his company. BBI charged that Clancy had used as many as thirty reporters to watch as BBI's daily trash was thrown out by janitors who cleaned BBI offices in downtown Boston; the reporters would then follow the garbage truck to a dumping ground located Quincy. (Clancy admitted to assigning nine reporters to the task.[5]) BBI officials were also convinced that their offices were being bugged. The paranoia was palpable, with their attorneys warning, "Watch your phones! They're being tapped. Watch whom you talk to in bars. You're probably being tailed. Don't talk to strange women."[6]

7

Finally, by early March of 1972 and by a vote of four to one, the FCC ordered WHDH to go off the air on March 19, at 3 o'clock in the morning, with permission granted for WCVB-TV as the new station's call letters. Leo Beranek, BBI's president, came up with the station's new call letters, having drawn them on a cocktail napkin during a lunch at Locke-Ober—"C" as in channel, "V" as in the Roman numeral for five, "B" as in Boston.[7] Not even a last-ditch appeal to the U.S. Supreme Court by Clancy, which failed, could change the outcome. The only negative for the new station owners was that CBS, fearing a wave of network preemptions on what would have been its second-largest affiliate and its largest affiliate on the East Coast, switched its affiliation to WNAC-TV, leaving WCVB to affiliate with a reluctant ABC.

If euphoric was the word to describe the new station owners, Harold Clancy and his legal team were devastated. The handover of the station to BBI revealed the level of their anger and resentment with Clancy, dogged as ever, going down fighting to the bitter end. WHDH's final movie airing on its last night was called *Fixed Bayonets*. WCVB signed on at 3:05 a.m. with a brief "Hello World." Still, the new station officials weren't taking any chances. Before going on the air, they made sure that armed police were placed around the new station's Needham headquarters—just in case.[8]

Historically, the FCC decision was important on several counts. It struck a blow against unsavory ex parte meetings, of which there had been all too many by government regulatory officials; it established the importance of media diversification during a time of growing multiple ownerships; and it set a precedent that FCC renewals should not be automatic, but should include assessing a station's performance. But perhaps its greatest significance was discerned by Nicholas Johnson, then a young, reform-minded, highly independent FCC commissioner. Issuing his own "concurring statement" in the FCC's decision, he wrote, "In America's eleven largest cities there is not a single network-affiliated VHF television station that is independently and locally owned. They are all owned by the networks, multiple station owners, or major local newspapers."[9]

He added that it would be "healthy" to have "at least one station among these politically powerful thirty-three network-affiliated properties in the major markets that is truly locally owned, and managed independently of the other local mass media." In the ensuing years, WCVB (Channel 5), Boston's new kid on the block, would prove the wisdom of those words.

CHANNEL 7 LICENSE CHANGE (1982)

The WNAC-TV case was marked by double irony. It denoted only the second time the FCC had ever denied a license renewal, both in Boston—the first involving WCVB in 1972. And while WNAC-TV was number seven on the TV dial, it had to be one of the unluckiest stations ever. Owned by General Tire, Channel 7 made its debut on June 21, 1948, just twelve days after WBZ (Channel 4), Boston's oldest TV station, signed on the air. From the beginning, its corporate owner had high ambitions, expanding its media properties to include WOR-TV and WOR AM-FM radio stations in New York, KHJ-TV in Los Angeles, and RKO Radio Pictures. In 1959, the company changed its name to RKO General when it closed down its film division.

The circumstances concerning the loss of Channel 7's license in 1982 were quite different from those of Channel 5—though just as prolonged and convoluted. In addition to its power to award, renew, and revoke a local station's license, the FCC was given the authority to assess the "character . . . of the applicant to operate the station," and ensure that the "public interest . . . would be served by the granting" of a license. As usual, the stakes were high—with the possibility that a broadcaster could lose its license worth millions of dollars.

By 1969, RKO was under challenge by two competing investor groups from Boston, Dudley Station Corp. and Community Broadcasting of Boston, Inc., initially for its programming, but later facing serious legal questions about its tax and accounting irregularities and improper reciprocal trade practices, and for acknowledging corporate bribery and corruption by General Tire, its parent company. In June 1974, a preliminary FCC finding indicated that General Tire was, indeed, engaging in such practices, but also that RKO did not deserve to be disqualified as a licensee because of it. While the case was pending before the FCC, the Securities and Exchange Commission (SEC) also opened its own investigation, one that eventually would cast doubt on General Tire's character, and by association, RKO's. As part of settling the case with the SEC, General Tire was forced to admit that it had committed financial fraud over illegal political contributions and bribes.

One of the investigations at this time involved Terry Lenzner, a relentless lawyer and private investigator, hired by David Mugar, a local multimillionaire businessman and philanthropist (his father founded the Star Market grocery chain). With Mugar the driving force behind Community Broadcasting, it proved a shrewd move. Earlier Lenzner had gained national attention as assistant chief counsel on the U.S. Senate Committee investigating the Watergate scandal, beginning with the burglary and cover-up at the Watergate Office Building. And it was Lenzner's law firm that drew up a massive report about RKO's alleged improper and illegal activities, delivered to the FCC in 1975. In the meantime, Community Broadcasting and Dudley Station Corp., the two investment groups that originally challenged RKO's license, in 1978 merged into New England Television Corp. headed by David Mugar.

In 1980, the FCC, in a narrow 4 to 3 vote, revoked the license of WNAC-TV, a property reportedly worth between $100 and $200 million. Of particular concern was RKO's "lack of candor" in reporting its lengthy list of wrongdoings to the FCC. It also left the door open to taking away the licenses for thirteen other RKO broadcast properties, including radio stations WRKO-AM and WROR-FM in Boston. At the time, William A. Henry 3d, the *Boston Globe*'s Pulitzer Prize–winning TV critic, called the decision "the most sweeping in the 46-year history of regulation of broadcasting by the FCC." But in a decision that underscored the confusing nature of this case, on December 4, 1981, the U.S. Court of Appeals for the District of Columbia Circuit affirmed WNAC's license revocation, but threw out most of the FCC's original findings, except for the charge of "lack of candor." Calling RKO General's conduct "so egregious and so conspicuous," the court suggested it wasn't the wrongdoing per se, but rather the dishonesty about its misconduct that cost the station owner its license.[10]

RKO appealed this decision, but in April 1982 the FCC denied its appeal and ordered the company to surrender the station's license. In a last-ditch effort, RKO, joined by the National Association of Broadcasters, which feared a chilling effect on the broadcast industry, appealed to the U.S. Supreme Court. But on April 19, the court turned down RKO's petition for a full-bench review of the Boston license revocation. And so, the previous federal appeals court order, issued in December upholding the FCC license revocation, was sustained. Apparently, everyone, even the high court, had had enough. The FCC then granted a license to Mugar's New England Television, with the new station, now called WNEV-TV, scheduled to launch on May 22, 1982.

It had been an exhaustive legal battle, lasting an interminable thirteen years, with the Mugar group accumulating 16,000 pages of testimony and $15 million alone in legal costs. "We all should have invested in Xerox," Mugar quipped to the *Globe*.[11] *Broadcasting*, a leading industry publication, sounded a note of finality—and relief. "It's all over for Boston's WNAC-TV" the magazine declared.[12]

But WNAC's license revocation was not merely a story about an important case in broadcast history, with the loss of a local TV station valued at between $100 and $200 million in a major television market. It was also about how a corrupt and irresponsible corporate owner, with little regard for the local viewers, could nearly run a local TV station into the ground. It was a sordid story about maximizing profits and minimizing public service commitments. Throughout its history, the ill-fated station would be plagued with severe ratings woes, management problems, inadequate local programming, poor promotion, low staff morale, and a litany of embarrassing episodes that would severely tarnish its image. Except for a few times in its history, WNAC was last in the ratings, usually coming in a distant third behind Channel 5 (WCVB-TV) and Channel 4 (WBZ-TV), the other market powerhouses.

The new ownership came with some impressive assets. Besides the usual complement of well-heeled, well-connected businesspeople, the board of directors featured distinguished academics and journalists, such as MIT President Emeritus Jerome Wiesner; historian Doris Kearns Goodwin; Martin H. Peretz, owner of the *New Republic* magazine; and Mortimer ("Mort") Zuckerman, businessman and owner of the *Atlantic Monthly*. Further, in a town that, historically, had more than its share of racial troubles, the group was also notable for its diversity, with the board including prominent African Americans, such as Bertram M. Lee, NETV's senior vice president and the president

of Dudley Station Corp.; Ruth M. Batson, former Boston NAACP official and Boston University associate professor; and Melvin B. Miller,
president of Banner Publications, Inc. Indeed, WNEV now had the
largest concentration of minority ownership at a VHF station in a
major city in the United States. As with BBI-owned WCVB-TV, localism was another important element, with most of WNEV's fifty stockholders from Greater Boston. Indeed, the fact that each station was to
be locally owned might have been factored into the FCC's decision to
grant each one a license. Ironically, three days before WNEV went on
the air, Metromedia, the country's fourth-largest broadcasting chain,
announced that it had acquired WCVB from BBI, thus leaving WNEV
as the Boston market's only locally owned station. It was a very good
sign.

THE "MASSACHUSETTS MIRACLE"

By themselves, the two license changes in the Boston market
would not have been sufficient to usher in a Golden Age of local television. Which brings us to still another factor—the economic boom
in the early 1980s, known as the "Massachusetts Miracle." It was a
period of remarkable growth and expansion for many companies,
including the local TV stations, which, after all, were in business to
make money.

When Michael Dukakis was first elected governor in 1975, Massachusetts was already in the throes of economic stagnation. The unemployment rate was at 11.2 percent, while the state's textile, leather,
and apparel industries, long an important part of the state's economy, had fled to the Sun Belt. In addition, the oil embargo imposed
by the OPEC nations in the early 1970s resulted in skyrocketing oil
prices, sending the United States into a recession, resulting in a near-
depression in oil-dependent Massachusetts. In Boston alone, the
number of jobs peaked in 1969 at 564,906, after which the city was
beset by a seven-year recession lasting from 1970 to 1976. During the
lowest year of the recession, in 1976, there were 518,513 jobs, a loss
of more than 46,000 jobs from 1969. In 1977, the number of jobs in
the city began to rise, and employment numbers reached their 1969
levels by 1981. Employment held steady at this level until 1983.[13]

By the early 1980s, coinciding with Dukakis's second and third terms in office (1983–1991), Massachusetts would experience a striking turnaround. Beginning around 1983, the state had a six-year period of phenomenal growth and prosperity, thanks to an explosion of technology companies along Route 128, a more than 180-degree arc around Boston, bearing names like Digital Equipment, Data General, and Wang Laboratories. The regional economy was also helped by the steady growth of the service sector, with an emphasis on finance, insurance, health care, and consulting. In "Higher Skills and the New England Economy," John C. Hoy, an expert in higher education, noted that more than one in three jobs in the region were in a health-related field, with more than 15 percent of the population employed in education.[14] Massachusetts was now leading the nation into the information age. And, with a reconfigured and revitalized economy, the state's unemployment, which had been at more than 11 percent—the highest for any industrial state when Dukakis first took office—declined in 1988 to less than 3 percent, the lowest of any industrial state. State and local taxes, which had been the highest per capita of any of the states—dubbing the Commonwealth "Taxachusetts" in some quarters—were reduced to the eighth lowest. And personal income in Massachusetts increased faster than in any other state during the 1980s. To spread the word, the state's Chamber of Commerce even produced a schmaltzy TV commercial in the early 1980s, called "Make It in Massachusetts," complete with T-shirts and bumper stickers. (You can see the commercial at youtube.com, "Make It in Massachusetts-early 1980s TV campaign.")

Economists and other experts still argue about how much credit Governor Dukakis deserves for the Massachusetts success story, whether it was through his initiatives—such as providing loans and grants to older depressed cities and towns like Lowell, Worcester, and Springfield—or simply the result of favorable market conditions, such as the convergence of academic and financial forces that made the Boston area the perfect site for the newly emergent high-tech industry. Perhaps the best answer can be found in the question posed and answered by Richard Manley, president of the Massachusetts Taxpayers Foundation, a civic watchdog organization and, incidentally, no friend of the governor. "Did he (Dukakis) engineer it? No," Manley said. "Did he recognize it and build on it? Yes, he did."[15] In any event, the "Massachusetts Miracle" propelled Governor Dukakis into the national spotlight. In 1988, he became the Democratic candidate for president, an election he would eventually lose to his Republican opponent George H. W. Bush.

Indeed, the times were looking good for the country itself. This was the first decade since the 1930s in which the United States was not engaged in a war. And, unless you happened to be poor, or an early AIDS sufferer, or an autoworker feeling stiff competition from the Japanese automakers, people were feeling optimistic. It was "Morning in America," as President Reagan's legendary campaign commercial told us in 1984. How perfect that Bobby McFerrin's 1988 cheerful little ditty called "Don't Worry Be Happy" later won a Grammy Award for Song of the Year. And, during this time, Boston local television stations, as we will see, would embark on their own grand adventures, with local television viewers the ultimate beneficiaries.

THE EFFECT OF CABLE ON THE BOSTON MARKET

Boston's Golden Age didn't occur in a vacuum, but was additionally affected by national forces and trends. In a perceptive *New York Times* article in 1982, taking the measure of the exciting developments in the Boston market, TV reporter Tony Schwartz took note of the rise of cable television and how it would affect local television markets: "What's happening in Boston is a mirror of the direction local television has begun taking in cities throughout the country. . . . (T)he attention to local programming reflects a recognition that original programming will be the best way for local stations to withstand the coming challenge from cable."[16]

The rise of cable in the late 1970s, which only intensified in the early 1980s, provided new competition for both the broadcast networks and local TV stations, including those in Boston. Beginning in 1972, in an effort to protect smaller, less powerful, independent stations (stations not affiliated with any broadcast network) and public television stations within a cable provider's service area, the FCC issued "must-carry" regulations that forced cable companies to deliver all local and public television channels within a 50- to 60-mile radius of the cable company's service area, which made it possible for such stations to provide improved reception and reach a wider audience. (However, by the late 1980s, as a result of challenges by cable operators, the courts struck down most carry rules as a violation of the First Amendment.)

As of 1976, most local areas only had stations affiliated with ABC, NBC, and CBS. But as independent stations became more profitable and the FCC began to allow more station licenses and frequencies per market, their numbers surged. According to the Association of Independent Broadcasters (INTV), "In 1978, only 91 independent stations aired programming, but this mushroomed to 321 by the close of 1988."[17]

In the meantime, new networks were created on cable aimed at specialized audiences: Time Inc.'s Home Box Office (HBO) in 1975; Ted Turner's "superstation,"[18] WTBS, in 1976; as well as C-SPAN (live coverage of the House of Representatives), ESPN (sports), and Nickelodeon (children's programming), all in 1979. At the national level, additional sources of news were also opening up. In 1980 alone, Ted Turner launched his Cable News Network (CNN) and ABC introduced *Nightline*. Three years later, PBS expanded *The MacNeil/Lehrer Report* to an hour, renaming it *The MacNeil/Lehrer NewsHour.*

The television news marketplace was getting increasingly crowded, with implications for the local TV stations that didn't want to lose out—and, besides, news could be highly profitable. In 1980, Channel 38 (WSBK) briefly ran Independent Network News (INN), a nationally syndicated newscast for independent stations. But up against the other local newscasts at 11 p.m., it fared poorly in the ratings and was soon dropped. Even Channel 25 (WXNE-TV), then owned by the Christian Broadcasting Network, launched an early morning half-hour newscast in 1983 called *Wake Up Beantown*, with a focus on "upbeat" news, information, weather, and sports. Two years later, Channel 56 (WLVI-TV) started up a half-hour broadcast called *The News at Ten*, on weeknights (then weekends as well), which was later expanded to a full hour. In 1987, Channel 7 launched *Live at 5*, to begin at 5 p.m. And, a year later, *World Monitor* on Channel 68 (WQTV), owned by the Christian Science Church based in Boston, was added to the scene. Anchored by John Hart, a respected newsman who earlier worked at NBC and CBS, *World Monitor* focused on national and international news, and was also available to a national audience, having partnered with The Discovery Channel. Though the ratings were extremely low locally, the program stood out as a prestige vehicle. "The sheer integrity of *World Monitor* is invigorating," wrote *New York Times* TV critic John J. O'Connor. *Time* magazine praised the program for its "meaty content and sober style of an earlier, less frantic TV era." And, in 1988 and 1989, Hart was named to *TV Guide's* all-star team (best anchor: cable).[19]

Talk about an abundance of riches! By 1988, the Boston market had no less than six stations with nightly newscasts.

With increasing competition in the area of news, the locals in Boston began to look more like mini versions of the national networks. All three major news stations set up Washington, D.C., bureaus. They also began dispatching their reporters abroad to various international trouble spots. Channel 7's R. D. Sahl went to the Soviet Union in 1985 to cover the first summit meeting between President Ronald Reagan and the Soviet leader Mikhail Gorbachev. Channel 5's Clark Booth accompanied Boston's Archbishop Bernard Law on a four-day visit to Cuba—the first such mission allowed during Fidel Castro's regime. Channel 4's Dan Rea filed stories from Ireland for a series about illegal Irish immigrants finding their way to Boston. Channel 4's Brad Willis went to Afghanistan. Channel 7's Dave Wright, a Canadian, was able to wangle his way into Iran. And, so it went. There were times, or so it seemed, when reporters and anchors spent more time abroad in hotels than in their own newsrooms. Recalls R. D. Sahl from his days as a Channel 7 anchor: "Photog Andy Dubrovsky and I made several trips to the USSR/Russia: one during Perestroika and the early days of (Mikhail) Gorbachev. Another during one of the Reagan-Gorby arms summits. Another during the early (Boris) Yeltsin period—we were in Moscow the day price controls were removed from staples like bread and milk."[20]

Channel 5's Martha Bradlee (now Martha Raddatz) was another well-traveled reporter, whose assignments included the Ethiopian famine (1983–1985), the Geneva summit meeting between Mikhail Gorbachev and Ronald Reagan (1985), and the crucial election in the Philippines that marked the downfall of Ferdinand Marcos and Corazon "Cory" Aquino's ascension as president (1986). Raddatz later joined NPR as its Pentagon correspondent (1993–1998) and then in

1999 joined ABC News, where she has been since. Presently its high-profile Chief Global Affairs Correspondent, and a moderator of both a presidential and a vice presidential debate, she recently recalled her earlier globe-trotting days at Channel 5:

> We did what I considered a remarkable story on the Beirut hostages ... an hour special ... it was one of the best things we did. And we did a lot on terrorism during the '80s with trips to Europe and the Mideast. But the story that has remained incredibly relevant even today is the series I did on the intifadah of 1988. I found people on all sides of that conflict. I went back in 2000 (as an ABC News correspondent) and found all of them (which took a major detective effort!) for a *Nightline* half-hour special—and then again two summers ago for a *This Week* piece, ... which was so eye-opening. I found the nineteen-year-old Palestinian woman ... now a mother of young children who lives behind a wall. And the Boston transplants in a massive settlement (Efrat) in the West Bank who have all but given up on a peace they had hoped for so long ago.[21]

Asked if there was always a local angle, Raddatz replied, "No, definitely not. If there was an obvious one (Corazon Aquino and her husband lived in exile in Newton before returning), we would certainly explore. And yes, we looked for Boston transplants for the intifadah story, but it was never a 'local' story in the way some people make it all about that. We had people from the area who we would interview or profile, which I think helped make these important international stories more relatable but also expanded the knowledge of these issues."

Queried as to whether Boston's TV reporters at the time were comparable to the network correspondents, Raddatz replied: "Well, that is quite a question to a network reporter who started in local TV! I think everything I did in local TV helped me be a better reporter for the network."

THE RISE OF THE INDEPENDENTS

The rise of cable also helped make the independent stations in the Boston market more of a force. WSBK (Channel 38), owned by Storer Broadcasting, and WLVI (Channel 56), owned by the Gannett Company, were not in the same league as the three major network affiliates in terms of ratings and revenue. But during the Golden Age, these top two independents were successful in their own right and made their presence felt. (Not until the late 1980s and 1990s would WFXT-TV Channel 25 assert itself in the market when it was bought by Rupert Murdoch's News Corporation in 1987.) Both stations made their mark in sports programming, theatrical movie repeats, and off-network reruns in the lucrative 6 to 8 p.m. time block. Each had a dependable block of movies in the 8 to 10 p.m. time period. "During the important rating periods, we'd simply roll out *Casablanca* or Charles Bronson's *Death Wish* movies," recalls one Channel 56 insider. But Channel 38 additionally became a brand builder by having deep-voiced Dana Hersey as the host of *The Movie Loft.*

Boston has long been a sport-crazed town. Even today, fans remain obsessed by the New England Patriots' "deflate-gate" scandal and still argue over who was greater—Larry Bird or Magic Johnson, or whether Big Papi ever used steroids. Acquiring the rights to televise the games of the various teams turned into a financial bonanza. By virtue of carrying many of the Boston Bruins and Boston Red Sox games, Channel 38 emerged as a sports juggernaut and was arguably the stronger of the two stations. The ratings for the "Bs," as they were often called, climbed during the 1980s, when the team made the playoffs every year. And when Channel 38 acquired the television rights to the Boston Red Sox in 1975—the same year the team won the American League pennant—the ratings soared. In addition, given the Red Sox drawing power, other Boston stations were angered when the games ran into the 11 o'clock news, taking a chunk out of their own ratings. Once in 1984, Channel 38 even threatened to sue Channel 4 over its use of Red Sox highlights on its late-night news.[22] With the popularity of the Red Sox picked up by nearly every cable provider in New England and as far west as Buffalo, New York, Channel 38 eventually became a national superstation in the late 1980s, when it worked out an agreement with Eastern Microwave to distribute its signal outside of New England.

Though not the sports powerhouse that Channel 38 was, Channel 56 did carry some sports programming of its own, principally the Boston Celtics road games from 1966 to 1969 and later from 1985 to

1990 during the wildly popular Larry Bird era. The franchise was so valuable that Gerry Walsh, the station's feisty general manager, was willing to shell out an unprecedented $15 to $16 million to get the second five-year contract. By 1988, the Celtics' drawing power was such that it boosted Channel 56's cable connection to 128 systems throughout New England, with the station able to reach nearly 1.2 million cable subscribers.

The independents impacted the market in still another way. Syndicated programming in the 6 to 8 p.m. slot cut into the numbers of other stations carrying local and network news. *Boston Herald* TV critic Greg Dawson, obviously not a news junkie, had this to say about the news stations during one important May "sweeps" ratings period in 1986: "The ratings for TV news generally get more attention than they warrant. According to Arbitron (ratings service), for example, the combined audience for reruns of *Hart to Hart* (Ch. 38), *Benson* (Ch. 56) and *Gimme a Break* (Ch. 25) from 6:30 to 7 is larger than the audience for either the *New England News* (Ch. 7) or *NewsCenter 5*."[23]

With Boston's three major television stations attracting some $40 million a year in advertising for its various newscasts, Gannett, which had recently bought WLVI (Channel 56) from Field Communications, decided to launch a newscast in 1984 called *The News at Ten*. With Jack Hynes and Julie Emry as its first anchors, Channel 56 was now the first independent commercial station in Boston to involve itself in the news area. Underscoring Gannett's serious commitment, the company budgeted $3 million alone for the first year and in time expanded the weeknight newscast to an hour and eventually extended it to weekends. Though *The News at Ten* never quite garnered the big ratings the officials had hoped for, it remained a credible alternative to Channel 2's more highbrow *Ten O'Clock News* and, among the independents, helped Channel 56 forge a clear identity. In the past, most of its reputation had come from movies and syndicated programming, but, as general manager Gerry Walsh once mused, "In a city like Boston, you don't have an image unless you broadcast news."[24]

WGBH-TV (CHANNEL 2): A UNIQUE FORCE

Boston's public television station occupied a unique place during the Golden Age. Unlike the other local stations, WGBH (Channel 2)[25] was much more of a national than a local player. Indeed, it was and remains PBS's single largest producer for television, producing shows out of Boston such as *Frontline*, *Nova*, *Masterpiece*, *American Experience*, *Victory Garden*, and *This Old House*. And let's not forget *The French Chef* with the legendary Julia Child from 1963 to 1973.

Over the years, Channel 2 was never as productive *locally* as Boston's other major stations. However, by virtue of its important leadership role in public television and by its very physical presence—located not far from the other stations—WGBH served to elevate the rest of the market. Still, the station had its share of locally produced shows and specials—more so than most other public TV stations. Down through the years, it had a lengthy list of informative public affairs shows, from *The Reporters* (1970–1973); to *Evening Compass* (1973–1974), which evolved into *The Ten O'Clock News* (1976–1991); and more recently, *Greater Boston* (1997–present), hosted by Emily Rooney until 2015, when she was succeeded by Jim Braude. Its lively edition on Friday night called *Beat the Press*, still hosted by Rooney, remains must-watch TV for media junkies.

The Ten O'Clock News was by far the station's most ambitious, most expensive, and longest-running (fifteen years) news program. Anchored by Christopher Lydon for most of its history, though later paired with Gail Harris (1984–1987), then Carmen Fields (1987–1991), the Channel 2 news was something of an oddity in the market—a genuine alternative to the other commercial newscasts—not necessarily superior to, but vastly different from, the others.[26]

The ratings were usually quite small (about 55,000 households), and for a long time the program had virtually no promotional resources. So when Channel 56 launched its own 10 p.m. newscast, in 1984, complete with a promotional budget of $300,000, the station hyped the program with a radio spot that had the show's anchor, Jack Hynes, saying, "I think the time has been right for quite a long while here in Boston for a 10 o'clock news. I'm surprised no one's done it before."[27] Ouch! The folks at Channel 2 were not amused. Their own newscast had been a local fixture at 10 p.m. since 1976. A new executive producer named Alan Foster was hired in 1985 to freshen up the news, with items like a new set that cost $10,000—actually, not much by commercial standards. (Five years earlier, Channel 4 paid the same amount for just the black-tile floor of its news set.) Yet, it was a newscast that had a fanatically loyal audience, and one that defied easy categorization, dared to be different, and wasn't afraid of being called offbeat or intellectual. Where else would you get a newscast whose idea of fluff was a lengthy report on an exhibit of *New Yorker* cartoons, featuring Chris Lydon and John Updike talking about the magazine while strolling through the Boston Athenaeum? For the most part, it turned its back on murders, three-decker fires, armed robberies, drug busts, and cutesy features like the one about Larry the Bear that got stuck in a tree in Lawrence. And, despite its elitist reputation, it probably devoted more time than its commercial counterparts did in covering minorities and neighborhood concerns.

But there were also problems. The show's puny $1.8 million budget (roughly one-fifth of the amounts each spent by Channels 4, 5, and 7) put severe constraints on the news operation. Having two camera crews (and only one on Monday and Friday) was absurd. An in-house joke had it that if the Massachusetts State House burned down, Channel 2 wouldn't have a crew to cover the story. Then there was the program's host Christopher Lydon, who was something of an acquired taste. This is how Lydon, as intelligent and literate as he was pompous, deigned to deliver a brief item on the weather: "The weather tonight—on what would have been the Beat novelist Jack Kerouac's 65th birthday—feels like a deeper relapse into winter." And when was the last time a newscast opened as follows? "Good evening, I'm Christopher Lydon. Boston bird-watchers, look for the migrating nighthawk these evenings in nocturnal pursuit of insects."[28]

But at its best, *The Ten O'Clock News* provided a thoughtful alternative to the gimmickry and shallowness of the other newscasts, and had the courage to do stories the other stations were too skittish to cover. For example, on the eve of an exhibit of Robert Mapplethorpe photos at Boston's Institute of Contemporary Art in 1990, a local controversy erupted over some of his sexually explicit, homoerotic shots—one showed two men, one black, one white, embracing; another, among his most famous ("Man in Polyester Suit"), revealed a gentleman in a three-piece suit exposing his penis. Most of Boston's news stations ignored or downplayed the story. Channel 4's "solution" was to do a brief story and insert black tape over the men's private parts. By contrast, Channel 2 devoted almost its entire newscast to the exhibit, which included a debate over whether the photographs were obscene and a six-minute report showing the controversial photographs. Such was the value of having an unconventional voice on the scene not subject to commercial pressures.[29]

WBZ-TV: CHANNEL 4 LAYS THE GROUNDWORK

Until the 1940s, radio had been king, but that was about to change. In Boston, by 1948 there was only talk about "T-Day," short for "Television Day." An unwieldy *Boston Globe* headline said it all: "'T-Day' is Wednesday—WBZ-TV to Open Television Era in New England."[1] At 6:30 p.m. on June 9, 1948, Arch MacDonald, broadcasting from a makeshift studio in the Bradford Hotel, delivered the news to Boston-area viewers by way of television for the first time. WBZ-TV (Channel 4) had just made history as the first commercial television station to begin operations in New England—beating WNAC-TV (Channel 7), which went on the air twelve days later, on June 21, 1948. Thirty years later at a WBZ nighttime anniversary special in 1983, Mac-Donald recalled the station's first night on the air:

> All of a sudden we realized it was time for the news. The saws were sawing; the hammers were pounding. . . . I screamed and hollered aloud for "Quiet! Quiet! Quiet on the set!" So everybody stopped hammering; everybody stopped sawing. (But) there wasn't any furniture in the building, which was still under construction. So we had a piece of plywood and I sat on a keg of nails, and that's how we got on the air. A little uncomfortable, but we made it.[2]

It had not been the smoothest transition. A severe snowstorm in March had set the plans back by several months. The Westinghouse Broadcast Center, as it was initially called, to be located in the Allston-Brighton section of Boston, wasn't quite ready (which was why the early broadcasts were staged from a hotel). Getting a nearly 600-foot tower built seemed to take forever. Besides which, *Variety*, the show business trade weekly, estimated that the Greater Boston area only had around 100 TV sets at the time (though obviously that would quickly change).[3]

With Channel 7 saddled with ownership and management problems and Channel 5 (initially called WHDH-TV) not on the air until 1957, Channel 4 for many years pretty much had the field to itself. The station's early accomplishments and aggressive moves would help set the tone for the marketplace in the coming years. Keep in mind that because television was so new, there were really no programming playbooks at that time. Thanks to the earlier research on Channel 4's history compiled by Donna Halper, a broadcast historian, now an associate professor of communication and media at Lesley University, here are some of the station's early initiatives:

August 19, 1948: The first televised weather reports are presented by a professional meteorologist—MIT professor James Austin, who appeared on the show *Weather or Not*.

August 28, 1948: The first live local sports show on Boston TV—*Sportstime*—features Irving "Bump" Hadley, a former ballplayer and popular personality on WBZ Radio.

September 2, 1948: Boston's first live local children's show makes its debut with Carl DeSuze's *Surprize Package*.

September 26, 1948: Channel 4 expands its hours of operation to seven days a week (it had been off the air on Mondays and Tuesdays at first).

October 6 to 7, 1948: Channel 4 and the *Boston Post* newspaper provide rows of TVs on the Boston Common so people can watch the World Series between the Boston Braves and the Cleveland Indians.

October 20, 1948: Channel 4 debuts an educational show called *Living Wonders*; the host Norman Harris presents different live animals each week.

October 27, 1948: Channel 4 is on hand when presidential candidate Harry Truman comes to Boston to speak at Mechanics Hall.

November 2, 1948: In what is a Channel 4 exclusive, the presidential election returns are televised for the first time from the newsroom of the *Boston Post*. Arch MacDonald and Streeter Stuart are the announcers/reporters for WBZ.

August 27, 1950: A new talent show, *Community Auditions*, is launched that would run for thirty-seven years—twenty-five of them hosted Dave Maynard.

September 10, 1950: *Starring the Editors* makes its debut. The program features editors from the *Boston Post, Boston Globe, Christian Science Monitor, Boston Record*, and *Boston Herald* discussing the news of the week. The public affairs program aired intermittently until 1975.

July 28, 1951: WBZ-TV begins a major series of Public Service Announcements (PSAs) in support of Westinghouse's anti-drug campaign; in addition to the PSAs, WBZ-TV produces a documentary about the dangers of narcotics.[4]

There were some lighter moments along the way. After winning the presidential election on November 4, 1952, President-elect Dwight D. Eisenhower spent an eventful day in Boston. First, his motorcade got lost en route to the Channel 4 studios for a live appearance. Then, while posing for a photograph at the station, a clock (which had been taped to the wall to serve as a prop) accidentally fell on his head. Thank goodness the incoming president had a sense of humor and was not seriously hurt in the accident.

Much of the station's early success can be attributed to its owner, Westinghouse Broadcasting Co. (later called Group W), which by the 1950s had emerged as a powerful force in broadcasting as distinct from the three major networks. Westinghouse also owned radio stations[5] (plus FM radio stations in the 1940s) and television stations as the FCC began to issue permits for those services. The company owned five TV stations, all with network affiliations, in major markets: KYW-TV in Philadelphia, KPIX-TV in San Francisco, KDKA-TV in Pittsburgh, WJZ-TV in Baltimore, and of course, WBZ-TV in Boston. In addition, the company produced and syndicated successful shows, such as *Mike Douglas, Merv Griffin*, and *David Frost*.

Donald McGannon, who enjoyed a twenty-six-year tenure as its president and later chairman, beginning in 1955, was responsible for many of Group W's initiatives. Over the years, McGannon emerged as a forceful and unusually progressive voice in the broadcasting business. In his authoritative *Encyclopedia of Television*, Les Brown (also a *New York Times* TV reporter) called him "a model broadcaster" and "an industry statesman."[6] Under McGannon's leadership, Group W created all-news radio stations (including Boston's powerful WBZ, which is still going strong)—the first station group to create its own worldwide news organization. He also fought the networks on the issue of gratuitous sex and violence; required Westinghouse stations to carry fewer commercials than allowed then by the National Association of Broadcasters; and banned cigarette advertising from his stations before it was officially outlawed. He will long be remembered as a relentless opponent of what he viewed as the networks' excessive control over affiliate programming. Indeed, he helped lead the way for the FCC's historic Prime Time Access Rule (PTAR) in 1970, under which the networks were required to return a half hour of prime time to local stations.

Small wonder that *Variety* called Group W "the Harvard Business School of Television," since so many of its former employees headed other broadcast groups or assumed leadership roles at the major networks. Of course, there were some negatives. With good reason, staffers complained that Group W stations tended to overwork and underpay their staffs; others chafed under strict budgetary controls that at times prevented WBZ and other Group W stations from competitive promotion campaigns.

The remarkable success of *Evening Magazine*—an industry breakthrough in the area of local programming—provides a perfect example of Westinghouse's big-picture thinking. Indeed, Channel 4's *Evening Magazine* and later Channel 5's *Chronicle* had a lot in common. Both shows used a half-hour format and were aired nightly in the 7:30 slot; both featured locally produced segments; both were well produced; both represented major station expenditures and had large staffs; and both at their peak were ratings' winners and moneymakers for their respective stations. Yet each show rested on a very different concept. *Evening* was about "infotainment," a combination of information and entertainment, while *Chronicle*, at least initially, was more about news and public affairs. But unlike *Chronicle*, *Evening* never really got its due from the TV critics. "A collection of cotton candy features that will tax neither your imagination nor your intellect,"[7] sneered *Boston Globe* TV critic Jack Thomas. Noting the show's absence of controversy and hard edges, *Boston Herald* TV critic Monica Collins simply dismissed it as "fluff."[8]

But if *Evening* was "fluff" and "cotton candy," it never pretended to be *Nightline.*

It was a charming, slick, fast-paced, show that dealt with lifestyles, leisure, pop culture, interesting people and places, and tips on everything from backaches to backpacking. Typical segments involved a bull-riding orthodontist who worked for the Harvard Health Plan, a blind student-gymnast from Fitchburg State College, a seventy-year-old cheerleader at Tufts, and a promising local comic from Andover named Jay Leno. But its most important contribution was its focus on the local community and celebration of Boston and New England in its own bright, breezy, boosterish way. People saw their homes, their families, and their friends on television. The *Evening Magazine* van, with its distinctive logo, was a ubiquitous presence in the neighborhoods, warmly greeted by curiosity seekers who had never before seen a TV camera or crew. Indeed, in order to save valuable time, the van would flash two signs to local residents: "No, you can't be on TV" and "No, we don't know when the story is going to air."

The show's dozen or so tipsters were another local ingredient. If the information dispensed was often shallow or obvious, the tipsters were at least real people from the community, not polished professionals. The original tipsters included Maggie Lettvin, who taught an exercise class at MIT; Nancy Glass, a Tufts University graduate from Newton, on lifestyles; Linda Harris, a Beverly homemaker, on travel; and Joyce Kulhawik, an English teacher from Brookline High School. This motley crew of nonprofessionals helped infuse the show with a whimsical, offbeat flavor. Nat Segaloff, a movie tipster for *Evening Magazine*, who later became a freelance film critic for the *Boston Herald*, laughed recalling some of the hokey bits he did. "For the movie *The Greatest*, on Muhammad Ali, I fought my way out of a huge paper bag on Tremont Street and the Boston Common," he said. "For a film called *The First Nudie Musical*, with Cindy Williams, I took my clothes off and paraded around Harvard Square in a barrel."

Evening Magazine was also the first magazine show in the country produced outside the studio, entirely on location. It was the first to introduce electronic newsgathering technology (minicams and computer editing) to local programming. But most significantly, *Evening* was the first show to fulfill the spirit of the historic 1970 prime-time access rule for which Donald McGannon had lobbied so hard to encourage local programming.

First launched in 1976 by KPIX-TV, Group W's San Francisco station, *Evening Magazine* was picked up a year later by WBZ and the other Group W stations. Each local station produced its own nightly edition with its own staff, hosts, and contributors. In Boston, the best-known cohosts were Robin Young and Marty Sender, and later, Sara Edwards and Barry Nolan. At the time, it was unheard of for a local TV station to spend such big bucks on a local venture. Recalls Sy Yanoff, then Channel 4's general manager, "It was very expensive initially, about $750,000 (a year). In time, we spent well over $1 million. But it could also generate a couple of million in sales or more."[9] By 1978 the show had become so successful that it was picked up by twelve non–Group W stations, which called it *PM Magazine*. By the fall of 1979, *Evening/PM Magazine* was carried by forty-nine stations across the country. And even when the show peaked, in the early 1980s with close to 100 stations, the cornerstone of *Evening/PM* remained local involvement and commitment. Each local station produced its own nightly edition with its own staff and hosts. Advertisers had to be beaten away with a stick because of the show's attractive demographics, which tilted toward females aged eighteen to forty-nine who were well educated and often members of two-income households. The help-wanted pages of broadcasting trade magazines swelled with ads from stations in the process of building staffs for their own *Evening/PM* programs around the country.

In time, however, the *Evening/PM* phenomenon fell victim to its own success and changing viewer tastes. As it became more of a national success, it increasingly pulled away from local stories. Once drawn to simple, colorful characters from the local community, it now went in for Hollywood celebrities and glitz—Robin Williams one night, Vanna White the next. Say good-bye to Boston baked beans; say hello to books on dead stars. Scratch the crusty old sea captain, but get a load of those sun-kissed bikini beauties on a remote Caribbean island. The shows were also beset with internal problems as a growing number of cost-conscious stations became unwilling to pay for the crews, hosts, and equipment needed for the shows' local elements. In the mid-1980s, a number of *Evening/PM Magazine* stations dropped the show in favor of glitzier syndicated shows like *Entertainment Tonight* and tabloid shows, such as Fox Television's *Current Affair* and King World's *Inside Edition*. By 1986 the number of *Evening/PM* stations had declined to fifty and by 1989, was down to just twenty-three stations. The following year the show was canceled.

Looking back, perhaps the greatest tribute paid to *Evening* came from Paul LaCamera, Channel 5's vice president/station manager, whose own show, *Chronicle*, had competed against *Evening* for so many years. "*Evening Magazine* is at the root of much of the success of local programming," he said. We never would have tried a *Chronicle* without Group W's success in first testing the waters."[10]

SPECIAL LIVE COVERAGE: *YES, WE CAN!*

The kind of bold, innovative spirit evident in the creation of *Evening Magazine* was also apparent when it came to some of Channel 4's smaller-scale projects. For example, at a time when the women's movement was in full swing, Channel 4, working with the Governor's Commission on the Status of Women, sponsored a televised women's fair in 1974 called *Yes, We Can!* The station donated sixteen (!) hours of its airtime, beginning at 7 a.m., for the event, which was held in the John B. Hynes Veterans Auditorium in Boston, and attended by some 20,000 women. The night before, Channel 4 kicked off the event with a nighttime entertainment special starring Helen ("I am Woman") Reddy, Anne Murray, and Jaye P. Morgan. For the main event, the station set up thirty-five booths inside the convention center, providing reams of literature and referral information to women on issues such as contraception, adoption, investment counseling, and employment discrimination. Panel discussions were held on stage, hosted by station personalities Sonya Hamlin during the day and Pat Mitchell at night, while broadcast to thousands of viewers watching at home.

At one point, the event was interrupted by about fifty chanting women, some holding signs like "Liberation, Not Tokenism" and "Free Abortion on Demand." One of the leaders objected to booths that dealt with food, fashion, and beauty tips, along with the participation of big corporations such as DuPont and Westinghouse. The television cameras were briefly turned off and order quickly restored. Recently, Hamlin recalled the incident:

> I was hosting the program all day and suddenly the WBZ program manager called me aside and said there was a large protest going on outside Hynes Auditorium (about seventy-five women—Bread and Roses and others) who threatened to charge in and destroy the TV equipment and that he was calling the riot squad (batons, shields, etc.) to come scatter them! I argued with him, saying, "If this program is for and about women, let us see if WE have another solution. Please ask them to send in a couple of representatives and I'll put them on the air and find out what their anger and objections are about."
>
> Amazingly, I convinced him and instead of a couple, all seventy-five marched in and up onto the stage! I had been interviewing Flo Kennedy, a brilliant, feisty, outspoken black lawyer when they all appeared. So I interviewed a couple of them and the gripe was that at lunchtime we had a fashion show—"Stereotyping, putting us right back in the old empty-headed vision of females, this whole exercise is a fake etc.!" When I explained that the "fashion show" was to help women who had made their own clothes lines and were showing them as a possibility for starting up their own business in their homes or stores, wanting critique and information about what steps to take etc., they calmed down.[11]

If the unusual event underscored the cultural divisions of the time, it also showed that women could come together to find common ground, and that a local TV station had a valuable role to pay in the country's marketplace of ideas. The event made it to the front page of the *Globe* the next day.

THIRTY YEARS OF NEWS DOMINANCE

Which brings us to the important area of news. In terms of "firsts," as noted earlier, Channel 4 was the first Boston station to have daily newscasts, starting with the station's very first night on the air on June 9, 1948; the first to broadcast a half-hour special on *Sputnik 1* in 1957, featuring footage shot by sister station WJZ in Baltimore as it passed over the city; the first to expand its news from fifteen minutes to a half hour; the first to expand its news to an hour, and later to ninety minutes; the first to create an investigative unit known as the I-Team; the first to hire a consumer reporter; the first to purchase a helicopter for the news department; and, in a racially troubled city, the first to hire African American anchors. On the other hand, the station did have one dubious "first," when on May 11, 1948, a month before WBZ went on the air, a couple of Harvard students thought it would be fun to climb to the top of the station's new 585-foot tower. As a stunned crowd gathered, the police were summoned and the two were let go with a warning.[12]

In any event, WBZ's enterprise and penchant for innovation propelled the station's *Eyewitness News*, as it was called, to dominate the Boston market for nearly three decades. Its hold on viewers and deep roots in the community were so strong such that even in the early 1980s, when the CBS *Evening News* (aired locally on Channel 7) and ABC's *Good Morning America* (aired locally on Channel 5) were leading the national ratings, NBC's *Today* and the NBC *Nightly News* were number one on Boston's Channel 4 (WBZ being the NBC affiliate).

TEXAS TOM: BOSTON'S FIRST SUPERSTAR

One other factor in the station's news success should be mentioned, for it foreshadowed the evolution of the modern-day anchor. In 1982, at a time when news was becoming a major profit center, a *New York Times* story about Boston's anchors noted: "Because a station's local news programs already provide as much as 50 percent of its profit, such broadcasts are increasingly packaged and promoted like prime-time entertainment—with high-priced anchors in the starring roles."[13]

Thus, when local TV news was in its infancy and just emerging as an important source of information, a young Texas dude named Tom Ellis from a San Antonio TV station rode into town in 1968 to coanchor Channel 4's *Eyewitness News*. For the next seven years, Texas Tom proved to be ratings gold. He was colorful, he was charismatic, he was controversial, he was good copy. And, perhaps most important, he quickly became this town's first bona fide media star.[14]

The first anchor in Boston to capitalize on television as a personality medium, he combined a flashy display of animal magnetism with show-business savvy. He was also the first to be the centerpiece of the news operation, with the reporters cast in the roles of supporting players. And he was the first to demonstrate that the anchor could be the single most important factor in attracting viewers. Mel Bernstein, who ran Channel 4's news department in those days, recalls that "there were no personalities before Tom Ellis. Boston news was conservative. Viewers grew up on Arch MacDonald and Jack Hynes. The coming of Tom Ellis made TV news important. He was the first anchor who had charisma and shook you. He had a great ability to jump through the TV set." Tony Pepper, who was teamed with Ellis from 1972 to 1975, praised Ellis's ability to relate to the camera. "Tom learned his craft well," Pepper said. "He knew how to use body language. If you want to be attentive, you lean into the camera. If you look toward the bottom of the camera lens, it helps you to communicate more effectively. He would bite his lower lip during a sad story. He taught me how to bite my lower lip."

Channel 4 quickly learned that it had more than a news anchor in Ellis—it had a star. In what represented the first tentative steps in the direction of personality packaging, Channel 4's management took Tom to Milton's for a new wardrobe. The station, Ellis says, "worked out a deal with Milton Katz. I got twenty suits, forty shirts, and eighty ties. That's a lot of clothes. All the latest styles," he recalled proudly. Tom became the prototype of the local TV anchor. Tall, trim (six foot two, 190 pounds), and ruggedly handsome, he came across more as a Hollywood matinee idol than a journalist. Stories circulated that he and actor Robert Stack were brothers (not true). In addition, with his bulging muscles, macho swagger, and Texas background, he became a sex symbol: the town's first and only anchor-stud. During his Channel 4 days, Texas Tom played to the women on the anchor desk, flirting shamelessly on camera with entertainment reporter Pat Mitchell, consumer reporter Sharon King, and any other pretty young filly in sight. Tony Pepper recalls that Ellis could create intensity and feeling through his eyes. "I was the guy next door," says Pepper. "Tom's job was to make love to the audience through the camera. He had fun with (reporter) Barbara Marshall, who was the Dragon Lady. She wore black leather miniskirts even a year after they went out of style. But Tom worked best with Pat (Mitchell) because she smoked back. She had smoke in her eyes as well."

Although he had since settled down with Arlene, his third wife, Texas Tom reveled in his earlier reputation as a ladies' man. "That's part of the legend," he boasts. "I went through separation and divorce in those days. But I never took an oath of celibacy. I wasn't a womanizer, but that didn't mean I didn't take advantage of a few opportunities."

If Texas Tom was drawn to the ladies, it was equally true that they found him attractive. Sonya Hamlin, Channel 4's former cultural reporter and talk-show host, remembers him as "a big hunk of man" who had female fans waiting for him outside the station after the news. "At 11:30, they used to whisk him out of the parking lot, where women would be waiting. The letters he got in the newsroom were very inflamed," she says.

Despite spending the bulk of his adult life on the East Coast, he remained a good ol' Texas boy at heart. His favorite heroes in history were Sam Houston and Sitting Bull. He grew up riding horses (and was known for riding around on Cape Cod, where he still has a home). When he was relaxed, distinct echoes of his Texas drawl would come back. Over the years, Ellis evolved into a news version of the Marlboro Man, boasting a pair of tattooed arms and a son named Duke. He enjoyed talking about his physical prowess: "I was such a jock, you wouldn't believe. I got out of the Big Thicket (area in Southeast Texas) at sixteen and played football with the big guys at Arlington State College." He loved telling stories—such as the one about the time he paid a visit to a tattoo shop called Painless Nell's, in San Diego. "I got fascinated by a guy with a tattoo on a motorcycle in Woodville, Texas. I followed him around a store. I was three years old. At eighteen, I was in the navy reserve boot camp. When I got my first pass, I went to Painless Nell's. She gave me an innocuous little snake on my right arm. Nell charged me $12.50."

The performer's instinct had developed early in his life, with his stepmother pushing him into the limelight when he was still a young boy. "I always had to perform—playing the piano or singing—for an audience." As a young Texas dude he had a series of jobs, from boxing to sideshow barking. By the time he came to Boston in 1968, he was a seasoned veteran who knew how to play a crowd. Personal touches were important. He started with a wink "now and then" at Channel 4. "I'd get letters. People would say they liked my smile, liked me, liked my wink," he says. Then he added a thumbs-up sign. According to Tom, "Sometimes I gave a thumbs-up sign at Channel 4. . . . As a kid, I watched the aviators in World War II movies where the crew chief would give the thumbs-up sign meaning 'ready to go.'" If Dave Garroway had his peace sign and Walter Cronkite had his "And that's the way it is," then Texas Tom would not be found lacking. "Have a good one" became his personal signature. Finally, the trademark vest was added as Ellis became even more fashion-conscious. "In 1971," he says, "I went to Mr. Sid's [in Newton Centre]. The Italian tailor said, 'Tom, you should be in three-piece suits. You have a good body.' He put a vest on me, then snugged it up with a few stitches. Nobody in television was wearing those suits."

Along the way, TV critics and colleagues sniped at the Big Guy's limitations. Stories circulated saying that he couldn't speak without a script, and he wasn't regarded as much of a reporter. But Tom's intellectual and journalistic limitations didn't matter; the jabs from the critics didn't matter. Back then, charisma was more important than competence and credibility, or at least the present-day illusion of these qualities.

It has long been rumored that Channel 5's Bob Bennett, frustrated by Texas Tom's soaring popularity at Channel 4, which had kept Channel 5 mired in second place, was the architect of a plan to get Ellis out of the Boston market. He reportedly sent a tape of the star anchor to his friends at WABC-TV in New York. The plan worked, with Ellis leaving Boston for the Big Apple in 1975. Ironically, three years later, when things didn't work out for Ellis in New York, Bennett was the one who lured the Big Guy back to Boston—this time to Channel 5.

Ellis confirmed the story during a recent telephone interview. "I remember when he [Bennett] was courting me to come to Channel 5 [in 1978], he took me to lunch at a hotel near the Braintree Mall." That's when the general manager confessed. "You know Tom, I was the one responsible for getting you to New York. I wanted to get you out of Boston. I was the one who sent your tape to WABC." Ellis said he just chuckled.[15] Ultimately, he did sign with Channel 5 and when teamed with Natalie Jacobson, *NewsCenter 5* overtook Channel 4 in the 6 and 11 p.m. ratings. Texas Tom had done it again.

LIZ WALKER: A RACIAL BREAKTHROUGH, THEN CONTROVERSY

It is fair to say that during Boston's Golden Age, none of the local TV stations covered themselves with glory when it came to the matter of race. Boston was always considered a very conservative town in this respect. Minority reporters were hired, but only now and then. Given this context, Channel 4 fared better than the other stations. Notes Garry Armstrong, an African American reporter at Channel 7 for more than thirty years (1970–2001), "Channel 4 had the best shop for minority reporters. Black, Asian, and Hispanic. Sarah-Ann (Shaw), Walt (Sanders), Charlie Austin, and others were very, very supportive during my early years, even when we were chasing the same stories. While I always admired Channel 5 for its journalistic excellence, they lagged behind Channel 4 during the early '70s with minority hires."[16]

Sarah-Ann Shaw, Channel 4's first female minority reporter, deserves special mention. Hired in 1969, not long after the Martin Luther King assassination riots, she worked at 'BZ for thirty-one years, and during that time, effectively functioned as the station's moral conscience. A former colleague, who greatly admired her, recently said, "Sarah-Ann was a real champion inside the newsroom. She was such a pain in the ass at the assignment desk—always pressing us to cover this community event or that."[17]

Still, if there were any doubt that Channel 4, like the other stations, didn't have a perfect record on matters of diversity, we need only look at the fate of Terry Carter, a handsome black reporter and weekend anchor at the station from 1965 to 1968. Well before Carter's personal services contract was up, the station let it be known to the press that it wanted to reassign him to Group W's Washington bureau— supposedly a promotion. But Carter clarified the situation, telling the *Boston Herald-Traveler* that while he was about to go into the third year of his five-year contract, the station had decided not to renew its option. Carter's explanation was a lot more plausible:

I think the reason they dropped me was because I had become active in community affairs in Roxbury and they felt many viewers in the television audience might be alienated because of my involvement.

They had spoken to me about it several times but, as I told station officials, I feel that because I'm a Negro I don't have to become a dummy in a store window—I should have the opportunity of becoming involved and helping my people whether I'm on television or not.[18]

But Boston's insensitivity and lack of inclusiveness in local television was most glaringly evident by the absence of high-profile weeknight anchors. By 1980, other markets—large and small, North and South—had long since desegregated their weeknight anchor teams. New York, Los Angeles, Chicago, Philadelphia, Detroit, Pittsburgh, Washington, D.C., Atlanta, Houston, Dallas, and San Francisco all had minorities in weeknight anchor slots. (And let's not forget Max Robinson, who, in 1978, became an anchor on ABC *World News Tonight*.) By contrast, Boston's African American anchors were traditionally confined to the "weekend ghetto," as it was commonly called—beginning with Terry Carter in the 1960s, Jim Boyd (Channel 5), Jim Scott (Channel 4), Lyn Vaughn (Channel 7), Pam Cross (Channel 5), and Liz Walker (Channel 4). Indeed, Maurice Lewis, who did weekend anchoring at both Channels 4 and 7, did not hold back his frustration:

> For years, we tried to break the race barrier. We anchored on weekends to work our way up. It was no secret I was willing to work my butt off. But other people would get the weeknight anchor jobs. At WBZ I wouldn't shut up about it. In 1976, the station official told me, "You people want too much. The town is not ready. People do not want to see a black face Monday through Friday." I would go out and do a story on the desegregation of schools and then ask the boss, "Why is our own station segregated?"[19]

A breakthrough of sorts—at least by Boston standards—took place in 1981 when Channel 4's news director Jeff Rosser decided to take Walker off the weekend desk and pair her with Tony Pepper on the nightly news at 11 o'clock—the first time a major Boston TV station had an African American weeknight anchor. (He later placed her on both the 6 and 11 p.m. newscasts.) Interestingly, his decision had nothing to do with race; it was all about ratings, with the news director seeking to blunt Natalie Jacobson's enormous popularity over at Channel 5. A tall (six foot one), attractive woman whose imposing physical presence was enhanced by an irrepressible manner, Walker had the necessary attributes for achieving success. She had solid news credentials, beginning as the public affairs director at KATV in her hometown of Little Rock, Arkansas, and working her way up to reporter/early morning anchor and host of a daily magazine show at KRON-TV in San Francisco. A year earlier, she had won a regional Emmy at KRON for a three-part series on the Jonestown tragedy in Guyana.

Yet, arriving in Boston six months earlier, she was still adjusting to the peculiarities of its racial climate. She learned that certain stories in hostile white neighborhoods were off-limits for black reporters— for their own safety. She was also taken aback by the large number of racially motivated incidents. "Coming from San Francisco, Boston is a rough city," she said. "Every weekend last summer, it seemed that some kid was getting beaten up because of his or her color. It was new to me. San Francisco has bizarre stuff like Jonestown and Patty Hearst—but not a racial beating a week." Then she added: "My mom said that when she thought of Boston, she thought of the Kennedys and Harvard. But the city has a lot of Archie Bunkers no one ever told us about. You come into this city and you're always on your guard."[20]

From the standpoint of ratings, Rosser's gamble proved successful. In the years to come, Channel 4's Liz Walker and Channel 5's Natalie Jacobson would establish themselves as the market's most popular anchors (market surveys seesawed between the two). This would continue until one day in the spring of 1987, when Walker and her station would be forced to confront a personal issue that would later rock the town and become an inflamed public issue—a referendum on her character and her race—that eventually went national.[21]

The crisis began when Walker discovered that she was pregnant. Although she was single and knew that marriage, for whatever reasons, was not in the offing, she was committed to having the child.

Aside from the reaction by her highly traditional Southern family—they were shocked—Walker's biggest fear was that she would be fired. For there was literally no way her pregnancy could be kept from the public. When the story broke that Liz Walker (a) was pregnant and (b) would not be getting married, she knew her morals and values would become matters for debate, and her race would additionally become an issue. She and her agent Bob Woolf arranged a meeting with Tom Goodgame, her old general manager at WBZ to whom she had been close and who had since become president of Group W's Television Station Group. What now? A lecture? A scolding? A forced resignation?

Goodgame, a Southern gentleman, a man of conservative values, a shrewd businessman, was surprisingly calm. "Tom did not miss a beat," recalls Walker. "He just said, 'Well, we'll just have to figure out a way to work with this.' To me, it was like, Jesus, aren't you going to react? I thought he would faint and then say, 'We'll get back to you.' And he went on to say, 'The station has made a commitment to you. And we're going to back you up.' It was the first consoling conversation I had had. One thing he said was: 'The worst that can happen to you is some real negative feedback. But that can only last a few months. And then life will go on.'"

Initially, she and her station management decided to hand the story to the *Globe*, which obligingly ran a discreet story on a Saturday, traditionally the slowest news day. Instead of being plastered on page 1, it was placed in the Living section. The headline, "Liz Walker Is Expecting," was tactful, if a bit confusing. Expecting what? A network offer? A new multimillion-dollar contract? But if the *Globe* underplayed the story, the *Boston Herald*, predictably, went wild. The following day's *Sunday Herald* had a page-one story by gossip columnist Norma Nathan headlined, "Liz Walker: Why I'm Becoming a Single Mom at 36." The article, which the paper hyped as an "exclusive interview," was based on a five-minute phone conversation between Nathan and Walker. If Walker and the Channel 4 management had thought that handing the story to the *Globe* would succeed in playing down the issue, they were naive. In fact, it was the *Herald*'s reporting, not the *Globe*'s, that set the tone for the citywide debate on the pregnancy.

A three-ring circus took place on the radio talk shows the next day. Walker was skewered. As but one example, WRKO's Gene Burns spent the better part of his four hours of airtime attacking Walker's sexual behavior. He accused her of "celebrating" her pregnancy. He advised her to get out of town and have her baby ("Maybe go right now"), adding that it might be a good idea to "move out" of Boston. And he demanded that she publicly acknowledge that "she has made a mistake."

The story took on a life of its own. It was written up in a host of national publications, including *USA Today* on June 15 ("Newswoman's Pregnancy Angers Clergy") and the *New York Times* on July 12 ("Pregnant, Unmarried and Much in the Public Eye"). "I got articles from as far away as Sydney, Australia," says Walker. "The headline was, 'Could It Happen Here?'"

The syndicated talk shows—*Oprah Winfrey, Geraldo*, and *Donahue*—all wanted to book Walker. Who knows? She might have been better television than the segment with two-headed twins or the South Carolina woman who claimed she lived with a Martian for twelve years. Of course, *People* magazine wanted a story. Mike Wallace, who was vacationing at his home on Martha's Vineyard, placed a call to Walker on behalf of *60 Minutes*. In this case, Walker returned the call. "He said, 'How are you? How are you getting through it?' He said he wanted to do a story. The one thing he said was, 'If we do the story for *60 Minutes*, we don't want you to be on anybody else's show." Her answer was thanks, but no thanks.

The dividing line between a public figure and his or her right to privacy grows murkier every day. Liz Walker had no desire to "go public" any further than she had, and proceeded to turn down almost every request. Nevertheless, Walker's pregnancy unleashed a heated public debate full of racial, social, moral, and religious questions. Some thought that it was a private, not a public, matter; that she was being singled out because she was black; and that for a mature, successful thirty-six-year-old woman with an annual income estimated at $500,000, the issue was one of choice. But the most vocal reaction was negative. A number of people argued that Walker had compromised her position as a local celebrity and, more important, her responsibility as a role model for black teenagers. The loudest, most disapproving voices came from the black clergy. The Reverend Earl Jackson, pastor of the New Cornerstone Baptist Church in Roxbury, sharply criticized Walker on a WEEI radio religious-affairs show: "At a time when we struggle in our community with teenage pregnancy and unwed motherhood . . . and we are trying to create proper values, this is precisely the wrong kind of signal to send." Walker was further castigated in a nationally syndicated column by Carl Rowan (an African American), which ran in the *Boston Herald*. "This black TV celebrity," he wrote angrily, "obviously counts herself among the Jerry Halls, Mia Farrows, and others who have thumbed their noses at the old social and moral conventions without fear of losing their jobs or their stardom."

To be sure, it was a great story in the old tabloid tradition, to which even the stuffiest broadsheets were not immune. Celebrity. Sex. The mystery of the father. Perhaps a dash of scandal. It was an irresistible mix, and the *Herald* even assigned reporters to find out who the father was. Inquiring minds wanted to know, after all. The whole controversy was tinged with irony. Since her arrival in Boston more than eight years ago, Walker had been very active in community affairs. However, as some of Walker's critics pointed out, certain facts couldn't be ignored. Around the time of the controversy, a report issued by the Massachusetts Caucus of Women Legislators on pregnant teens found the birthrate among black teenagers in Massachusetts was disproportionately high.

Both as a person of color and as a local celebrity, Walker had always believed that she had a special responsibility to the black community. Even as a youngster in 1963, she was one of a handful of students who helped desegregate the junior high schools in Little Rock. "In a way, you're a kind of conduit for them. You're a conduit for everybody, but particularly for the black community," she said. But as a prominent public figure and role model, had she unwittingly sent "the wrong kind of signal," as the Reverend Jackson charged, to young people, especially to black teenagers?

Walker answers the question by recalling the time when she spoke with some high school students from a poor Boston neighborhood. "I had done my little thing on television news. The first question (from a student) was asked: 'You got that baby? You the one with that baby?'

The next question was, 'You got a husband?' My only answer to them was: 'I have a child, I am single, I'm thirty-seven years old, I've worked for fifteen years, I have a degree and half a degree, and my child will never be on the public rolls if I can help it. Other than that, I have no answer for you. It doesn't mean I think that every teenager should go out and have a kid. God, how absurd!' And with that, those kids went right on to another question. It was apparently answered enough for them." Of the hundreds of letters that poured in, Walker estimates that 90 percent were favorable. But the other 10 percent hurt.

On Sunday, November 29, 1987, at 8:31 p.m., at Brigham and Women's Hospital. Nicholas Charles Walker, 5 pounds and 15 ounces, made his entrance into the world. Two months later, on January 25, 1988, Liz Walker returned to work. On her first 6 o'clock newscast she read her copy flawlessly but was noticeably subdued. The media, as usual, waited breathlessly for quotes. A word about Nicholas. Those black ministers. Anything. They were greeted with silence. Beneath the *Boston Globe*'s headline, "Liz Walker: Boston's Single Parent of the Moment Is Returning to the Channel 4 Evening News Tonight," Bruce McCabe, a *Globe* TV critic, managed to write an entire article about the anchor's return without a single quote from the anchor herself, who declined to be interviewed. With Walker back on the air but unavailable for interviews, the controversy eventually subsided.

In time, a measure of tranquility and sanity replaced the turmoil and hysteria of the previous year. In a very public sense, Walker had been welcomed back into the family fold. The vast majority of people admired the dignity and class she displayed during the long period in which she was under fire. Her popularity was never greater. Both she and her station had weathered the crisis.

Years later, Walker's life took a different turn. In 2001, traveling as a reporter to Sudan, which was in the throes of a civil war, she learned firsthand about some of the world's worst human rights abuses, which included the wanton killing of civilians, rape as tool of war, torture, and the use of child soldiers. Appalled by what she witnessed, she helped cofound My Sister's Keeper, a women-led, women-focused humanitarian organization, which later built a first-of-its kind girl's school in a Sudan village.

Eventually, Walker made a life-changing decision to leave the

TV scene. In 2005, she completed her master's degree at Harvard Divinity School and was subsequently installed as pastor of the Roxbury Presbyterian Church. Today, she remains highly active in civic affairs. Indeed, when President Barack Obama and his wife Michelle traveled to Boston in the aftermath of the Boston Marathon bombings in 2013, Rev. Walker was among the dignitaries who spoke at an interfaith prayer service and welcomed the Obamas to the traumatized city.

LOCALLY PRODUCED TALK SHOWS

These days, it is at once both a fact and a sad commentary on the state of local television that not one of Boston's three major stations currently has a daily, locally produced talk show. Alas, they have long since been mostly replaced by syndicated programming, which is generally far more profitable for the locals. Hence a proliferation of shows like *Judge Judy* ("Boyfriend dumps girlfriend; she keeps car") and *Dr. Phil* ("My transgendered son is ruining his life"). No mess. No bother. No employees to pay. No health benefits to worry about. And, bottom line: no local angle.

But it wasn't always this way. During the Golden Age, all three major stations (and for a time one independent, Channel 38) had their own daily talk shows, which were plugged into the community and enlivened the local scene. Most of the shows were standard talk-show fare—an eclectic mix of celebrities, book authors, politics, social issues, how-to segments, and entertainment. Each had its own host(s), many of whom came from or were active in the community.

Over the years, Channel 4 had a variety of shows that followed the standard talk-show format. But coinciding with the burgeoning women's movement, at least four of them had an unabashed feminist bent: *The Sonya Hamlin Show* (1970–1975), and a series of daily talk shows called *Women '75*, *Women '76*, *Women '77*, etc.

Sonya Hamlin broke new ground in the area of women's programming. At a time when women's consciousness-raising groups were all the rage, other shows contained on-camera encounters, including one in which a female college student took on a truck driver in hopes of finding common ground. Another important show on breast cancer featured a film clip of a woman giving herself a self-exam, with her breasts discreetly covered. (Remember, this was the '70s.) And among her most memorable moments was the first-ever broadcast of a natural childbirth after following a pregnant woman throughout her pregnancy. According to Hamlin's website, "The effect of the series was feedback from thousands who then had the courage to try natural childbirth and to gain insight into the whole process of parenting as a result of this series."

Purely in terms of longevity, *People Are Talking*, a live, early afternoon talk show, was the station's most successful. But it got off to an extremely rocky start. When the show initially premiered in 1980 amid anemic ratings, a decision was made to go tabloid. In a 1981 *Boston Globe* column, I outlined the station's strategy:

> Keep the standard stuff like supermoms and celebs. But also go for broke with socko subjects on the sensational side. Never mind the news in Poland. Forget the state of the economy. Go for the audience-grabbers: a ghost-hunter who comes complete with audio tapes; a "vampirologist" who claims that there are forty vampires living in North America; a woman who believes she is the reincarnation of Queen Isabella; a soap opera psychic who predicts storylines; the author of a book called *The Mistress Survival Kit*, [written by] an ex-madam who was once sentenced to thirty days in a nunnery.[22]

Fortunately, *People Are Talking* eventually found its footing and was transformed into a lively and entertaining show. It achieved not only high ratings but also respectability in the marketplace. The show was initially hosted by Nancy Merrill and then Buzz Luttrell, but its last host turned out to be its best known—Tom Bergeron. Boyish and blessed with an easy charm, he went on to host *Hollywood Squares*, *America's Home Videos*, and *Dancing with the Stars*. As the Boston market declined, the show was canceled in 1993, but not before it had a healthy thirteen-year run.

SPECIAL PROGRAMMING

Channel 4 shined brightly in the area of special programming. Here are some of the highlights:

This Secret Should Be Told (1984). Several months after *Something*

About Amelia, ABC's groundbreaking 1984 TV movie that dealt with incest, and starred Ted Danson, Channel 4 aired a remarkable special of its own about sexual abuse—this time aimed at very young, innocent children who are also potentially at risk. The challenge was daunting: how to deal with one of society's greatest taboos in a tasteful, sensitive way that would inform kids without terrifying them. Producer Garland Waller, working with Susan Linn, a nationally known child psychologist and puppeteer, came up with a novel solution. Two puppets, a girl duck and a boy lion, tell a story about a friend who has a secret—that she is being molested. The puppets encourage children to "tell a trusted adult" if ever they have been touched in an odd way. The response to *This Secret Should Be Told* was immediate, with the station reinforcing the program's core messages through editorials and a news series. It also prepared a pamphlet on hotline help for individuals and organizations. A week later, *Time* ran an item about the show titled "The Message: Hands Off." By then, the story had gone national. Letters and calls from the Boston area and well beyond poured into the station from school professionals and parents seeking information. It was a long way from *Captain Kangaroo*—a breakthrough in children's television.

Whispering Hope (1984). It is terribly easy to look away from the more unpleasant aspects of life. Perhaps that's why, historically, the media were so slow to pick up on Alzheimer's, one of the cruelest of brain diseases. It also remains one of the leading causes of death in the United States. As of now, it is the only cause of death among the top ten in the United States that cannot be prevented, cured, or even slowed. No one is immune, though the disease is much more common among women. The subject had special resonance for me, because both my mother and my grandmother succumbed to this cruel disease. It can claim the lives of once-glamorous Hollywood stars, such as Rita Hayworth, and television pioneers, such as Donald McGannon, the head of Group W. Indeed, it was McGannon's illness that inspired a month-long special project at WBZ, culminating in a two-hour event: *Whispering Hope: Unmasking the Mystery of Alzheimer's Disease*, a one-hour documentary centered on the lives of the sufferers and the latest medical research.

This was among the earliest television efforts to draw attention to the disease and was in keeping with an innovative idea by Group W president Lawrence Fraiberg, who favored wall-to-wall, heavy-saturation coverage for its campaigns, which meant involving various departments within the station—news, talk shows, specials, and PSAs. The documentary was immediately followed by an unprecedented hour-long live teleconference orchestrated by WBZ, beamed to Boston and the other Group W stations around the country: Philadelphia; Pittsburgh; Baltimore; San Francisco; and Charlotte, North Carolina. On hand were medical experts, relatives of sufferers, and members of Alzheimer's Disease and Related Disorders Association (known now as the Alzheimer's Association). On a personal note, I was allowed to sit in the control room that night and got to observe Francine Achbar, the show's executive producer, expertly coordinating the discussion, with viewers from one city posing questions to experts in another. Exactly one month and one day before this impressive event, Donald McGannon died, lending a bittersweet note to the proceedings.

Jenny's Song (1988). There were no souped-up car chases or steamy love scenes in this TV movie to make sure we stay tuned. Nor would the drama conclude with the obligatory happy ending. Only in Hollywood could a Bobby Ewing on *Dallas* be brought back to life. Once again, a local station, this time WBZ, would show the networks how to produce a thoroughly professional ninety-minute original drama called *Jenny's Song*. The plotline was refreshingly simple, centering on the recent death of a family's father. And, with young people in the most vulnerable position dealing with the death of a loved one, it was appropriate to have the story told through the eyes of fourteen-year old Jenny Shields, played by a seasoned actress named Jennifer East. The production credits were notable. Kenneth Cavander (who had previously written for PBS's *Great Performances* and *American Playhouse*) wrote the teleplay, with Boston author Caryl Rivers serving as a consultant. Well-established actors Ben Vereen and Jessica Walter were hired for key roles, though local actors were also part of the cast.

The production was not without problems. For instance, a wood-frame house in Somerville originally selected to serve as the Shields's home burned down the day before shooting. A house in Newton was lined up as a substitute. *Jenny's Song* was part of the *For Kids' Sake* public service campaign developed by Channel 4. (Another component was a poignant, thirty-minute drama the station produced about divorce written by a twelve-year-old boy who had experienced divorce in his own home.) And, with Group W, wbz's owner, having established itself as a pioneer and national syndicator of public service campaigns, *Jenny's Song* was additionally sold to more than 100 tv stations around the country.

You Gotta Have Arts (1981–1984). Too little has been written about public service campaigns (such as *For Kids' Sake* just referenced), which have long been a staple of local tv stations. At their best, they provide useful information to the public on subjects such as drugs, health, and drunk driving. To be sure, such campaigns are not done purely for altruistic reasons. Falling into the category of enlightened self-interest, they also contribute to a station's identity and positive image in the community. Typically, such campaigns take the form of special programming and public service announcements (psas); they can last a few weeks, or even a year or more. At their most ambitious, they may involve a total station effort—news, editorials, programming, special projects, sales, and public relations. Unfortunately, too often such campaigns fall into the category of bland "do-gooder" efforts that are safe and risk-averse. After all, is there anyone out there who is *for* drunk driving?

Which brings us to Channel 4's *You Gotta Have Arts*. The campaign's purpose was twofold: first, to counter the image of rival Channel 5, which was regarded as "the classy station," and second, to meet a public need during a time of severe federal and state cutbacks for the arts. And so, Channel 4 (wbz-tv), with the backing of Group W president Lawrence Fraiberg, created a plan that would raise money for Massachusetts artists through a $1 million charitable trust called The Fund for the Arts, while also providing exposure for the arts through a televised campaign. According to the *Christian Science Monitor,* "wbz was the first station in the country to undertake such an endeavor."[23]

Joyce Kulhawik, the station's arts and entertainment reporter and a tireless advocate for the arts, was the face of the campaign and host of several specials. The station also forged links with arts organizations, businesses, and local communities. For star power, well-known celebrities, such as Geraldine Fitzgerald, Geoffrey Holder, and Marcel Marceau, were enlisted to appeal for money in charming PSAs, each announcing "You gotta have arts." (A stickler for correct grammar, Lillian Gish insisted on saying, "You've *got* to have arts.") The station also held free workshops to help community arts organizations put together promotional spots on which to advertise their events.

Much of the money was raised through a unique arrangement: the often cash-strapped organizations would get promotional airtime in exchange for a percentage of the gross from the events. As but one example: the Boston University Celebrity Series was in need of greater exposure for its subscription package of the Alvin Ailey American Dance Theater and the Joffrey Ballet. The Fund for the Arts received $56,000 (10 percent) from the promotional effort, while the dance companies were able to add to the number of their performances and more than double their grosses from the previous year. After only one year, the arts fund had raised $800,000 and was able to give out sixteen grants to local artists to create public works of art. By the end of its third year, it had met its $1 million goal.

With Channel 4 early on laying much of the groundwork, it truly was the beginning of a new era, a Golden Age of local television.

WCVB-TV: CHANNEL 5 BLASTOFF!

In 2013, Bob Bennett, who joined the Boston Broadcasters, Incorporated (BBI), investment group and later became the new station's celebrated general manager, co-wrote a memoir titled *How We Built the Greatest Television Station in America*. Though the book was largely a slapdash, self-serving affair, it nevertheless contained some wonderful anecdotes. In one such passage, Bennett candidly wrote about his personal misgivings when BBI was applying for the license, suggesting that the group was posturing—grandstanding in order to acquire the coveted license. Calling the plans "almost impossible to attain," he wrote: "I can tell you this. If I had been around when those promises were made to the FCC, I would have advised BBI not to make them. They were too ambitious."[1]

Too ambitious? He need not have worried, and fortunately, he was a man who loved a good challenge. Under his extraordinary leadership, coupled with BBI's impressive commitment to local programming and the station's willingness to spend money in pursuit of its goals, Channel 5 (now called WCVB-TV) would help set the pace for the rest of the Boston market over the next decade.

Just how did the station do it? We begin with Bennett himself, who remains a revered figure in the television industry, particularly in the area of local programming. By the time he became Channel 5's general manager in 1972, he was a seasoned broadcaster, having worked his way up in sales at KTTV in Los Angeles, then going on to become the general manager of two independent stations, first at WTTG-TV in Washington, D.C., and later at WNEW-TV in New York.

Early on, it was clear he adored being in charge of a local station—

to the point that he turned down an offer by board chairman and CEO Leonard Goldenson in the 1970s to become the president of ABC. Besides, in his memoir, he confided he didn't want to put up with the independent, freewheeling ways of Roone Arledge, the flamboyant president of ABC News—a man who favored safari jackets and hanging out with sportscasters, and who used to head ABC's sports division. One night, during a dinner meeting with Leonard Goldenson and ABC president Elton Rule in Manhattan, Bennett expressed his misgivings in no uncertain terms: "'Leonard, in thinking about me for the President of ABC,' I said to him, 'I think there is something you should know about me first. If I take the job as President of ABC the first thing I will do is fire Roone Arledge.'"[2]

So Bennett stayed put at WCVB and, I suspect, never regretted his decision. Always the mover and shaker, Bennett also became the founding president of the New England chapter of the National Academy of Television Arts & Sciences and chairman of the Board of Governors of the ABC Television Network Affiliates Association.[3]

Bennett was also a born leader. Blessed with good looks and the build of a fullback, he was the whole package, a real charmer, and charismatic to boot. No one would call him an intellectual; he attended UCLA, but, drawn more to the business world, he never graduated. Yet he was smart and savvy, and not afraid to take risks. And, unlike many bosses, his staff adored him, while rival general managers liked and respected him. "He could sell ice to Eskimos if he put his mind to it, and truth be told, they would be happy with their purchase," recalls Maria Morales, his former secretary.[4] In a *New York Times* article lavishing praise on WCVB, the legendary producer Norman Lear hailed Bennett as "the best local broadcaster in the nation."[5]

GOOD DAY!

Bennett's launch of a daily talk show called *Good Day!* (originally called *Good Morning!*), was one of his signature accomplishments. For several reasons, I'll spend a little more time on this show. First, it serves as a textbook case on how to go about creating a phenomenally successful talk show that, in short order, would dominate the Boston market, expand into the reaches of New England, and later catch the eye of the networks.

It was also a show in which I had a personal interest, for I was present at the creation, so to speak, hired as one of the show's staffers. During the past seven years, I had been a research associate at Brandeis University's Lemberg Center for the Study of Violence, mostly writing about race and the media. But when the center closed its doors in 1973, I was ready for a change and decided, given my interest in media, that it might be fun to work in television. As fate would have it, I was hired as an associate producer on Channel 5's new talk show shortly before it went on the air. My job, usually called a "talent coordinator," involved booking celebrities, musical performers, and people in the news. This was where I got much of my "basic training" in television, which proved invaluable when I became a TV critic. Finally, by working backstage I learned firsthand how decisions were made, what really went on behind the scenes, and how a local talk show was also a microcosm of the culture at that time.

There I was in my very own *Mary Tyler Moore* world; the timing couldn't have been better, since that classic CBS sitcom, which ran from 1970 to 1977, coincided with my time at *Good Day!* Like Mary Richards, the lead character on the show, I was a single, independent, career-minded woman in her early thirties. Both of us worked at a local TV station—she, an associate producer in news at WJM-TV in Minneapolis, and I, in the same position, on a talk show at WCVB-TV in Boston. But oh, the rookie mistakes. I once turned down a largely unknown singer/composer piano player named Billy Joel, because our show would have had to pay the New York-to-Boston airline shuttle ticket—I recall it was about $49—and, besides, I thought his "Piano Man" song too schmaltzy. Another time I turned down a local kid from Andover, a young comic, a recent Emerson College grad named Jay Leno. (I always wondered what happened to him.)

Bruce Marson, a former producer at *Zoom*, an Emmy Award–winning kids show on PBS produced out of WGBH in Boston, was hired as the show's producer. Low-key, with a mischievous mustache and droll sense of humor—you need that in the frenetic world of television—he was also skilled at managing the staff, including the "talent," as on-air people are called (which, I suppose, made the rest of us "non-talent"). With each of our roles clearly defined, there was remarkably little backbiting, which is unusual in television. Bruce used to joke: "If the show is a hit, it'll be called 'Bennett's Baby'; if it fails, it'll be 'Bruce's Baby.'"

His diplomatic skills played well in dealing with mercurial, often temperamental celebrities coming on the show. On one occasion, we managed to book the legendary Sarah Vaughan, a supremely gifted singer known for her smoky voice, three-octave vocal range, and enchanting scat singing. It was something of a coup, since "the Divine One," as she was known, rarely did television, much less local talk shows. Because of the show's early hour (9–10:30 a.m.) we agreed to tape her in the afternoon the day *before*—a rare departure from our "only live" booking policy. (You can be sure we didn't do this for Barry Manilow, whose people made a similar request.) All this, and a specially constructed set built for her on which to perform. Unfortunately, when she arrived at the station in a sullen mood, she announced that she would sit for an interview but would not perform. It was only after a lengthy discussion with Bruce that she relented and the segment came off as originally planned. And, yes, she was truly "divine."

John Willis and Janet Langhart were hired as cohosts, both of whom turned out to be inspired choices. Though utterly mismatched in terms of politics and personality, their on-air chemistry proved irresistible to the viewers. He was white, she was black; he was a staunch Republican, she was more liberal, especially on social issues; he was straitlaced, perhaps a bit stodgy, she was freewheeling and unpredictable. Lured from *Panorama*, a popular talk show on WTTG in Washington, D.C., Bennett's old station, Willis was a serious news guy; Langhart, a former model and Chicago "weather girl," was not always well informed, but, frankly, was the more interesting of the two. Drop-dead gorgeous and loaded with personality, she gave the show its oomph, though some were put off by her unrestrained ego. On one occasion, when Tennessee Williams was a guest, she asked the playwright if he would please put her in his next play. Dick Cavett once sized her up during an interview: "You're insatiable," he mused. Yes, but never dull.

The show was additionally helped by Bennett's bold thinking. If the competition—two well-established local talk shows, *Sonya Hamlin* on Channel 4 and *Paul Benzaquin* on Channel 7, each had a single host, *Good Day!* would have two (actually three, in the beginning); if the others were taped, *Good Day!* would be live; if the others were low-budget affairs and studio-bound, *Good Day!* would shell out big bucks on the latest technology for live remotes all around Boston. Quentin Crisp, the British writer and raconteur, once disparaged talk shows—ironically, during an interview on one—as nothing more than "amiable fatuousness." True, *Good Day!* wasn't *Masterpiece Theatre*, nor did it pretend to be. Still, within the talk-show genre, *Good Day!* would emerge as one of the best of its kind.

Making its debut on September 24, 1973, the show got off to a mildly awkward start when the station delayed the beginning of the televised Watergate coverage, eliciting angry viewer complaints. But month by month, *Good Day!* climbed steadily in the ratings and, within a year and a half, knocked both of its competitors off the air. Soon to follow were occasional nighttime versions of the talk show—highly rated specials called *Good Evening, Good Morning!*, which garnered critical praise. After the first one, the *Globe* gave it a rave review: "Live variety television returned with all the class and professional polish of national productions as WCVB-TV's *Good Evening, Good Morning* crew moved into the prime-time spotlight Thursday night and showed they can and will stay."[6]

At its peak, *Good Day!* was syndicated throughout New England, and with Bennett the prime mover, was eventually carried by seventy-one stations around the country, according to the Channel 5 website. Perhaps most impressive, *Good Day!*, along with Cleveland's *Morning Exchange* at WEWS-TV, became the prototype for ABC's *Good Morning America*, which made its debut in 1975. Even the name of the new ABC show came by way of Boston. In a 2015 phone interview, Bennett recalled the time when ABC executives came to Boston to look over his local show. "Dick O'Leary (head of ABC's owned-stations division) came up with a couple of producers to see our show. After returning to New York, he contacted me and asked: 'Would I consider renaming our show?' I wasn't happy about it, but agreed to do it."[7] And so, *Good Morning!* was renamed *Good Day!*, and the new ABC show, which is still going strong, was called *Good Morning America*.

Good Day!'s uncanny ability to generate news was a real strength. The events could be large or small—convicted Watergate burglar

James McCord making his first public appearance, or the disclosure by Maggie Lettvin, the show's physical fitness guru, that she regularly fed her family Milk-Bones. Its unorthodox booking strategy made for an eclectic mix of celebrities, newsmakers, homey regulars, and assorted weirdoes. Would you believe Nguyen Cao Ky, the former South Vietnamese Air Force commander and once his country's wartime leader, and Mister Rogers, the sweet-tempered host of a PBS children's show, both on the same stage?

The show could also be delightfully unpredictable, which only added to its appeal. Take the accordion segment involving that much-maligned instrument, mostly good for weddings and bar mitzvahs. One day, we booked not one accordion player, but an entire orchestra comprised of about fifteen passionate accordionists. Another time, we had on a Cuban band, with instructions to play three songs to be interspersed throughout the show. Unfortunately, the musicians' grasp of English wasn't very good, so they played the same song three different times. The qualities that made *Good Day!* so much better and more successful than its rivals and most of the country's other local shows involved the producers' keen understanding of the way television works—the need to be live and play off current events; the know-how in generating publicity; and perhaps above all, an early appreciation of how important celebrities were to attract viewers. For the most part, the show's rivals were a bit late in learning these lessons and paid the ultimate price—cancellation. Here are the kinds of things I learned:

LESSON #1: YES, TELEVISION IS A VISUAL MEDIUM. While this is not exactly a news flash, it was hard for me as a print person who thought in terms of ideas, to think in terms of moving images and pictures. And looking back at my time in television, I don't think I ever really grasped the difference; my mind was analytical, not visual. But Bruce Marson, our fearless leader, did understand. With a background in television, his brain was programmed to think in terms of pacing and movement. Or, as one of the station's directors used to say, "If it don't wiggle, it ain't TV."

LESSON #2: COSMETICS ARE IMPORTANT. While TV critics like to carp about the overemphasis of style over substance, cosmetics do have their place, whether it was the hosts' clothes (though Bruce could do nothing about John's dated white patent-leather shoes) or the delightful studio set that served as the show's backdrop. The overall "look" was important. On one occasion, Bruce looked up at a TV monitor in our office area that was airing *Sonya Hamlin* on Channel 4, our competitor's show (something we all watched daily). There she was, this highly intelligent woman, a former chairperson of Radcliffe and Harvard's dance department, sitting on a sofa, wearing a dated, bouffant hairdo. "Look," he said, shaking his head in disbelief. "It's a morning show, and yet Sonya has a black background and she's wearing a long gown. That's crazy." By contrast, our set featured light, warm-colored woods, comfy chairs, and separate components that could be moved around, all of which created an atmosphere that was relaxed, informal, and in keeping with the show's format.

LESSON #3: THEY DON'T CALL IT *SATURDAY NIGHT LIVE* FOR NUTTIN'. For whatever the reasons, our competitors' shows were mostly taped. It may have been easier and more convenient. No do-overs with live television, but the tradeoff was taped shows had a static quality. By contrast, *Good Day!* was live, giving the show energy and spark. On-location segments were a regular feature. One favorite was "Sidewalk Sam," an engaging street artist and social activist; Sam (real name Bob Guillemin) brought art to the public by chalk-painting his creations in places like Boston's Public Garden. (Known to thousands of Bostonians who enjoyed his work, Sam died in 2015, at seventy-five, some months after a roofing accident had paralyzed his legs.)

Even when something went terribly wrong, it could work to the show's advantage. Take the incident involving Lauren Hutton, the famous "cover girl" model, with a lucrative contract with Revlon, and sometime actress who was on hand to plug *Welcome to L.A.*, her new movie. For some reason, our cohost Janet Langhart, also a former model, asked her guest how it was she made it to the top—a question that had a certain undercurrent. "I just fucked around," Hutton shot back. Oops! Langhart quickly changed the subject. John Willis later issued an on-air apology; the Revlon people called for the tape; and the station phone lines were clogged with about 400 callers, a few expressing amusement, but most critical, some threatening to go to the

FCC. Of course, the next day's papers had a field day, including the *Globe*, which put its story on page 1, under the headline: "Bite Your Tongue, Cover Girl!"[8]

And, oh the excitement and backstage drama. Daniel Ellsberg, best known as the author of the Pentagon Papers and famous Vietnam War critic, was a coveted guest. But he once threw a temper tantrum while waiting in the Green Room, threatening to walk out because he was scheduled to appear *after* "Professor" Irwin Corey, the double-talking comic. Didn't "Mr. Pentagon Papers" understand? It wasn't personal; it was simply showbiz. Then, there was the time when one of the members of the Fifth Dimension—Ron Townson, the portly guy—wouldn't go on stage unless somebody put his hair up in rollers. (Of course, we obliged.) And, during a live nighttime special, a student intern had a seizure. Shirley MacLaine, on hand as a guest, raced to the poor kid who was out cold on the floor, just off the set, and applied mouth-to-mouth resuscitation. When the young man woke up and saw the famous movie star standing over him, he thought he was dreaming.

Finally, there came an off-stage drama that would spill onto the set of a live nighttime special. Looking for a headliner for a special, I booked the one and only Martha Mitchell. In 1975, the effects of Watergate were still newsworthy, and as the outspoken ex-wife of former Attorney General John Mitchell, who later went to prison, Martha seemed like a terrific booking. She was colorful, outrageously funny, and controversial. Still, it had been widely reported that she had a drinking problem, and it was jolting when she claimed that Nixon aides were out to shut her up because she knew too much. "I've been persecuted more than anyone since Jesus Christ," she once told syndicated writer Marian Christy.

Was she a truth-teller or crazy as a loon? Was she a victim or was she psychotic? We weren't quite sure; all we knew was that she would be "good television"—and wasn't that what it was all about? As a precaution, I was dispatched to New York to pick her up at her Fifth Avenue apartment overlooking Central Park, with instructions to escort her back to Boston. But as our train made its way through Connecticut en route to Boston, she suddenly jumped up in horror upon hearing a loud noise. Mistaking the sound for gunfire, she thought Nixon cronies were on her trail. As it turned out, her "persecutors" were a couple of kids throwing snowballs at the train.

Once in Boston, I dropped her off at the Copley Plaza and returned to my apartment to get some rest before driving to the station for the evening show. I thought we were home free. As it turned out, it was a mistake to have left her by herself. By the time a limo picked her up and whisked her to the Needham studio in the evening, she seemed dazed, erratic. Spaced out. Pills? Alcohol? Who knew? When the show began, John Willis delivered a gracious introduction, and then posed some routine questions; instead, she clammed up and would not respond. Silence. This went on for several minutes, which felt like an eternity on live television. Suddenly she rose from her chair, started waltzing around the stage, turned to the host, and said, with a flirtatious air: "Oh, let's dance, John." It was funny, it was sad, but it was good television—no, it was great television.[9]

LESSON #4: WE LIVE IN A CELEBRITY CULTURE—GET USED TO IT. In his book *Intimate Strangers: The Culture of Celebrity*,[10] Richard Schickel, a perceptive film critic and historian, had an interesting theory about the factors that brought about our celebrity culture. Advances in communications technology (the rotary press, still photography, movies, and later television), he argued, coupled with an expansion of mass media (from *Look* and *Life* through *People*, and more), helped create the modern star system, thereby heightening the public demand for celebrities. As the public had a closer view of stars, on the big screen, later on the small one, and in the pages of glossy magazines, people hungered to know more about them. What were they really like? Were they as appealing and physically attractive as they seemed? What about their private lives?

As television took hold in America in the 1950s it is hard to overestimate its place in the celebrity culture. Because television is such "a close-up medium," as Schickel called it, its power stemmed from its intimacy and accessibility, its ability to come into our homes, its focus on personality, and its capacity to reach millions of people at the same time. As David Blake, an English professor at the College of New Jersey, in Ewing, has written: "Television, more than any other cultural development, has radically changed our experience of celebrity," adding, "television has made celebrities both prevalent and ubiquitous, and with the rise of television came a whole new branch of the public relations industry. Public relations once focused on preparing accomplished individuals for the interest and scrutiny that had come to them. Now it involves manufacturing celebrities to meet the culture's seemingly insatiable desire for them."[11]

In other words, television now had the power to create or *manufacture* celebrities—from Lucille Ball, to Johnny Carson, to Walter Cronkite, to Oprah Winfrey, to Jon Stewart—all to satisfy the public's unquenchable thirst for stars. Oh, how we longed to know these people—to gaze at them, love them, worship them, resent and even hate them—we just . . . *wanted* them. And, of course, the Internet and social media have created still more platforms and demand. Calling Perez Hilton, TMZ, anyone?

In the early 1970s, celebrity bookings were considered nice but not absolutely necessary for local TV talk shows to thrive in the ratings. But the times were changing, along with the nature of celebrities. The movie-star magazines that had grown out of the Hollywood star system—the *Modern Screens* and *Photoplays*—were in decline, as well as mass-market magazines like *Life*, which ceased to be a weekly in 1972 and *Look*, which folded in 1971. Writing about the evolution of the celebrity culture, Kurt Anderson pinpointed 1974 as a turning point: "Then came the new zero year, 1974. *The Enquirer* went legit, the *National Star* was launched, and Time Inc. created *People*. *Us* and *Entertainment Tonight* followed soon after."[12]

"Public relations once focused on preparing accomplished individuals for the interest and scrutiny that had come to them. Now it involves manufacturing celebrities to meet the culture's seemingly insatiable desire for them," wrote Howard Altman.[13] In other words, television now had the power to create or *manufacture* celebrities— from Lucille Ball, to Johnny Carson, to Walter Cronkite, to Oprah Winfrey, to Jon Stewart—all to satisfy the public's unquenchable thirst for stars. Oh, how we longed to know these people—to gaze at them, love them, worship them, resent and even hate them—we just . . . *wanted* them.

New kinds of celebrities were emerging and *Good Day!* alertly seized on these developments. Besides movie stars, we began to expand our sights and aggressively hunt for celebrities well beyond Hollywood. The stars, after all, were the ratings grabbers, the "hook" to get viewers to watch. Initially, as the new kid on the block up against two well-established local shows, we were at a severe disadvantage. But if we couldn't compete with our rivals directly, we decided to go around them and find new sources for bookings. If we couldn't get the usual stars, we would redefine the notion of "headliners" to include news personalities, politicians, well-known book authors, sports figures—or anyone who was famous for fifteen minutes.[14]

Our goal was to have at least one celebrity or entertainment segment per show. Management was supportive, opening up its purse strings so that we could afford to fly in more stars from both coasts. We also established a special working relationship with the American Program Bureau, a prominent lecture agency located in nearby Chestnut Hill. As part of our working agreement, we absorbed the travel and hotel expenses of their better-known clients coming to Boston in return for an appearance on *Good Day!* One after another of the Watergate figures, looking to cash in on their notoriety, signed up with the lecture agency. After all, even famous ex-jailbirds qualified as celebrities. The list of Watergate characters making their way to *Good Day!* included John Dean, Jeb Magruder, James McCord, and Senator ("I'm just a country lawyer") Sam Ervin, best remembered for his investigation into the Watergate scandal.

Other lecture agency bookings included David Frost, Germaine Greer, Dick Gregory, Julian Bond, Alex Haley, Ralph Nader, and Seymour ("Sy") Hersh, a Pulitzer Prize–winning investigative reporter who had exposed the My Lai Massacre and its cover-up during the Vietnam War. The Sy Hersh booking underscores the lengths to which we would go to snare "name" guests. The main purpose for his Boston visit was to meet with his representatives at the American Program Bureau. But when I followed up with a phone call to invite him on *Good Day!*, he was none too excited. "Why would I want to come on your show when I could be out playing tennis?" he asked. Assuring him that I was a pretty decent player, I offered to make a reservation for the two of us at the Cambridge Tennis Club, where I was a member. He agreed; we played, though he seemed mildly chagrined when we split sets. Long story short: Sy got his tennis and I got my booking. We also set up a special relationship with the Copley Plaza Hotel, which had recently started booking musical acts for its Merry-Go-Round Room. This is how we were able to book first-rate performers such as B.B. King, Earl Hines, and Bobby Short.

As our ratings grew, more A-list celebrities began coming our way, with the notable exception of Warren Beatty. Our competition over at Channel 4 had begun to realize that celebrities, for better or worse, were the lifeblood of talk shows. Thus, the race to "get" Beatty, in town to promote his film *Shampoo*, was fierce. I had managed to book him first. But enter a new talk-show competitor on Channel 4 called *Women '75*, hosted by Pat Mitchell,[15] who was also the station's arts and entertainment reporter—and who no doubt would be reviewing Beatty's movie. She and her staff used their clout to get him abruptly "unbooked" from our show onto theirs. Though crushed at the time, I had learned another lesson. This was not just showbiz; this was war.

LESSON #5: IN TELEVISION, YOU CANNOT TELL A LIE—EXCEPT SOMETIMES. There is a special bond between the fans and the stars they adore. Richard Schickel regarded this relationship as "intimate," which explains why we often call them by their first names, such as Beyoncé, Bono, LeBron, Adele, and Oprah. And, as with any close relationship, it is based on trust and shared values. Unfortunately, in the case of the bond between a talk show and its audience, that faith can be violated or at least compromised by lies and deceptions—large and small—either to maintain a certain image, which is so crucial in television, or simply because of self-interest. As an example, one day John Willis arrived at the station with his arm in a sling from a minor injury—he needed it only to drive. Just as he was about to go on the air, he took the sling off. But our wily producer Bruce Marson instructed him to put it back on, which he did; it was good for "host talk" and made for "good television." A small fib? Yes, but did it matter? Should it matter?

Other forms of deceit were more blatant. Management executives are perfectly within their rights to terminate on-air people. Things don't always work out. But given the strong emotional ties between the TV personalities and their fans, those in charge may be loath to level with them lest it hurt the relationship, causing angry viewers to turn away. Case in point: Martitia Palmer. When *Good Day!* made its debut, the show actually had three hosts—John, Janet, and a nice young woman named Martitia Palmer. A model with some acting credits, Martitia had been living in Italy for the past seventeen years, but in her audition had impressed station officials. She was pretty, with finishing-school looks and a pleasant personality. Besides, as some of us liked to joke around the office, the new host spoke fluent Italian.

But after Martitia got the job and shortly before the show went on the air, our on-location producer Dick Mallory was assigned the job of picking her up at Logan Airport. Upon reporting for work the next day, he expressed concern. "You know," he said, "on the way back from the airport, we were talking, and it turns out this woman had never heard of Howard Johnson's or *Sesame Street*." What this says about television's values and priorities is a topic for another day. After all, in 1985 CBS News hired Phyllis George, a former Miss Texas and Miss America, as an anchor for its early morning news program. (The former Miss America lasted about six months.)

Martitia's learning curve proved too steep and she was fired after three months. No on-air explanation was given to the viewers; Martitia simply vanished from the TV screen, as if she never existed. And when the viewers called in to the show, they were told, "Martitia is traveling." Months later, when the calls had dwindled down to a trickle, the station line continued. "As far as we know, she's still traveling." To this day, this kind of charade continues to be played out over and over in television whenever "talent" is let go. Can't break that bond between the fans and their favorite personalities—the viewers could be mad and turn elsewhere. Gotta maintain the sense of intimacy between the two, or at least the *illusion* of it.

Years later, history would repeat itself in a very unkind way. In 1983, the Channel 5 management decided to terminate its longtime host John Willis and replace him with a younger man. Martitia was fired after only three months, but John had been with *Good Day!* for a decade and he was a genuinely nice guy. So how to finesse this unpleasantness? This time, the show staged an elaborate on-air party, complete with presents, nostalgic clips, Champagne toasts, and lots of hoopla and applause, all to celebrate John's "retirement." Long since having left the show, I was now the TV critic for the *Patriot Ledger*, and felt some sort of response was needed after watching this farce unfold on television. I sat down at my computer and angrily tapped out the words for my next day's column, which bore the headline: "Ah Yes, the Indescribable Joy of Being Kicked Upstairs." (That one was for Martitia.)

Which brings us to "plugola"—a more serious form of deception, which was all the more insidious because it didn't just involve *Good Day!* but rather many of the local talk shows around the country. Unbeknownst to the general public, Big Business had entered the talk-show arena via "plugola"—the use of promotional and sales techniques under the guise of public-service information and consumer advice. The viewer, with increasing frequency, was being sold a bill of goods by the corporate suppliers of just about everything—food, clothing, household goods, appliances, cosmetics, pharmaceuticals, metals, and fuel.

This is how the system worked: a guest would come on the show and be introduced as, say, a nutritionist, or chiropractor, or scientist, to extol the virtues of a particular product. For instance, Maria Rama, an attractive-looking, personable woman, identified simply as "a pastry chef," would perform a "cooking demo" involving the uses of chocolate, complete with mouthwatering displays of Black Magic cake with sour-cream frosting and chocolate gifts for the holiday season. But what the viewers were not told was that "the Chocolate Lady" was actually in the employ of the Chocolate Manufacturers Association of the U.S.A. At least with the Man from Glad, we knew where the guy had come from.

And so, over the years scores of talk shows were now basically fronts for companies and industries selling their products through pleasant-sounding "experts" in what was really a form of covert advertising. Hence the International Breakfast Lady (Quaker Oats), the Aluminum Foil Lady (Reynolds), the Pronto Camera Man (Polaroid), the Energy Lady (Shell Oil), and so on. Should the reader think this was a fairly harmless ploy, consider that on a single promotional tour, the Pronto Camera Man appeared on twenty-three talk shows in eighteen cities, all to push the latest Polaroid gadget. It was a long way from the good old days of candor when Ernie Kovacs had a cash register ring offstage each time there was a hint of a plug on his TV show. Having been an eyewitness to dozens of such segments, I was appalled, and after I had left *Good Day!* I wrote about it in a *Columbia Journalism Review* piece called "Plugola: What the Talk Shows Don't Talk About."[16]

LESSON #6: IN TELEVISION, IT'S ALL IN THE FAMILY. The notion of "family" is a precious one—not only in real life, but in television as well. Television plays to this impulse. Mary Richards's "family" included Lou Grant, Rhoda Morgenstern, Ted Baxter, and the rest of the gang. In Boston, Channel 5, once playing on this notion, had a clever slogan saying, "Five Is Family to New England."[17] And today, notice how often on-camera people invoke the same folksy image—whether it be George Stephanopoulos welcoming a guest to the *Good Morning America* "family" or Judy Woodruff alluding to the *News-Hour* "family."

In reality, of course, it's all quite contrived. These TV "families" are bogus; they are not our nearest and dearests. But the "family" image serves everyone's agenda—viewers can indulge their fantasies about their favorite stars, while the marketing departments of networks and local stations can count on our undying love and loyalty, along with an implicit promise not to click on the remote to find another program. Paradoxically, the staff working behind the scenes on a TV show (or in any high-pressure setting like a political campaign) can feel like "family"—close-knit, intense, fun-filled, competitive, gossipy, rife with petty rivalries and personal agendas. But as with fictional shows on TV, be it *Mary Tyler Moore* or *Modern Family*, they also reveal much about the culture, including the "family values" of the time.

This was certainly true at *Good Day!* By and large, our staff was a happy one, with lots of camaraderie and kidding around. Still, this being the 1970s, and despite the women's movement in full swing, not all the "family" members were treated with respect. At times, even by famous guests. One time, George Jessel, the former vaudevillian, actor, and comedian now in his late seventies, was booked for the show. But while he was waiting to go on for his segment, our pretty, young production assistant came running down the stairs to where our offices were located. She was obviously upset: "That man just stuck his tongue down my throat!" she told us. There were no consequences. Neither she, nor the rest of us, complained to any of the higher-ups. The dirty old man got away with it. (Et tu, Donald Trump.)

It was all part of the culture and—many would say—still is. Too often our boss Bruce Marson, someone we all liked, provided the women on his staff with unsolicited back rubs[18] while we all worked away in our tiny cubicles. God knows why "Take your clothes off" was his favorite greeting to us. He thought it was funny; we found it weird. Yet, none of us had the nerve to speak up or tell him to knock it off. He was our boss, after all. With some reluctance, I must confess that on one occasion, after a night of good food and lots of drinking with our staff at a local restaurant, Bruce did make a pass, literally sweeping me off my feet, as he walked me to my car. Nothing more happened and, in all candor, I was flattered. Besides, wasn't there an episode where Mary Richards and her boss Lou Grant briefly toyed with getting romantically involved? They, too, thought better of it by the end of the show.

But let me offer one caveat before climbing back onto my soapbox. Some of the antics referred to above may be traced to the television culture itself—television being a much more visceral, touchy-feely medium as compared to, say, newspaper newsrooms, where journalists tend to be more restrained and less demonstrative. Television jargon is revealing: a "tease" is a brief line or two to seduce the viewers into staying around for the next segment; a "kiss-off" refers to the payoff for a segment; an appealing or exciting topic is regarded as "sexy"; and let's not forget all that incessant, phony kissy-poo on-camera between hosts and guests. Ultimately, it is difficult to assess to what extent some of the *Good Day!* high jinks around the office were due to television norms or simply the sexist values of the culture—most likely, both.

On the other hand, something else occurred in our "family" that should be noted because it so clearly epitomized women's second-class status in the workplace at the time. Betty Levin, a large, maternal woman (she once played Abraham Lincoln's mother in a school play), was the show's coordinating producer—second in command to Bruce. Intelligent and extremely hardworking, Betty quietly went about her job of dealing with book authors and the show regulars; she also functioned as a kind of COO, making sure the operation was running smoothly, especially when Bruce was upstairs schmoozing with the big boys. So when Bruce received a much-deserved promotion, rising from producer to executive producer and then to the station's program manager, the expectation was that Betty would move up into Bruce's job. Only it didn't happen—she was passed over. In a totally unexpected move, Bruce's job was split into two positions, to be shared by Bob Loudin, the show's director, and Bob Raser, the show's on-location producer. Both were good at what they did, but so was Betty, who had more than paid her dues and who knew more about actually running a show. No one in management ever explained to us the reasons for this apparent slight.

Finally, a few words about race. Typical of the times, the station's management people—general manager, program, news, and sales directors—were all white, but for one African American man who was put in charge of paper clips. At *Good Day!* one of our two hosts was African American, and out of a full-time staff of about eight or nine employees, one, an associate producer, was black. As far as booking African American guests, our record wasn't all that bad, with a list that included Bill Cosby, Alex Haley, Julian Bond, Senator Edward Brooke, along with minority leaders from the local community, such as Elma Lewis and Melnea Cass. Still, I can also appreciate the anger lurking beneath the surface felt by black people working at the station—which extended to Janet Langhart, the show's popular black host. I am reminded of a conversation we once had during the time we all traveled to Portland, Maine, for a special July Fourth extravaganza. It was a gorgeous sunny day, perfect for an outdoor show, complete with red, white, and blue balloons and American flags strewn about the grounds. But before she had put on her makeup and happy face for the show, Janet turned to me and, in no particular context, her voice dripping with sarcasm, said: "You know, this is *your* holiday, not mine."

Despite many changes in personnel and numerous ups and downs in the ratings over the years, *Good Day!* stands as an incredible success story. The show became a vital part of Boston's television history, complete with a remarkable run that would last for eighteen years. Even *Mary Tyler Moore* only ran for eight!

NEWSCENTER 5: THE LEGEND OF JIM THISTLE

If WCVB was the House that Bennett built, his news director Jim Thistle was the man who put together his important news operation. Local news was a major profit center as well as the place where, as Bennett put it, "news made your reputation and set the tone for the station."[19] Dissatisfied with Larry Pickard, his first news director and an original BBI stockholder, Bennett replaced him in 1974 with Jim Thistle, who would turn out to be the most-respected, best-liked, most-honorable TV newsman in the town's history. *Globe* TV critic Bruce McCabe once wrote that Thistle might be "the most significant figure in broadcast journalism Boston has had for the past 25 years."[20] In a profile written for *Boston* magazine, I dubbed him "Boston's version of Edward R. Murrow."[21]

More than anyone else, over the next eight years Thistle transformed *NewsCenter 5* at 6 and 11 p.m. into the most thoughtful and classiest news operation in the market. By 1981, Channel 5's news would also become Boston's most popular newscasts in these key time slots, dethroning Channel 4's *Eyewitness News*, a formidable competitor that had previously reigned supreme for years. By the end of his lengthy, distinguished career, Thistle would have worked at four different Boston stations—Channels 4, 5, 7, and 56. But it was during his Channel 5 years where he had his greatest success.

A news junkie, Thistle began his career at Channel 4 (WBZ-TV), starting out as a student intern in 1963. Three years later, he became the station's assistant news director. By 1969, the news director's spot opened up. Thistle wanted it, but management wanted him to get more seasoning at another Westinghouse-owned station. His response was to walk away—a pattern he would repeat over and over during his broadcast journalism career whenever he found himself in an untenable situation. Later that year, he joined Channel 56 and created Boston's first 10 p.m. newscast, anchored by the late Arch MacDonald. But two years later, shortly before Kaiser Broadcasting, the station's owner at the time, pulled the plug on the newscast, an unhappy Thistle gave his notice.

Returning to Channel 4 as news director in 1971, he was promoted a year later to executive producer in charge of programming. "I hated programming," he says of his decision to leave in 1974, when Sy Ya-noff was Channel 4's general manager. At Channel 5, Thistle profited from having a boss like Bob Bennett, who not only gave him a great deal of freedom, but who understood, as the old entrepreneurial saying goes, "to make money you have to spend money." During the Bennett-Thistle years, Channel 5 had a news staff of seventy people, then the largest in the country. Looking back years later, Thistle said, "I had freedom at Channel 5 unlike any other news director in town. I was known as 'Little Roone' [as in ABC News president Roone Arledge] because I spent so much money. In 1980, the year Teddy (Kennedy) ran (for the presidency), I went over budget by $600,000. But that was the year we really solidified our hold on first place."[22]

In many ways, Thistle was an anomaly. In a high-glamour industry, he was refreshingly unslick, unflamboyant, and unpretentious. Gaunt-looking in appearance, low-key and reserved in manner, he seemed more like a political science professor than the news director of an important station. And in an upwardly mobile world where success is equated with a network job, he spurned the CBS and NBC news divisions, perfectly content as the local kid who made good. To be sure, his lifestyle was unique—at least by television standards. Born in Malden, raised in Everett, he graduated from Boston University in 1964. Married to Jeanne DeNapoli, whom he met at Everett High, the two had three children and remained longtime Everett residents. "I live in the same house I bought when I was making $120 a week as an overnight editor at Channel 4," he proudly recalled. But having worked his way up from an overnight editor to Channel 5's vice president of news, making about $70,000 a year, wasn't it about time he moved to a more affluent suburb? "I really like Everett," he replied. "I walk down the street and know the kids. My wife's and my own family live in Everett. I like to be among good, hardworking people."

A devout Catholic churchgoer who was active in local civic affairs, Thistle played in a local country music group every Friday night. Staffers at the station chuckled when he mispronounced unfamiliar-sounding words like "Izod LaCoste." And while other TV executives were drawn to Cadillacs and Mercedes, Thistle drove around in a Plymouth Voyager. "He's not a Champagne guy. Strictly beer and peanuts," mused Channel 5 reporter Ron Gollobin. Clark Booth, a Channel 5 colleague and a close friend of Thistle, noted: "Jimmy never gets on a soapbox or puts out lofty memos. People are charmed by that. TV is so full of so many peacocks."

But more than anything else, Thistle placed his personal stamp on the news. He had a knack for finding first-rate people. Earlier, as news director at Channel 4 (WBZ-TV) from 1971 through 1973, he named Bill Wheatley as his number two man. Wheatley joined NBC News as an assignment editor in 1973, and from 1995 to 1990 served as the executive producer of the NBC *Nightly News with Tom Brokaw.* At Channel 5, Thistle assembled the strongest bench team in the city. His hires often flew in the face of prevailing news values and assumptions, where too often bones, not brains, were the governing principle. Journalistic competence, not cosmetics, was what he valued above all else. During a recent telephone interview, Clark Booth broke into laughter recalling his old boss. "Jimmy used to say, I've got the five ugliest guys in television—Joe Day, Mike Taibbi, Ron Gollobin, Chuck Kraemer, and Clark Booth."[23] Thistle's heart was also in the hard news area, with a passion for politics and issue-oriented stories. Typical were his "Checkpoint" reports at Channel 5—in-depth stories that might run as long as seven minutes. And for years, Channel 5 was the only station in Boston with a reporter assigned full time to the State House.

In handpicking reporters to work alongside seasoned veterans like Chet Curtis, Thistle frequently disregarded a person's lack of television experience. Reporter Anne McGrath was stolen from WBZ radio; consumer reporter Paula Lyons used to work for Boston mayor Kevin White as a liaison to the federal government; Ron Gollobin, a former Nieman Fellow at Harvard University, was strictly a print journalist. "I came to the interview planning not to take the job," said Gollobin. "My print friends said, 'Don't do it. Television will make a whore out of you.' But Jim said, 'Ronnie, why don't you try it for a year? If you don't like it, you can go back.'" Gollobin signed a contract in 1975 and worked as a Channel 5 reporter for the next thirty years—along the way racking up five New England Emmy Awards for outstanding news coverage.

Thistle also had a penchant for idiosyncratic reporters who didn't fit the mold. He found Joe Day—a former *Providence Journal* reporter—languishing in the station's pubic affairs department and made him "chief correspondent." He hired Chuck Kraemer, balding and bearded, from the *Real Paper* who turned into an extremely witty and literate critic-at-large. (General manager Bob Bennett's personal choice was Channel 4's competent but perkier entertainment reporter Pat Mitchell.) From Channel 4, he snatched Clark Booth who, complete with a pronounced Boston accent, blossomed into a poet laureate of sports and later a dark, brooding essayist with the title of "special correspondent." And after Channel 4 fired Jack Borden, a popular twenty-two-year news veteran with a whimsical, offbeat style, Thistle signed him on a part-time basis.

To be sure, he made some concessions to the show-business realities of news. His decision to hire Tom Ellis, formerly a star anchor at rival Channel 4, was a tacit acknowledgment that sex sells, even in news; while "Dickie" Albert, complete with a joke bag of weather quizzes, was hired to act as a comic foil for the anchors, replacing Bob Ryan, a more serious-minded meteorologist. During the 1970s, he once had Chet Curtis and Natalie Jacobson hold up a Doris the Energy Duck T-shirt to remind viewers to conserve energy. It was all an obvious attempt to lighten up the format. "What we were trying to do was hang on to our image of being serious and credible and turn around our image of being dull and boring," he explained candidly.

An intense, driven man, Thistle regarded news as a calling. Years later, he bristled at the depiction of the television newsroom in the 1987 film *Broadcast News*: "What a crock," he said, branding the William Hurt bimbo-anchor character as "an insult" to local newscasters. And as for the portrayal of news executives: "The news directors were like animals. That's not how we behave," he said.

But Thistle did have a playful side. He was known to do mean impressions of Tip O'Neill and the late President John F. Kennedy. And years later, when he became the Channel 7 news director, he played a hilarious prank on his serious-minded anchor R. D. Sahl. Returning from the 1988 Democratic Convention in Atlanta, the anchor found a real-life donkey strapped to his desk.

Aside from Thistle's shrewd, if not unorthodox professionalism, members of his staff appreciated his thoughtfulness and integrity. "Jim always leaves you a little note. He never forgets who edited a story, who wrote it, who did the supers (name I.D.s)," said Channel 5 reporter Martha Bradlee (now Martha Raddatz). "During the last snowstorm, when the news van had blown a piston, Jim picked us up in Winchester." She and Clark Booth, her Channel 5 colleague, each recalled Thistle's role on a major story one dark and tragic night in January 1982. "During the night of the World Airways crash, our equipment broke down for a live segment from Logan Airport. Jim was on top of a truck in front of the terminal, with a screwdriver in his hand, dismantling the whole microwave unit," she said. Booth also remembered that despite near-freezing temperatures and a ferocious January wind, Thistle clung to the satellite mast of a television truck in 1982, in a last-ditch effort to air images of the World Airways plane crash. "We had been at his house eating supper that night when we got the call. He's out there holding this thing, and people were saying, 'That thing's radioactive, Jimmy.' . . . He was just determined and willing to do the hard work."

Such selfless acts inspired a general attitude among his employees bordering on adoration. "I signed my last contract in three minutes," said Ron Gollobin. "Coming over from Channel 4 to Channel 5 was like going from Buchenwald to Disneyland," quipped Jack Borden. "Like Bird or Orr," said Booth, "he lifts the level of play. It's an exalted feeling to be on the same court or ice with him."

Channel 5 reporter David Ropeik had similar sentiments. At the time of the shooting of Levi Hart, the Roxbury teenager killed by a white Boston policeman in 1980, Ropeik visited the area and filed a story containing the statements of irate residents predicting a race riot. "The next day," recalled Ropeik, "I got a call from Jim. He was upset I had so strongly suggested a riot. He was calm, reasonable, explaining to me why the way I reported the story was a problem and how I might better have phrased it. And, in passing, he mentioned [that] Mayor Kevin White or his office, the cardinal or his office, the governor or his office, had all called expressing outrage at the report. Here he had the mayor, the governor, and the cardinal on his ass. He didn't lay their anger on me. He dealt with the whole thing in a supportive way. He had legitimate points to make. There is no insecurity in the man."

But Thistle was not completely without faults. He freely owned up to his difficulty in delegating authority. Ropeik mused that in some ways Philip Balboni, Thistle's successor, was a more effective manager. "Jimmy is more at home writing lead-ins for the B section in the newscast than working upstairs with management, lobbying for his department. Sometimes management has to manage," Ropeik said. At times, Thistle's democratic style encouraged his subordinates to ignore proper channels and to take little problems directly to his desk. "I really do beat up on Jimmy for that," said Booth. "If a fire broke out on a Saturday night, they'd call him and ask, 'Should we have to pay overtime?' He became a father figure who inspired a worshipful attitude. I wish he was tough enough to say, 'We have a chain of command.'"

Thistle also admitted that he had trouble firing people. On one occasion, he was forced to terminate State House reporter Bill Harrington for his involvement in a car insurance lobby group. Recalling the "awful episode," he quickly shifted the conversation. "We had a cameraman with an attitude problem. Everyone wanted him fired. I told him, 'One more time.' Today, he's one of the best guys in the field. Sometimes you don't have to move quickly."

Looking older than his thirty-plus years, Thistle was a workaholic who, chain-smoking his way through the day, tended to drive himself to exhaustion. His one concession to his health was to add a little cream to his coffee. "The black stuff was getting to me," he said, laughing. No doubt his inclination to internalize his anger and frustration contributed to stomach ailments and occasional bouts of poor health. "He's frail," worried a friend. "He had a cold in January. Next thing they diagnosed it as walking pneumonia. The Boy Wonder is the skinniest son of a bitch." At one point, he actually resigned because of physical exhaustion. "By 1976, I had been through two years of busing," he said. "I was totally burned out. I gave my resignation to Bob Bennett, who suggested I take a five-week leave of absence." He subsequently agreed to stay. "How many news directors get a standing ovation at 5:45 in the newsroom?" asked Joe Day, echoing the collective relief of his staff.

By traditional news standards, Thistle's main weakness lay in a certain conservatism. Although Channel 4, under Jeff Rosser's aggressive news leadership, suffered from its superficial, souped-up approach to the news, his station was hungrier, more aggressive, and more experimental. Denying that he would rather be right than first—which would be news heresy—Thistle admitted that his chief competitor made quicker and more effective use of the latest technology. "Channel 4 is superior technologically. They have a lot of microwave equipment. The night of the World Airways crash, they got pictures from the field and beat us by forty-five minutes," he sighed.

Part of Thistle's legacy was his maintenance of unusually high newsroom standards, a tradition carried on by his successors Phil Balboni, Emily Rooney, and Candy Altman. As evidence, over the years Channel 5 is believed to have sent more of its on-air talent to the networks than any other Boston TV station. The list includes Martha (Bradlee) Raddatz, who went on to be a Pentagon correspondent at NPR, and since 1999, as noted earlier, has held a variety of senior-level positions at ABC News; and Jay Schadler (ABC), Ron Allen (NBC), Dan Lothian (NBC and CNN), Dawn Fratangelo (NBC), Dr. Tim Johnson (ABC), Paula Lyons (*Good Morning America*), Dr. Michael Guillen (ABC News science editor), David Muir (anchor of ABC's *World News Tonight*), and Arthur Miller (legal editor for *Good Morning America*). News director Emily Rooney left the station in 1993 to become the executive producer of *World News Tonight* with Peter Jennings—the first woman ever to hold that position at a network.[24]

In 2008, following Thistle's death at the age of sixty-six from cancer, and many years removed from his Channel 5 days, Natalie Jacobson, his former star anchor at Channel 5, offered some remarks that serve as a fitting epitaph. "He was just as comfortable changing a tire on a news vehicle as he was changing the lead to the 6 o'clock news thirty seconds before it went to air," she said. "We all felt we were doing God's work. . . . That's how a Thistle newsroom operated, full of passion, full of sense of purpose, the desire to get it right and to do it right."[25]

PROGRAMMING

Good Day! and *NewsCenter 5* were hardly Channel 5's only success stories. Historically, the station could also boast a number of "firsts": the first Boston station to produce live remote reports using portable cameras for inserts into the newscasts on a daily basis; the first to completely close-caption all of its newscasts for the benefit of hearing-impaired viewers; the first local station to carry CNN; and the first to produce an *ABC Afterschool Special* called *The Cheats*.

CHRONICLE

Launched in 1982, *Chronicle* is a nightly news magazine that, remarkably, after thirty-five years, is still on the air. The brainchild of Phil Balboni, then Channel 5's public affairs director, the show was intended to be more reflective and in depth than the nightly news. It was also in keeping with the FCC's "prime-time access" rule, which, hoping to encourage local programming, had set aside the 7:30 to 8 p.m. time period for non-network shows. Unfortunately, most of the country's local stations simply flooded their schedules with schlocky game shows and tired reruns—it was easier and potentially more lucrative. *Chronicle* stood out as one of the country's lone exceptions.

Even before the show's premiere, Monica Collins, TV critic for the *Boston Herald American*, hailed it as "a Boston television milestone, a project worthy of praise and support."[26] Some station officials even suggested that what *60 Minutes* did for the country, *Chronicle* would do for New England. The station's strong commitment was underscored by its initial investment of $1 million for the new show. More than twenty producers, correspondents, editors, and photographers made up the staff, churning out roughly 130 episodes a year. Over the years, the show has had a long succession of cohosting teams, including Mary Richardson and Peter Mehegan in the 1980s and 1990s, and presently Anthony Everett and J. C. Monahan.

At times, *Chronicle* could be wishy-washy on issues; some of the shows were uneven or even dull. But more often than not, *Chronicle* represented "quality television," as general manager Jim Coppersmith, Bob Bennett's successor, liked to say. Many of the subjects were important and timely: the state of the Massachusetts economy, Chelsea's urban makeover, sexual assaults on campus, depression, homelessness, growing up biracial, the challenge facing gay Latinos and black youths in Boston, and whether to legalize marijuana.

On some occasions, the program itself would make news. One of the most ambitious and high-minded episodes was a live one-hour televised forum with all seven declared presidential candidates in 1983,[27] including former Vice President Walter Mondale and Senator

Gary Hart, that dealt with the timely Cold War issue of arms control. The event went page 1 in the *Boston Globe* the next day. Sponsored by the Massachusetts Citizens Coalition for Arms Control and the Kennedy School's Institute of Politics, the debate was beamed from Boston to most of the residents of neighboring New Hampshire, site of the nation's first presidential primary. Besides Channel 5, now owned by Metromedia, the event was televised by way of a satellite to seven other Metromedia-owned stations, thus making the debate available to 25 percent of the nation's homes.

Another memorable show, this one in 1988, took a critical look at our criminal justice system, which included an on-site visit by host Mary Richardson and a camera crew to the severely overcrowded Salem House of Correction. Ten minutes after the show aired, which the inmates had been allowed to watch, violence broke out at the prison. Heavily armed police marched into the prison; an ambulance arrived on the scene to take away an inmate suffering from smoke inhalation; and inmates set fires and ripped out wall railings and pipes. Four of Boston's TV news outlets made it the lead item on their late-night shows. A few viewers may have blamed the show itself for "causing" the disturbance. But it's always easy to blame the messenger. In this instance, *Chronicle* was drawing attention to a chronic problem too often ignored by the media, including the Boston press.

When *Chronicle* first began, up against stiff competition from shows like *Evening Magazine, Entertainment Tonight,* and *Barney Miller* reruns, it badly trailed in the ratings. But eventually, the show found a winning formula—an eclectic mix of hard news and public affairs, in combination with soft features, more than purists would like, with topics such as maple sugaring, pumpkin carving, and, let's not forget, "Wilma the Whale," the lost Beluga, which washed up on the Nova Scotia shore. But let's be realistic. In the world of commercial television, which is ever more competitive and volatile than ever, such compromises simply represent the cost of doing business and remaining viable. Besides, let the record show that while Peter Mehegan traveled around New England in his battered old Chevy for his *On the Road* shows, he was also the reporter who traveled to Africa to report on the Ethiopian famine.

Over the years, *Chronicle* has performed well in the ratings, these days usually finishing a solid second to Channel 4's *Jeopardy*, while on occasion beating the game show. It continues to be a revenue generator, still finishing in the black, and has won just about every award, including two prestigious Columbia duPonts, a Gabriel for communication arts professionals, and numerous New England Emmys. Several attempts were made to expand the show nationally, with short runs on cable's A&E and the Travel Channel. And there are regional versions of the show on two Hearst-owned stations: *New Hampshire Chronicle* on WMUR-TV and *WTAE Chronicle*, consisting of a series of news specials on the Pittsburgh station. It never quite achieved the heights of a *60 Minutes*. But even after all these years, *Chronicle* holds a special place in television history as the country's longest-running local magazine show that, somewhat amazingly, has managed to retain both its audience and its New England identity.

PUBLIC SERVICE: *A WORLD OF DIFFERENCE*

Could there be anything more noble or ambitious than for a local TV station to create a public service campaign designed to combat prejudice, particularly in a town that historically has had such well-advertised problems in this area? One Boston station did—WCVB-TV.

The idea grew out of a lunch Paul LaCamera, Channel 5's vice president of programming, had with the late Leonard Zakim, director of the New England chapter of the Anti-Defamation League of B'nai B'rith (ADL). This led to both joining forces with the Greater Boston Civil Rights Coalition and Shawmut Bank in 1985 for a campaign designed to heighten public awareness and mitigate the insidious effects of prejudice. The cleverly titled campaign, called *A World of Difference*, was announced at a news conference with Channel 5 officials, Governor Michael Dukakis, and Mayor Ray Flynn in attendance. Over the next year or so, the station aired documentaries, special news reports, live event coverage, locally produced dramas, and PSAs featuring celebrities such as Bill Cosby, Stevie Wonder, and Rene Enriquez of *Hill Street Blues*. Within a year, Channel 5 had broadcast its eighth prime-time special dealing with racism. The creation of a 326-page course of study for teachers and junior and senior high school students around the state was the campaign's most important component.

To be sure, there were bumps along the way. After three months, Ed Siegel, a *Boston Globe* TV critic, expressed disappointment, sharply criticizing two back-to-back specials. He charged that *Franklin: From Santo Domingo with Love*, a documentary, was guilty of "trivializing" the immigrant issue; the other, an original drama called *Blind Alley* about an American of Japanese ancestry, was chided for having "nothing to do with prejudice." The review was headlined "So Far, a Weak Ch. 5 Campaign."[28] Some of the station's efforts seemed more geared to entertainment than enlightenment, as when Rory O'Connor, who produced a live televised benefit show, *Rock Against Racism*, tried to explain the concert's purpose to the *Boston Herald*: "Anyone who is really into music can't be a racist."[29] (Really?)

But overall, in terms of its high-minded goals and elaborate efforts, the campaign should be judged a major success. Big topic. Big effort by a local station. Among the many awards the station received for this campaign was a coveted Peabody, which underscored the station's goal of "trying to do something about prejudice rather than just talk about it." The ADL was so pleased with the campaign that it eventually took it over and rolled it out nationally, as an antibias educational training program for high school students and others. Reflecting on *A World of Difference* many years later, LaCamera calls it "certainly one of the most significant, important, and impactful of WCVB's varied local programming and community service initiatives, if not the most so."[30]

"Significant" yes, but how "impactful"? Tough question. For other than testimonials, the outcomes of this laudable campaign by independent researchers were never measured in a scientific way, according to Donna Latson Gittens, the former Channel 5 executive who oversaw the campaign. In the final analysis, though, Channel 5's ambitious antidiscrimination campaign serves as a potent reminder of just how deeply rooted the race issue is in this country's DNA, and how much work remains to be done.

SPECIALS

Over the years, Channel 5 turned out hundreds of ambitious and well-produced specials, many of them award winning and critically acclaimed. Here are some of my favorites:

No Place Like Home: Foster Care in Massachusetts (1980). In terms of having a tangible impact on public policy, *No Place Like Home* qualifies as a superb example. This program took a hard look at the 1978 case of Baby Jennifer, a two-year-old child from Somerville whose beaten and dismembered body was found in a local dump. Her parents, Denise and Edward Gallison, were later convicted of manslaughter and also found guilty of physically abusing their three-year-old son. The public outcry in the aftermath of Channel 5's powerful, award-winning documentary helped pave the way for sweeping state reforms of the state's foster care system.

A Day in the Life of Massachusetts (1985). On a late summer day, the station dispatched ten camera crews and eight still photographers to 200 locations all over Massachusetts over a twenty-four-hour period. The result was a stunning visual portrait of our daily lives: horses in Foxboro put through their early morning paces; an artist in Woods Hole putting the finishing touches on a watercolor; an earnest young man in Lynn signing up for the Marine Corps. Along with Tony Kahn's understated narration, cameras lingered on the bits and pieces of our everyday lives, as distinct from the death and destruction featured on the nightly news. Not everything was perfect. We learned that over the course of the twenty-four hours, 217 people were born, 165 people died, and the Central Artery was never not clogged with traffic and loud, obnoxious drivers. These things, too, are part of life. Would that we could all take a break from our frenetic, overprogrammed lives to understand that life's simple pleasures are often the most beautiful. That was the message of this exquisite special, produced by Jerry Kirschenbaum.

Summer Solstice (1981). On the basis of its sheer ambition, the use of an original script by a Massachusetts native, a cast headed by two Hollywood screen legends, and the purchase of the film by a major network, this locally produced TV film project was considered by some the station's crowning achievement. Designed to seek out creative TV talent in areas outside of New York and Los Angeles, this experimental project was conceived by Bruce Marson, now the station's vice president of programming, working in partnership with a gifted producer named Stephen Schlow. It began with a screenwriting contest, resulting in more than 400 submissions; the winning script was by Bill Phillips, originally from Brockton, Massachusetts. Henry Fonda, Myrna Loy, Lindsay Crouse, and Stephen Collins were hired to star in the film. Ralph Rosenbloom, who previously had worked on several Woody Allen movies, directed. At the time, Fonda happened to be in New Hampshire filming *On Golden Pond*, and after reading the script, agreed to star on condition Myrna Loy would play opposite him. General manager Bob Bennett remembered his last telephone conversation with the elderly actor who was not in good health. "Don't ask me why I'll do it, but I'll do it," he grumbled.[31]

The result was *Summer Solstice*, which centered on Joshua and Margaret Turner, an elderly couple who travel to Cape Cod, where they first met and fell in love, and now assess their lives after fifty years of marriage. The production, which cost $450,000 to $500,000 to make—a relatively modest sum—was filmed on Cape Cod and in Boston. Forty-four members of the crew were from Massachusetts, as were eight members of the cast. The film received rave reviews from the local TV critics. Meanwhile, ABC optioned the film, then preempted a block of programming to air it for a national audience. While expressing a few reservations, *New York Times* TV critic John J. O'Connor concluded: "*Summer Solstice* would represent an outstanding credit for any producing organization."[32]

Given these and so many other of the station's exceptional accomplishments, the national press was beginning to notice. Under the headline "Some Say This Is America's Best TV Station," a memorable *New York Times* story in 1981 opened with the following question:

> Can a local commercial television station afford to originate dozens of hours of its own shows, offer regular prime-time programs on health, the law and minority issues, feature five separate newscasts a day and spend $500,000 on a series of Saturday-morning children's programs? . . .
>
> The quality, quantity and diversity of its local programs have prompted people ranging from producer Norman Lear to ABC News President Roone Arledge to suggest that WCVB may be the best commercial television station in America. And in the past several years, it has begun to generate impressive profits as well.[33]

CHANNELS 4 AND 5 DUKE IT OUT

Over the years, Channels 4 and 5 would continue to duke it out for market supremacy. But just as the *New York Times* in 1981 had suggested that WCVB was quite possibly the country's best commercial station, the market conditions changed over the next few years, owing to two successive sales of WCVB to media conglomerates—first to Metromedia (1981), and then to the Hearst Corporation (1986). Channel 5 would still be very productive, though perhaps less of a charming and adventurous mom-and-pop store than when it was locally owned.

In the meantime, Group W's WBZ, perhaps tired of being outshined by its rival and sensing a changing television marketplace, enjoyed its own period of revitalization and growth. In 1986, the editors of *Channels: The Business of Communications*, an industry magazine, asked me to write an article assessing Boston's high-profile TV market. The piece was to be included in the magazine's annual "Salute to Excellence" issue, which honored various industry leaders in television, including CBS *Sunday Morning, Late Night with David Letterman*, director Jay Sandrich (*Mary Tyler Moore, The Cosby Show*), and *Cagney & Lacey*, the landmark female cop show. Taking note of various changes in the Boston market, my own conclusion was as follows: "WBZ has eclipsed WCVB as Boston's strongest station, and didn't compromise its values in the process. WBZ remains the jewel in Westinghouse's crown, and Boston is still the home of what may be the finest local TV station in America."[34]

And so, two Boston TV stations were now vying to be the best in America—further evidence of the market's glory days. Which was the greater station, Channel 4 or Channel 5? Tough call. My own view is that, at different times in their respective histories, each could lay claim to being Boston's (and the country's) best. There were advocates for both sides. In a lengthy 1987 *Boston Business* article, Caroline Knapp clearly favored Channel 5: "By 1982, Channel 5 was a humming machine. . . . Its news and programming departments brimmed with broadcasting awards—more than 300 of them, including national and regional Emmys, prestigious Gabriels from watchdog groups, the print press and academics, plus the first Peabody, the industry's equivalent of a Pulitzer, ever granted to a station for overall excellence."[35]

Not surprisingly, Francine Achbar, wbz's former executive producer of programming and later director of programming and client marketing, would beg to differ: "Back then we thought it was normal to receive a letter every couple of months from some prestigious award organization like the Columbia duPonts or the Gabriels or Action for Children's Television (ACT). I'd put on my black velvet dress and go off to yet another black-tie event to be honored for our own programming team's work! Those were the days."[36]

In any event, each station over the long haul would continue to challenge the other, while bringing out the best in both. And, in the end, as they say, "you pays your money and you takes your choice." My own view is that if there were any real differences between these two great stations it involved their respective sensibilities. Channel 4 was the slicker, grittier, and more aggressive; Channel 5, the more cerebral, laid-back, and thoughtful. Channel 4 would tend to do something first (*Evening Magazine*), while Channel 5 would come along later and do it as well, if not better (*Chronicle*). Also, Channel 4, located in the Allston-Brighton section of Boston, was more urban, more racially and ethnically diverse. Channel 5, located in Needham, outside of Boston, was primarily a bedroom community and had a more suburban outlook. At the risk of getting letters, I'd say that Channel 4 seemed a little more (liberal) Democratic, while Channel 5, a little more (moderate) Republican. In a broader sense, though, Achbar may have grasped the larger significance of these two worthy rivals, as they "duked" it out in the 1980s:

> The point is less who was better, wbz or wcvb, but rather that we were pretty much the only stations in the country doing so much creative local programming—producing nationally syndicated shows like *Evening/PM*, syndicated public service campaigns like *For Kids' Sake* that included programming, sponsorable vignettes, and made-for-TV movies—all revenue producing as well as tackling challenging issues like Alzheimer's disease, child sex abuse, and domestic violence in innovative ways.[37]

WNEV-TV: CHANNEL 7 DECLARES WAR

As we have seen, the Boston market was blessed with two great local TV stations during the Golden Age—Channel 4 (WBZ-TV) and Channel 5 (WCVB-TV)—both of which, justifiably, had earned national reputations.

And, then there was the market laggard—little, lowly, laughable Channel 7 (WNAC-TV). On the air since June 21, 1948, the station was owned and run by General Tire, which later purchased RKO Radio Pictures (and was subsequently renamed RKO General in 1959). But RKO proved an irresponsible and unethical owner, later admitting to federal charges of financial fraud over illegal political contributions and bribes, and all but running the station into the ground. As the years went by, Channel 7 emerged as the black sheep of the neighborhood, the market's also-ran. By 1969, RKO's fitness to hold a television license was under challenge by numerous groups in a bitter court battle that seemed to go on forever. Finally, on April 19, 1982, WRKO's license to operate WNAC-TV in Boston was revoked when its last-ditch appeal to the U.S. Supreme Court failed, and David Mugar's New England Television Corporation was subsequently awarded a license. After several weeks of negotiations with RKO, NETV announced on May 7 that it had purchased WNAC-TV's facilities, reportedly for $22 million, and would officially go on the air on May 22.

At long last, the bad guys had been run out of town. Time for a fresh start, a reversal of fortune, a chance to put the station's wretched past behind. The air was filled with anticipation, while 280 jittery employees wondered if they still had jobs—despite promises by the new management that no more than fifteen employees would be laid off.

The new station was issued a new set of call letters: WNEV-TV; a civic-minded board of directors was now in place. And as circumstances would have it, three days before WNEV went on the air, Metromedia, the country's fourth-largest broadcasting chain, announced that it had acquired WCVB from BBI—thus leaving WNEV as the Boston market's only locally owned station.

With WNEV officially signing on just before 6 a.m. on May 22, 1982, the stockholders, employees, and their families gathered together later that morning in the main studio for a Champagne brunch, dining on sausages, rolls, and pastries. Their excitement was punctuated by the station's quick launch of a $250,000 advertising blitz, complete with full-page ads in the *Boston Globe* and *Boston Herald*, proudly announcing, "There's a New Day Dawning."

Interestingly enough, before officially going on the air, David Mugar declined to reveal his new programming plans to the *Globe*. "Why let Bob Bennett at Channel 5 and Sy Yanoff at Channel 4 know what we're up to?" he asked rhetorically, noting that only one copy of the plans existed. "I keep it here in a safe in my office, which is locked every single night, and nobody but me has a key."[1] A little nervousness on Mugar's part may have been understandable. For despite the hope for "a new day dawning," the truth is that like many a "failed state" in the Mideast, the new owner and his associates had basically inherited a failed TV station—one that lacked a progressive tradition, or any sort of responsible leadership or accountability to its viewers.

The particulars of the station's troubled past are important, for they demonstrate what the new owners were up against and provide a context for the drastic, ill-fated actions yet to come. Traditionally, news was not only a local station's major profit center; it was the source of bragging rights and prestige in the marketplace. Yet over the course of RKO's thirty-four years of ownership, the station would commit one blunder after another, much to the delight of its competitors, while providing reams of delicious material for the town's TV critics and columnists. Except for a few times in its history, the old Channel 7 would remain in the ratings cellar, usually coming in a distant third behind the other two network affiliates, Channels 4 and 5. At one point, its 6 p.m. news even ran behind *Three's Company* reruns on Channel 56 (WLVI-TV), an independent station.

But the ratings were merely a symptom of more fundamental problems. With one personnel change after another, the station was a revolving door for its top management. During one five-year period, from 1976 to 1981, WNAC went through no fewer than five general managers, and at one point, had no top manager for a year. Following the departure of news director Mel Bernstein in 1977, for the next five years the station had no fewer than six people in that important position, counting Dick Graff and Jack Fitzgerald, each of whom held the job twice. With such a leadership vacuum, the station was forever playing catch-up. Around 1960, its 11 p.m. newscast was simply made up of an announcer reading the news, while the viewers saw "News," "Weather," and "Sports" slides on their TV screens. It wasn't until the other network affiliates—Channels 4 and 5—were showing up their rival that Channel 7 modernized its newscast, using an on-camera anchor and filmed stories from its reporters in the field. In 1975, Channel 7 expanded its 6 p.m. news from thirty minutes to an hour—the last of the "big three" affiliates to do so. Station executives once auditioned 400 young women before deciding on seven weather girls—one for every day of the week ("Miss Monday," "Miss Tuesday," and so on).

But that was nothing compared to the Jay Scott fiasco. In 1974, when news director Mel Bernstein was staying at a Ramada Inn in Denver, or so the story goes, he flipped on the local news and eyed a young, pretty boy on the screen. Thinking the kid—who looked like a surfer dude and appeared to be all of twenty-one years old—was the answer to the third-rate and third-rated station's prayers, he and his (then) general manager Jim Coppersmith hired the young man as an anchor for the 6 and 11 p.m. news. Then, they made a fateful decision to market him as a sex symbol. They changed his name from J. Hugh Sprott to Jay Scott and bleached his sandy-brown hair blonde. And finally, the pièce de résistance—they unleashed an advertising campaign with the now-infamous tagline in bold letters: "WE FOUND OUR ANCHORMAN IN A MOTEL ROOM IN DENVER."

Of course, the press had a field day. Even when the poor guy was fired ten months later, the *Globe*'s Jack Thomas couldn't resist one last swipe: "This is not meant to be catty or captious, but if you look carefully under Jay Scott's face, you'll notice the beginnings of a second chin, and while that may not be the reason he was fired last week from his $59,000-a-year job as anchorman at Channel 7, neither does it bode well for a 23-year-old boy who depends on his good looks for his income."[2]

Then there was the "alleged news" incident, involving Jack Cole, hired to anchor the WNAC news in the late 1970s. Though the newsman was a sharp, serious guy, he was also cursed with a loose tongue and a very large ego; wherever he went, he seemed to court controversy. One night around Christmas, the newscast featured a story about how to clean a chimney for Santa Claus. When the camera returned to Cole, he couldn't resist. "We'll be back with more alleged news," he sneered, his voice dripping with sarcasm. He was initially suspended for a week, and then the station declined to renew his contract in 1979—whereupon Cole turned around and formed a college campus and nightclub act called "Alleged News in Review." Unlike Jay Scott, at least Jack Cole was colorful and even had a law degree.

But WNAC did not merely report the news; on too many occasions, it *was* the news. The year 1979 was especially trying. On January 10, Stephen Guptill, hired to produce specials about the elderly, was forced to resign after admitting he falsely claimed to have two foreign degrees.[3] In April, Dr. Fred Ward, who held a PhD in meteorology from MIT and had been with the station since 1963, learned his contract had not been renewed, and that he was being demoted to working weekends; he was let go in January 1980. Earlier he had filed a complaint with the Massachusetts Commission Against Discrimination (MCAD), charging that he had been the victim of age discrimination. But his complaint was later dismissed. In October, Tanya Kaye, the station's consumer reporter who had worked at Channel 7 for six years, also filed a complaint with the MCAD, alleging she had been discriminated against because of her gender. After her termination in 1980, while her case was pending, the MCAD dismissed her complaint as well. As with Fred Ward, the MCAD sided with management, which claimed there were adequate reasons for each termination based on performance.

Still, such incidents continued to bring a barrage of unwanted publicity. As an example, on February 4, 1981, under the headline

"Women Battle 7," the *Boston Globe* ran a story about five women's organizations urging viewers to "switch off" Channel 7 for the month of February, as a protest against alleged discrimination against its female employees. As 1979 drew to a close, the station faced still another embarrassing incident when, in December, Charlene Mitchell, a news reporter and weekend anchor, and her sister were arrested for shoplifting in the men's department of a Lord & Taylor's store in Boston. Mitchell was later exonerated, though her sister was found guilty. Even so, it was one more headache for the station's beleaguered PR department.

Each fresh batch of bad news, and the attendant publicity that followed, added to the station's battered image. Indeed, one of the station's worst gaffes occurred several months later when, on April 1, 1980, April Fool's Day, the 6 p.m. newscast closed with a bogus bulletin reporting there had been a volcanic eruption in the Great Blue Hills area of Milton. With Jan Harrison reporting from the scene, the TV screen was filled with images of flowing lava and bright-red flames, courtesy of the active Mount St. Helens volcano in Washington, along with a dubbed warning by President Carter. At the end, Harrison held up a sign saying "April Fool."

Unfortunately, many viewers were apparently too frightened to laugh. After the report, some Milton residents fled their homes. The Milton Police Department received more than 100 calls from residents who thought the report was true, while the state civil-defense phones were flooded with calls from residents asking if they should evacuate their homes. One man, fearing that his house would be overwhelmed by lava, reportedly carried his sick wife outside in order to escape. An apology was offered on the 11 p.m. news and the producer Homer ("Skip") Scilley was promptly fired. But the damage had been done. The next day, the *Globe*'s Eileen McNamara had some choice words for the station management in a news story headlined "'Yuk-Yuk News' (on Ch. 7, folks) no joke in Milton." The story ran on page 1, and soon went national. But the real joke was on the station, which, by now, had become the laughingstock of the neighborhood.

I could go on, by citing other indignities, such as the 1980 drunk-driving arrest of Bob ("Two-Beer") Gamere, the station's talented but perpetually troubled sportscaster; or the station management's refusal to carry CBS's acclaimed *Sunday Morning* when it debuted in 1979—preferring to run a paid religious show, *Hour of Power*, produced in California, from which the station derived more revenue.

What is especially sad is that over the years, the station had some first-rate reporters and anchors in its ranks, including Chuck Scarborough, John Henning, Mary Richardson, and meteorologist Harvey Leonard, some of whom eventually sought refuge in other Boston stations; others, such as Mike Taibbi and Rehema Ellis, eventually wound up as NBC News correspondents.

Oh, what a sorry legacy overall. Thus, with the backing of David Mugar, the principal owner and board chairman, the station's fortunes were largely entrusted to two experienced executives. Winthrop Patterson Baker Jr. (called "Win"), a descendant of John Winthrop, the first governor of the Massachusetts Bay Colony, was named president and general manager. Critics warned about his abrupt, intimidating manner. But he came with lots of experience, having previously been Channel 4's general manager, and as president of Westinghouse Broadcasting from 1973 to 1979, was considered a trailblazer in the television industry. One of his early moves at the new Channel 7 involved the hiring of Bill Applegate as his vice president of news. Applegate, who had been the news director at KPIX-TV in San Francisco, another major market, had a reputation as a tough customer and fix-it guy. Both shared the same mindset—that given the station's history, they would have to move quickly, decisively, and boldly to make up for lost time if their station was to become a serious player in the market. Both were like-minded creatures of television, and together they would set the direction and tone for the new station. It's telling that on the bulletin board across from the elevator on the third-floor newsroom was a sign with a message: "They Don't Call Him Win for Nothing."

Applegate had his own message for his staff and, more to the point, for the rest of the market. A huge sign was posted in his newsroom for all to read: "THIS IS WAR!" A rather eccentric fellow, he was known to walk into the newsroom, shouting, "This is war!," only to turn around and walk back into his office. If nothing else, he was consistent. Years later when he became the general manager of a Cleveland station, a local writer noted his reading habits: "Applegate's favorite ancient text was *The Art of War*, the Chinese manual on combat strategy, which he was known to quote at length."[4]

At every level, Applegate felt compelled to show that he was the man in charge, treating his reporters as if they were green army recruits. Early on, he ordered veteran reporter Ron Sanders to shave off his beard. "Too unkempt," he told me. Channel 5 had a gifted critic-at-large named Chuck Kraemer who also sported a beard. He had worked at the station for twenty-seven years—apparently no one there was bothered by his whiskers.

Applegate took impish delight in taunting his crosstown rivals. Channel 5 was "lazy," "complacent," "soft and vulnerable." Channel 4 was "nervous, uncertain in its direction." With this added zinger: "I watched 'BZ at 5:30 the other day and one of their anchors was stationed at a fruit market, asking questions like, 'How do you feel about buying fresh avocados?'" I vividly remember the first time I met him in connection with a three-part series I was working on, interviewing Boston's TV news directors about their fall plans. There he was in his office—he called it "my bunker." Steely eyed, graying, looking much older than his thirty-six years, he puffed away on a cigarette, confidently predicting victory in the not-too-distant future. "It's going to be a three-way race. Now, there is competition. You bet it's war," he said. And he meant it.[5]

Given the station's long and unhappy third-place history, Baker and Applegate were convinced they had to move fast and come out swinging. "It takes time, though, because we start at a tremendous deficit. I always call it the hole that's thirty-four years deep, so I don't underestimate how long it's going to take us to climb out," the general manager told the *Globe*.[6] His statement reflected his belief that he was up against the clock and had to move at a frenetic pace—a mindset that would later result in rash decisions that had unintended consequences.

The station's ambitious promotion campaign was strictly soft-sell, complete with a sweet musical jingle and original lyrics, promising "A New Day Is Dawning."[7] But what the new leadership team meant was: "Watch it guys, 'cuz we're gonna beat the living daylights out of you!" A daring battle plan was drawn up designed to destabilize and demoralize the market, along with bold and aggressive steps to strengthen the new station. It was a multifaceted strategy, built mostly, though not exclusively, around news, a crucial profit center:

Spend millions of dollars on acquiring stars; acquire the most up-to-date technical equipment, costing more than $1.5 million; and build a splashy new set for the news.

Raid the enemy, that is, the other stations, of their talent— anchors, reporters, producers, and so on.

Launch a PR war that will throw the market into turmoil. The weapons used were radio and TV promos, print ads, and billboards, along with station officials trashing the competition in the press. The PR offensive would also include targeting TV critics deemed "unfriendly" to the station.

ENEMY RAIDS

The station had loaded its muskets; it was ready to enter the fray. Star wars. Salary wars.[8] PR wars. Suddenly, the market was under siege. The opening shot was fired on June 10, 1982, when Tom Ellis, Channel 5's star anchor, strolled into his small office at 4 p.m., cleaned out his desk, removed a picture of his wife from the wall, and then quietly unloaded the news—he was resigning. The bombshell came in the form of a brief note that he dropped off in general manager Bob Bennett's office. The note read: "I wanted very much to tell you first, and in person, that I am leaving the station effective immediately. I will be calling you."[9] Ellis, who had been on vacation that week and not expected in the office, next went to see Emily Rooney, the assistant news director. He told her he had worked his last day at WCVB after four successful years there. Then he quietly walked out the doors of the station. (Later, when asked about the bush-league manner with which Ellis made his exit, Win Baker, sounding like General Patton, replied: "He was under orders.")

Bennett had been out of the office and was just returning from a business trip to California. In a recent phone interview, he recalled the shock he felt when, after his plane had landed at Logan Airport, he was driving home that evening. "Going through the [Sumner] tunnel I heard the news on the radio—I almost wrecked my car," he said.[10] Meanwhile, just as Ellis was bidding farewell, rival WNEV was busy preparing a press release announcing that Ellis soon would join the new Channel 7 to coanchor the 6 and 11 o'clock news. Baker was so anxious about the release getting out prematurely that he ordered his publicity manager Jim Byrne not to leave his conference room. When Byrne requested a bathroom break, the general manager insisted his secretary walk with him to the men's room.

While Channel 7 was ecstatic over having a news star of Ellis's magnitude, Channel 5 officials were completely caught off guard. Jim Thistle, Channel 5's vice president of news, had taken the day off to give his mother and aunt a helping hand at their home in Gloucester. Having returned to his home in Everett later in the day, he received word of Ellis's defection from his assistant news director Emily Rooney while he was mowing the lawn. "I'm shocked, stunned, and personally hurt by the decision and the way it was rendered," said the soft-spoken Thistle, arguably the most respected broadcast journalist in Boston.

Never the darling of TV critics, Ellis was always popular with the TV news audience—as we have seen, a major draw on Channel 4's *Eyewitness News* from 1968 to 1975 and since 1978 on *NewsCenter 5*. Indeed, it is possible to document the impact of the man with the rugged features and the three-piece suit. Channel 5 overtook Channel 4 as the top-rated news station on the 11 o'clock slot in February 1979, only four months after Ellis joined Channel 5. In September 1980, when Ellis was paired on the 6 o'clock newscast with the stately Natalie Jacobson, dubbed "the News Madonna," the two proved a winning combination. Channel 5 began leading the early evening news race as well, thereby establishing market supremacy in news for the first time in years.

Still, Ellis was never completely comfortable there. His on-air relationship with Jacobson was cool; he was not regarded as a particularly strong reporter, and he fared poorly in ad lib situations— as evidenced by his being passed over for high-profile, live events coverage, such as the Tall Ships and the visit by the Pope. Given the circumstances, it was not all that surprising that Ellis could be lured to Channel 7 with a five-year contract that would increase his current $165,000 to $180,000 salary to one believed to be in excess of $500,000 a year.

But this was only the beginning. Fed up with television making stars out of newscasters and paying them super salaries, Jim Thistle made an agonizing decision to resign. His decision came only days after Tom Ellis bolted the station to sign a lucrative contract with Channel 7. "That was the straw that broke the camel's back. I didn't know anything about it," he said. "When that happened, I said, 'This is it!' The single thing that bothers me most has been the making of stars out of newscasters. The Star Wars game is crazy. TV takes three steps forward and two steps backward."[11] In an obvious reference to Ellis' salary, Thistle asked plaintively, "Do you know what you could do with $500,000—how many camera crews, investigative units, and documentaries you could get?" Citing "some extremely disturbing trends" within the industry, Thistle lashed out against the star system and its accompanying super-salaries. "The whole thing is ridiculous and it's growing. The spread between what the few and the many earn at a TV station is beyond all sanity or reason." Thistle's annual salary at Channel 5 was $70,000, though he did receive $215,000 for 200 shares of stock when Metromedia bought the station. By contrast, Channel 7's Bill Applegate received $140,000 for signing with his station.

The immediate reaction of Thistle's colleagues to his resignation was a deep sense of shock, sadness, and loss. "I'm in a bunker," said Bob Bennett, struggling to make a joke. "I love Jim. I didn't want to lose him. But he was so unhappy. He's upset, tired, and wrung out." Looking for some sanity, Thistle escaped to Boston University's broadcast journalism department. "I'm amazed," said Channel 5 reporter David Ropeik: "It's like a death in the family. I don't think I will ever work for as good a news director. He placed such a high priority on journalism—not show business or pizzazz." Thistle's health was also a factor, as the thirty-nine-year-old newsman had been plagued by recurring bouts of stomach ailments. "I'm just tired," he said. "My stomach uprisings have become more frequent." Some in the newsroom held out hope he might return at some point; but for now, he was gone. "I simply need a breath of fresh air," he explained.

But this was only the start of the market's media madness. Two weeks after snaring Tom Ellis, Channel 7 hired thirty-one-year-old Robin Young, previously a popular cohost of Channel's 4's *Evening*

Magazine and, more recently, an NBC correspondent working for *Today*, to coanchor the 6 and 11 p.m. news. Young, who was finishing up a two-year, $400,000 contract with NBC, was reportedly signed for over $500,000 in her first year at Channel 7. Pulling down a cool million dollars or so a year together, Tom and Robin were now believed to be the country's highest-paid local anchor team. At the time of his resignation, Thistle lamented the salary structure in which Boston's top TV reporters didn't even make $60,000 a year, while some local anchors—swipe!—were now set to pull down a half a million dollars a year.

Inside the Channel 5 newsroom, however, not everyone was pleased with his remarks. The next day, Joe Day, the station's chief political reporter and one of the market's most principled broadcast journalists, hung a sign over this desk that read: "This top reporter does not make $60,000 a year." Within a month, Day himself was gone, enticed by a five-year contract with Channel 7 that increased his Channel 5 salary from $52,000 to $97,000 the first year, to $127,000 in his final year. Channel 7 was basically using the same playbook super-sports agent Scott Boras would later employ in almost single-handedly driving up baseball's salary structure. Forced into paying higher salaries to retain their talent, the other TV managers were frustrated, but forced to play the game.

"Obscene" is what Phil Balboni, Thistle's Channel 5 replacement, angrily called the situation. Earlier, as the station's public affairs director, he was credited with making his TV editorial department the best in the city. A serious-minded, thoughtful man with a reputation for journalistic integrity, Balboni was deeply offended by Channel 7's moves. "It's certainly fair to try and hire a reporter from another station, but the sums of money involved are approaching the obscene level, and it can be corrupting," he said. "This is a sad day. The effect? It's too early to say, but we must get back to thinking about the news and not the money."[12] On the other hand, his boss, Jim Coppersmith, who was more pragmatic, wryly told the *Globe*: "The last person to turn down a raise," he said, "was St. Francis of Assisi."[13]

As the market's news leader at the time, Channel 5 was an especially inviting target. Natalie Jacobson, Ellis's partner at Channel 5, was contacted by Channel 7, but decided to stay with her current employer. The *New York Times* reported that the price tag for Channel 5 was steep, with Jacobson's new five-year contract "approximately five times her previous salary—and comparable to that paid Mr. Ellis and Miss Young."[14] Chet Curtis, Jacobson's husband and a Channel 5 reporter, was also signed on as her new coanchor for a slightly lesser amount. Meanwhile, Channel 5 political reporter Martha Bradlee toyed with, but rejected, an $85,000-a-year contract at Channel 7. Janet Langhart, formerly the popular cohost of Channel 5's *Good Day!*, joined Channel 7 to do pop culture features on its news.

Attempts were also made to raid the other stations. Channel 5 reporters David Ropeik and Kirby Perkins each had offers from Channel 7, as was true for Channel 4 reporter Charles Austin, who decided to stay put. But the Channel 7 management team was relentless, right down to sounding out Maria Morales, Bob Bennett's charming and efficient personal secretary, about switching sides. (Oh, the sensitive "intelligence" to which she had access!) Morales told the *Globe* she had been contacted by an employment agency asking about her going to work for Win Baker. "I felt a little flattered, then a little insulted, and it frightened me somewhat that people operate in this manner, especially with little people like me. It scared me."[15]

But Channel 7's spending spree was not confined to personnel. The newsroom was doubled in size; a state-of-the-art set was built, featuring an anchor desk that could accommodate six people (most anchor desks only sat four), along with the latest, most sophisticated technology at a cost of over $1.5 million. "There are thirty monitors," boasted one station executive. "It looks like an airport. It was designed so that no matter where you are in the newsroom, whenever you look up, you see a monitor."[16]

CASUALTIES OF WAR

Of course, in any war there are casualties, even on the home front. After years of stagnation, such changes were both predictable and necessary. And, with a new management team in place, some bloodletting at the fledgling station was inevitable. As Applegate and his managers went about hiring dozens of new staffers, the list of RKO holdovers forced to resign or fired included an anchor, an assistant news director, a sportscaster, a news writer, and no fewer than five reporters. Even the new guard wasn't spared. Nick Lawler, the new news director, was fired after only four months on the job.

The manner of handing out the pink slips was unusually callous, even by the brutal standards of television. On the Friday before Tom Ellis and Robin Young made their September debut, Brad Holbrook, a Channel 7 anchor during the WNAC years and during the transition period, was told he was gone—five minutes after his last newscast. On another day, Shirley McNerney was sent out to cover a story late in the day, only to be called back from the assignment and told she had been fired. Ironically, two days later, McNerney was nominated for a regional Emmy Award for reporting. Al Riley had been the executive producer on the 11 p.m. news—that is, until he got back from a summer vacation and learned via a bulletin board notice that he had been demoted to a weekend producer. A few months later he, too, was a goner.

Though it's not clear that either Win Baker or Bill Applegate had ever read *The Prince*, they and their henchmen seemed to embrace Machiavelli's dictum: "It is better to be feared than loved, if you cannot be both." As time went on, Channel 7's war against the other stations showed signs of degenerating into a reign of terror, even at home, where the newsroom felt more like a boot camp. Seasoned and respected professionals—on and off the air—were subjected to verbal abuse, harassment, and intimidation. Common standards of decency and simple courtesy were thrown out the window. One incident, reported by *Globe* TV critic Jack Thomas, illustrates the chilling environment:

> There was a lull in the Channel 7 newsroom one night a few weeks ago. It was 8:30, and Bill O'Connell was chatting with fellow sportscasters John Dennis and Roy Reiss and cameraman Jack Crowley when Win Baker, the general manager, burst into the room, clearly angry. As Baker strode past them to the assignment desk, conversation froze. Former news director Jack Fitzgerald was summoned, and the two men left the room. "What was that about?" one of the sportscasters asked. "He wanted to know who was driving the green and white Scout," said the assignment clerk. "It's blocking his car." "Oh, my God," said Crowley as he rushed toward the garage.

Baker was furious, and despite Crowley's apology, he belittled Crowley the way a Marine Corps drill instructor would a recruit who had just stepped on his spit shine. "What's your name?" said Baker, writing it down in a notebook. "Don't you know you don't do that to your general manager? Do you like working here?"[17]

MANAGING THE PRESS

But such tactics were hardly confined to the newsroom. The war was getting uglier. Another front was opened up—this time against the town's television critics. The first blow was struck when the general manager, in the face of an embarrassing situation, attempted to gag the press. A confidential memo containing a list of potential hires, including people's race and gender in some instances, had inadvertently been left on a Xerox machine over the weekend. By Monday, a lovely June day, the question for Baker was whether the press had gotten its grubby little hands on the memo.

Fearing the worst, the general manager summoned each of the local TV critics to his office late in the afternoon for private, one-on-one meetings. The *Boston Globe*, the *Boston Herald*, the *Patriot Ledger*, and the *Boston Phoenix*, a respected alternative weekly, were all present. Each of us was handed a copy of the memo, along with a request that we *not* publish it in our papers. (Ironically, while it was not clear who, if anyone, had the memo in the first place, all of us obviously did by the end of the day.) As I left Baker's office, I was not entirely unsympathetic to the general manager's dilemma. Actually, I was of two minds: Was he interested in protecting the names of the candidates, some of whom were up for the same job? Or did he simply want to avoid telegraphing his next moves to the other TV stations? And, finally, did it or should it matter?

Upon returning to the *Ledger*, I sought counsel from our executive editor Bill Ketter. "Of course we'll do a story," he said. "We're in the news business, and the memo is news. And make sure to make it clear that Baker tried to kill the story."[18] All four papers published all or parts of the memo.

Unfortunately, the whole episode only served to demonstrate Baker was not only arrogant, but also terribly naive. Later that week, he called a staff meeting, with about seventy-five news operatives in attendance, the main purpose of which was to formally introduce Bill Applegate. But the meeting began on a tense note, with the general manager angrily demanding that the person or persons who had leaked the memo stand up and resign. No one did. (The *Globe*'s Jack Thomas compared it to the scene in *The Caine Mutiny* where Captain Queeg launched his famous inquiry as to which of his men stole the missing strawberries.)[19]

As internal tensions inside the station grew concerning the management's tactics, some wondered how David Mugar, the station's board chairman—a nice, mild-mannered man—could sit on the sidelines, seeming to condone such roughshod tactics. Instead, he gave his management team a strong public vote of confidence, even reaching for a military metaphor to make his point. "It's like the old Army story," he told the *Globe* later that summer. "You want the boot camp sergeant along with you when you have a tough hill to take."[20]

Nevertheless, the station's first attempt to manage the news, which failed, was followed by a second memo in late August ordering the employees not to speak to the press without going through the PR department. No other TV station in Boston had such a policy forbidding direct communication between employees and the press. The gag order only had an unsettling effect on the already nervous staff, while increasingly alienating the media. Many staffers complained of being treated like POWs in an enemy camp. Communication between TV critics and employees was sometimes done by letter. Out of fear, critics' phone calls to station contacts often went unreturned.[21]

The station's bunker mentality asserted itself in other ways as well. While Channel 7's war against the other stations was now being covered by the print press as a legitimate news story, which it was, the station only seemed to further isolate itself, becoming increasingly inaccessible, especially when it was the subject of stories by Boston's other radio and TV stations. Locally, Channel 4's John Henning did a five-part series on the *Eyewitness News* called "Star Wars." *Chronicle*, Channel 5's thoughtful news magazine, devoted an entire show to the subject. And Hubert Jessup on WHDH radio similarly held a round-table discussion with local TV news directors.

Meanwhile, Channel 7 was behaving like North Korea. In every case, it was the only TV station declining to participate. But much to its distaste, the station itself was becoming a national story, with headlines such as "Boston TV Stations Battling Over News Anchors" (*New York Times*, August 30, 1982) and "The Battle of the Nightly News Anchors: 'Star Wars' Comes to Local TV" (*Christian Science Monitor*, November 24, 1982). General manager Win Baker and his news director, Bill Applegate, employed a double standard—speaking with some TV critics, refusing to talk with others. With paranoia gripping the station, the notion of "fair press" got equated with "favorable press."

There was more than a little irony about the station's PR stance. On one hand, it had the largest PR department of any TV station in town, sending out more press releases and spending thousands of dollars wining and dining members of the press. Yet it continued to have the worst image of any local station. In digging out one of my old columns, headlined "TV War: Dispatch from the Trenches," it was evident that some of us in the press had already soured on the station, well before the *Tom and Robin Show* had even made its debut: "The promise of a new day dawning has turned into an ugly nightmare. The forces of greed have been unleashed. Ethical standards have been thrown to the wind. And, the ruthless nature of the television industry—first and foremost a business—has been exposed."[22]

As the months went by, much of the initial goodwill by the press and public toward the upstart station would be frittered away; it was now perceived as the bully on the block, rather than a sympathetic underdog. And, by employing a hyperactive PR machine, the station inflated expectations—only to be angered when critics found the on-air product wanting. With all three affiliates gearing up for a ferocious three-way news battle in the fall when Channel 7's revamped newscast would be unveiled, its rivals were hardly standing still.

CHANNELS 4 AND 5 LAUNCH COUNTERATTACKS

Both Channels 4 and 5 looked for ways to build up their arsenals, while their rhetoric, with each passing day, grew more heated. "Yes, it's hard being Number 1," mused Channel 5's news director Phil Balboni. "Everybody is gunning for you. It is difficult to maintain that intense competitive edge when you've been Number 1 for a time. But there is not a complacent person in my newsroom. Everyone understands we are going to have to be competitive like never before."

He also disclosed upcoming additions to his already potent news operation. The *NewsCenter 5* newscast at 6 p.m. would be expanded by thirty minutes, or possibly an hour, in the spring. Investigative reporting was now a high priority, while (unspecified) specialty reporters would be added. Technology, sometimes considered a station weakness, would be upgraded. And Clark Booth, an unusually talented writer, would be taken off sports to write and produce what would become exquisitely crafted essays "inspired by his own insights." Balboni expressed respect for Channel 4 as a worthy opponent; however, he was openly disdainful toward Channel 7, dismissing its news operation as "a temporary challenge"—attacking its extravagant spending, its hiring policies, even its journalistic principles: "There is no love lost between us and Channel 7. I don't admire them . . . I have a total determination to win. I have no intention of being beaten by show-business news, if that's what they intend to put on."[23]

For his part, Jeff Rosser, Channel 4's news director, denied he was running scared, though some of his moves belied that assertion. He freely conceded he renamed his 11 p.m. program *Nightcast* several days after Bill Applegate was hired as Channel 7's news director. *Nightcast* just happened to be Applegate's name for his late-night newscast at KPIX-TV in San Francisco. He indicated his newscast would undergo cosmetic changes, such as a new set, "redesigned" theme music, and new opening animation, as well as a new but unnamed 5:30 p.m. anchor team to strengthen Channel 4's lead-in to its 6 p.m. news. Ever the wily tactician, Rosser also disclosed that John Henning would be added to the regular 6 o'clock news team of Liz Walker and Jack Williams, which meant that Channel 4 would now have *three* anchors. Henning had years of experience, having worked earlier at both Channels 5 and 7 as a reporter, anchor, and political analyst. And, with his graying hair, solemn demeanor, and impressive height, he was the personification of the credible newsman. To underscore his points, Rosser added: "Channel 7 has been dubbed the 'Dream Team'; Channel 5 has the 'Love Team' (husband and wife Natalie Jacobson and Chet Curtis). Well, Channel 4 has the '*News* Team.'" Then, a final swipe at *both* his rivals: "The most popular team was Tom and Natalie, but they no longer exist," he said.[24]

By August 1982 one thing was clear. Since changing ownership and now under a new management, Channel 7, the market's third-place news station, was on the warpath, and actually driving the market.

THE *TOM AND ROBIN SHOW* DEBUTS

Monday, September 13, 1982. It seemed like just another news day. The Dow, up more than 11 points, closed at 919.69; and, closer to home, the struggling Red Sox, playing at Fenway, were losing a doubleheader to the Cleveland Indians—what else was new? But when nighttime approached in Boston, it was showtime! All eyes, or so it seemed, were on Channel 7; the curtain was about to rise on the much-anticipated *Tom and Robin Show*. In the best of show business tradition, Robin Young received dozens of flower bouquets on the big day, while Tom Ellis got helium balloons from adoring fans before air-time. About the only thing missing was Joan Rivers on the Red Carpet trashing the anchors' outfits.

The sense of excitement was palpable, with hundreds of thousands of viewers at home awaiting the stars' entrance—not to mention an increasingly skeptical press lying in wait. Would Tom and Robin suffer from opening night jitters? What would be the response of the critics? And, of course, how would the "Dream Team" fare in the ratings?

A lot was at stake. For one thing, it is hard to overestimate the importance of the anchors. Not only were they considered a key factor in the ratings, but they also had come to symbolize a station's identity. With this in mind, Channel 7 spent a small fortune publicizing the new team in advance of "opening night," through station promos (which all but ignored the reporters), print ads, radio spots, and billboards. Quite literally, it was a full-court press, which meant full-page advertisements in *seven* daily newspapers, *TV Guide*, and trade weeklies, and heavy saturation on twelve of the area's most popular radio stations. Even Walter Cronkite was enticed to come to town for a black-tie affair at the Bay Tower Room overlooking Boston Harbor—complete with a spectacular fireworks display for the guests, courtesy of board chairman David Mugar, whose production company since 1974 had provided the fireworks display for the Boston Pops' July Fourth outdoor concerts.

Indeed, some would argue that Tom and Robin were worth the big bucks and hoopla because anchoring is actually harder than it looks. It requires a set of attributes and skills unique to television as a visual medium: good looks; a pleasant personality; a confident, pleasing voice; and an ability to project certain qualities, such as authority and credibility. And, while it's helpful for the anchor to be knowledgeable and well informed, too often it's more about bones than brains, especially at the local level. In the end, it's about things like "image" and "performance"—more about how one comes across than how much the person knows, or who the person really is. If the anchor can fake the essentials, he or she has just about got it made.

In her insightful book called *The Evening Stars*, Barbara Matusaw makes this point with reference to how the legendary CBS anchor Walter Cronkite appeared to millions of viewers every night—a kindly, calm, and reassuring presence—as opposed to the way some of his colleagues found him: "According to the conventional wisdom, television exposes people for what they are, but Cronkite was unusually adept at concealing certain parts of his personality. The benevolent persona that viewers saw was not a fabrication. . . . But viewers never saw the other side—the tough, Germanic stickler who was on the whole rather aloof, even forbidding—the Cronkite colleagues saw at work."[25]

So how did the new anchor team do? The reviews were out the next day—"mixed on the downside," as they say in the showbiz trade papers. All of us—from the *Herald American, Globe*, and *Patriot Ledger*[26]—had praise for the fast-paced newscast, the impressive set, the fancy graphics, and the razzle-dazzle technology. Meteorologist Harvey Leonard, showing off his new computer graphics, was like an excited little boy in a Toys "R" Us store.

But the reviews were most heavily focused on "the Dream Team." Both attractive people—Tom Ellis, the rugged Marlboro Man, and Robin Young, Snow White with a touch of funk—the two scored very high in terms of physical appearance. The *Herald*'s Monica Collins put it well: "Robin looked lovely, demure. Her hair was cut into an attractive cascade. She wore (a) no nonsense but feminizing string of pearls around her neck, a mauve, silky-looking boat-neck blouse and a nubby weave bluish suit. Her make-up was merely suggestive, not glaring."

Even so, Tom was well received, while Robin was not. As described in the *Ledger*:

> Tom turned in a masterful performance—smooth, forceful, polished. And oh so sexy! Nattily attired in a plain gray suit, with nary a hair out of place, he looked positively smashing.
>
> But in terms of "performance," Robin was at a serious disadvantage. Though she had lots of previous on-camera exposure, and was well-regarded, both as a producer and feature reporter, she had never been a news anchor. She may well have been the better journalist, but Tom was the more experienced anchor—and by far, the better actor.[27]

In the lede to her column, Collins was characteristically blunt: "Tom held his own. Robin bombed." Putting her evaluation in the form of a report card, she gave Ellis satisfactory or above average grades in Credibility (B+) and Delivery (B). By contrast, Robin, who seemed to have a case of opening-night jitters, received poor grades in Delivery (D), Credibility (C), and Composure (C-). Regarding that mysterious commodity known as chemistry, Collins was merciless: "Robin made Tom look like a venerable Edward R. Murrow. Tom was the one who put you at ease. Robin was the one who put you on edge. Her energy flagged. Her sense of timing was off. Her attempts at ad libs fell flat."

To which yours truly added in the *Ledger*:

> More importantly, her natural camera ease deserted her. At one point she couldn't find her copy; she fluffed a line about a Needham man charged with first-degree murder; she noted that Marvin Hagler was "headling" (sic.) for Italy. . . .
>
> Moreover, it's obvious it will take some time for the chemistry to develop between the two anchors. When Robin teased Tom about his pronunciation of the word "tornado" (he said "tornada"), she got the silent treatment from her partner.

The *Globe*'s Jack Thomas was more charitable: "Robin Young, who looks like the Queen of the Senior Prom, made it clear that she'll be no wallflower next to Tom Ellis. Despite a slip in reading here and there, she managed to out dance Ellis in the 'small talk department.'"

BOMBS AWAY!

Oh yes, the content. Politics is something of a blood sport in Massachusetts. So it was fitting that the new Channel 7 management aimed to create a strong political unit. They made a good start, hiring reporters Joe Day from Channel 5 and the feisty Howie Carr, late of Boston's *Herald American*. As it happened, the debut of the *Tom and Robin Show* came on the eve of the Massachusetts primary, ending a bitter, bruising gubernatorial campaign between Edward J. King, the current governor, a conservative, and former liberal governor Michael S. Dukakis. (Dukakis was the next day's winner.) But for Channel 7, it turned out to be a missed opportunity, as the *Globe*'s Jack Thomas wrote: "Nearly a quarter of the show was devoted to politics, but it lacked bite. Joe Day, for example, emphasized that the Democratic gubernatorial primary is up for grabs, a point that has been made on television and in newspapers for days."

Though not a total flop, the show was hardly a smashing success. Despite a brief uptick in ratings during the week, no doubt due to the curiosity factor by viewers, the station quickly settled back into its customary third-place ratings position, well behind Channel 5, the market's top-rated station, and Channel 4, a strong second. Even before the show's premiere, there was evidence that viewer resistance in the market was running high. In a letter to the editor published in the *Globe*, the very day of the first night's performance, one woman charged, "The forces behind WNEV are the callous megalomaniacs they appear to be. Perhaps they can buy the most expensive people to tell the news, but can they afford to buy an audience? WBZ and WCVB at least appear to have a genuine commitment to their staff and a desire to deliver the news without the need to acquire the best actor awards."[28]

As time went by, in an effort to gain traction, news director Bill Applegate, growing increasingly desperate, tried all sorts of gimmicks, resorting more and more to cheap thrills and sensationalism. Ron Sanders, a solid reporter, was sent down to Palm Beach to cover the tawdry divorce trial between Roxanne (nickname "Foxy Roxy") and newspaper tycoon Herbert "Peter" Pulitzer. Allegations of drug use, extramarital affairs, and kinky sex made for spicy tabloid fodder.

Cute and cuddly animal stories are often used by local stations and networks alike as the "kicker" at the end of their newscasts. But no other local station demonstrated quite the same zeal in terms of such trivial pursuits. My own favorite involved a pooch named Bo who had rescued his owners during a raft accident on the Colorado waters— not even the Charles River. In the aftermath, Ken-L Ration dog food voted him its 1982 "dog hero." A Channel 7 camera crew caught Bo arriving at Logan Airport and being escorted into a waiting limousine to accept his reward at a Boston hotel. At least newsman Mike Leavitt reassured the viewers: "The dog will not, however, be a guest in the Channel 7 studio."[29]

Which brings us to sports, another area where the station misread the market. In another ploy to counter the enormous popularity of Channel 4's super-duper sports anchor Bob Lobel, Channel 7 added the quirky, oddly named, soon-to-be-infamous Zip Rzeppa to its sports desk. Lobel just about owned the market, what with his naughty little-boy persona, his nightly banter with anchor Liz Walker, and his funny "Sports Spotlight" series about sports mishaps. Alas, Rzeppa did not possess Lobel's deft touch. (One glaring exception—the times Lobel dressed up in a reindeer suit for Channel 4's annual Christmas promo.) Some of Rzeppa's more outlandish antics involved his donning a skirt to play field hockey with girls, stripping to his waist to compare his skinny body to that of a wrestler's, and chatting amiably with a South American parakeet. But on the night of a Super Bowl, Zip would reach a new low. After picking the wrong team to win—the Washington Redskins actually beat the Miami Dolphins—he shamelessly cracked a raw egg on his face (Get it?), and continued to report the news, while the yolk dribbled down to his chin. By this time, even Jack Craig, the *Globe*'s mild-mannered TV sports columnist, had had enough, writing: "If there is a groundswell of acceptance out there, a mini-survey indicates it hasn't reached above Zip's shoelaces."[30]

The station's already-poor image suffered still another blow with an ill-conceived, sensationalistic four-part investigative series called "Death in the Nursery." With Bill Applegate hoping to make a national splash, the reports dealt with a thorny and highly complex medical ethics issue: Should newborns born with a life-threatening or life-diminishing disease or defect be kept alive at all costs? Or, in cases in which there is no hope, should physicians withhold or with-

draw "futile" life-sustaining treatment? At the time, the project, by reporters Mike Taibbi and Carlton Sherwood, was the most ambitious
undertaken by any Boston TV station in some time.

Unfortunately, it turned out to be little more than a biased, right-
wing diatribe. A Chicago lawyer interviewed called a decision to withdraw treatment "the road to the final solution in Germany . . . began
as a program of how to get rid of the problem of severely handicapped
children." Loaded language was used—"manslaughter," "homicide,"
"infanticide," and "murder"—to describe the physicians' actions. The
Boston Globe took the station to task, citing a variety of experts, including Boston University professor George Annas, a nationally recognized authority on medical ethics, who said there was never a law
against withholding treatment "as long as the action is considered
to be in the best interest of the child."[31] Carlton Sherwood,[32] one of
two reporters involved in the project, did get an invite to President
Ronald Reagan's conservative White House, but at home it was just
another black eye for the upstart station.

With all the excessive hype, inflated expectations, negative publicity, the "This is War!" stance, and countless other blunders, Channel 7 continued to sputter in the ratings. As of January 1983, Channel 7's 6 p.m. news, which mostly had been a third-place finisher
for years, actually sank to *fifth* among the stations—not only behind
the news on Channels 4 and 5, but also behind syndicated reruns
on the independent stations—*M*A*S*H* on Channel 38 and *Laverne
and Shirley* on Channel 56. A joke making the rounds was that the
safest place for a criminal to hide was behind Tom and Robin's anchor desk—because no one would be watching.

At this point, it might be worth noting the role of the press in this
saga. Geralyn A. White, an enterprising Harvard student who interned
in Channel 7's news department during this time, subsequently wrote
her honor's thesis about the station. Analyzing 400 news clips, she
concluded that the press had been too harsh in its coverage: "Even
though the Boston press helped Channel 7 become one of the biggest
media events ever to hit New England, it was also a facilitating factor
in Channel 7's failure."[33]

But she also noted that besides the comings and goings of personnel and the management's rough, often brutal tactics, the critics drew

attention to Channel 7's more substantive weaknesses: "The critics realized there were larger issues at stake. They understood that the race for ratings meant long term (sic.) survival, but ultimately maintained that the public need for information was being forsaken."[34]

The news operation was not the only problem. Baker and his cohorts felt that if the station couldn't beat the others into submission, to gain traction they would have to outspend them in the programming area as well. Which brings us to *Look*, the station's two-hour, live afternoon magazine show, featuring experts from a variety of fields, which launched in late November 1982. Touting itself as "the most expensive local program in television history," it had a staff of more than fifty people. (*Good Day!* had a staff of eight or nine.) The goal was to revolutionize afternoon television in the 4 to 6 p.m. slot, while functioning as a strong lead-in to the 6 o'clock news. Jeff Schiffman, the vice president of programming, and executive producer Raysa Bonow were put in charge of the show. Two driven, overwhelmed executives, they badly overreached. They hired and fired staffers and spent wildly, while their bloated show did diddly-squat in the ratings. Nor did their abrasive personalities help, with stories circulating that they practically came at their overworked and demoralized staff with bullwhips. Indeed, I once got a plaintive call from a South Shore woman. Worried about the physical and emotional health of her husband who worked on the show, she pleaded with me to write something about the way the staff was being humiliated and verbally abused.

After eighteen months of chaos at an astonishing cost of $10 million, mercifully, the show was canceled. The experiment had failed. In the long history of daily shows that had flopped, this one was a mega-bomb—the local equivalent of *Gigli*, the multimillion-dollar movie flop starring Ben Affleck and Jennifer Lopez. A far less expensive, more modest version of *Look*, called *New England Afternoon* and hosted by Bill O'Reilly, also tanked in 1984, after a brief run.

REGIME CHANGE: NEW LEADERS IN CHARGE

Within the station and in the Boston market itself, the situation seemed to be spinning out of control. In March 1983, Bill Applegate, perhaps sensing more chaos or knowing his own days were numbered, left the battlefield, resigning after only nine months on the job. He was off to fight another war, this time in Chicago as news director at WLS-TV, another third-place station. But Applegate's departure was only the beginning. Thursday, June 2, 1983, would be another day of high drama, with not one, but two explosive announcements involving *two* major Boston stations. At about 11:30 in the morning the entire Channel 4 staff was assembled for an unscheduled meeting. Larry Fraiberg, the president of Group W TV Stations, which owned WBZ, had flown up from New York that morning to inform the rank and file that Sy Yanoff, his longtime general manager in Boston, had just resigned. The staff was shell-shocked—the news totally unexpected. Among other things, Yanoff's departure from Channel 4 sort of blew out the candles on the cake of his now-former station, which was about to celebrate its thirty-fifth anniversary with much fanfare the following Thursday. About a half hour later, Win Baker, who, a year earlier, had signed a six-and-a-half-year contract to become Channel 7's general manager, informed his own staff that he was stepping down (though technically staying on as a consultant). According to *Globe* TV critic Ed Siegel: "Just after noon yesterday, Baker called his staff together in Studio B to tell them that he was leaving. Before he could announce his successor, in walked Yanoff. Baker didn't have to finish. The 200 assembled staffers let out a collective gasp and broke into applause."[35]

Around 2 o'clock, Channel 7 held a news conference for the two men—one newly hired, the other, newly leaving—no, obviously fired. It was quite the media spectacle—a packed house, attended not only by the TV critics and other members of the print press but also by TV reporters and camera crews from Channels 2 (WGBH), 4, 5, and 7. Once again, the media found themselves reporting on themselves. It was at once bizarre and ironic. Channel 4's John Henning, a seasoned pro, whipped out the needle, asking his now-former boss if he had a message for the troops over at WBZ. It was strange to see Win Baker introducing Yanoff as his successor. In the early 1970s, when Win Baker was appointed president of Westinghouse Broadcasting, one of his first moves was to hire Sy Yanoff as general manager at WBZ. But when Baker returned to Boston in the summer of 1982, relations between the two men were cool because of the warlike atmosphere. On this day, though, when Baker introduced his successor to the troops, the two embraced in a warm bear hug. Baker seemed oddly relieved and made a candid admission before the assembled media: "I can't honestly say it was fun for one day," he said. "But I gave it everything I had." While many had taken issue with his ruthless, strong-arm methods during his brief tenure, no one could quarrel with his intentions. It was a graceful exit.

Within a year, the architects of the new Channel 7 were all but gone, with misguided program executives Jeff Schiffman and Raysa Bonow shortly out the door as well. Haunted by the station's failed past, they had all badly miscalculated the market—overreaching, overspending, overpromising, and overreacting in a way that had proved disastrous. Somehow, they had managed to infuriate their rivals, antagonize the press, and turn off the viewers—all within an unusually short period of time.

So what now? At the strange news conference, reporters pressed Yanoff on why he was willing to move from a strong, well-established station to one filled with serious growing pains and uncertainty. At the age of fifty-one, the new general manager admitted that financial security was the major factor—having been given a five-year contract and stock worth as much as $2 million. In the high-stakes, high-risk business of television, the Dorchester kid who made good was now financially secure for the rest of his life. In his new position, Yanoff was expected to provide a different, more palatable style of leadership. A colorful, hot-tempered man with an earthy sense of humor, Yanoff was experienced and street-smart—a hardball player who had mellowed (a little) with the years. Having been WBZ's general manager for the past decade, he had emerged as something of an unpolished but successful elder statesman. Channel 7 staffers were surprised and delighted when he went around shaking hands with his new newsroom staff.

THE EMERGENCE OF CHANNEL 7

Yanoff moved quickly—in less than two weeks luring Jeff Rosser, his former news director at Channel 4, to Channel 7, where he became the vice president of news. By now, viewers were becoming used to such channel-hopping. Once again, money was a factor.

Rosser signed a five-year contract, reportedly given a salary upgrade from $80,000 to $120,000, a $20,000 bonus, and stock in the station, roughly half of 1 percent, worth about $500,000. In his three years at Channel 4, the thirty-five-year-old Rosser had managed to transform a lackluster news operation into a formidable one poised to challenge top-rated Channel 5. Though not universally liked around the newsroom, he was respected by just about everyone. His biggest assets were his steadiness under pressure, his willingness to take risks, and his ability to instill his troops with a winning attitude.

In short order, the new Yanoff-Rosser team began cleaning house. Within a month, the station announced that Robin Young, so miscast on the news, was being demoted, yanked from the anchor desk and reduced to producing special projects. (Her partner Tom Ellis would live to anchor another day—actually several more years.) By November, the mercurial Janet Langhart, who never quite fit into the news operation and whose contract with the station would shortly expire, resigned. As for the infamous Zip Rzeppa—well, in the end, Zip would get zapped, too.

For the moment, Channel 4 was rudderless, until Tom Goodgame, general manager for KDKA in Pittsburgh, another Group W station, was named as Yanoff's replacement, and Stan Hopkins, Rosser's assistant news director, moved up into Rosser's old position. Once again, the market was in the midst of uncertainty. It felt like the antenna on Boston's media roof was beginning to fall off—almost an instant replay of the previous year's events when anchors, reporters, and producers went hopping from one station to another. It punctured the illusion that any of the local TV stations could lay claim to stability—with Boston having emerged as the most volatile market in the country.

When Jim Kelly, a polished, former CBS sportscaster (and one-time Buffalo Bills quarterback) hired by Channel 7, abruptly left the station in October 1983, after only four months on the job, a media friend of mine expressed sympathy for the station's latest setback. "We might as well face the fact that Boston is simply a two-station town," he said, sounding more mournful than self-righteous. It reminded me that I had once written, "Channel 5 is classy; Channel 4 is flashy; and Channel 7 is trashy." Cheap shot, yes, but Channel 7 was such an easy target. But now, new guys were in charge. Sy Yanoff and Jeff Rosser, both of late of Channel 4, had brought with them to Channel 7 a keen knowledge of the market, a realization that the quick-fix strategy of their predecessors hadn't worked, and a strong determination to profit from the mistakes of the recent past. No more bellicose rhetoric, inflated claims, terrorizing the staff, or going after the critics.

News would be the first order of business and Jeff Rosser—shrewd, intensely competitive, and cool under pressure—proved the right man for the job. If Jim Thistle, during his Channel 5 years (1974–1982), was the standard-bearer for local news in the 1970s, then Jeff Rosser, at Channel 4 (1980–1983) and now at Channel 7 (1983–1988), was perfectly cast for this role in the 1980s. Indeed, they were polar opposites in just about every way—philosophy, style, and temperament. Yet the two were destined to become the market's most influential news figures during Boston's Golden Age. While Thistle was the traditionalist who favored hard news and issues, Rosser was the pragmatist in love with the latest technology.

Whereas Thistle remained the hometown kid who made good, Rosser was cut from a very different cloth. A product of Dallas, Texas, he graduated from Brigham Young University, and from an early age was the epitome of the ambitious, upwardly mobile professional. Going from one market to another, he continued to move up the corporate ladder. By the time he was twenty-seven, the whiz kid was already a news director at the ABC affiliate in Tulsa, Oklahoma; later, he became the assistant news director at WNBC-TV in New York, the country's largest market. Now he would make his mark in Boston, first as a Channel 4 news director in 1980, and presently as the vice president of news at Channel 7. Both news directors got the best out of their troops, though each had a very different management style. Were they football coaches, Thistle, whose caring and generosity were legendary, would be Pete Carroll, while Rosser, demanding and aloof, would be Bill Belichick.

But what ultimately mattered was that the world of television was changing and Rosser was more comfortable with the new realities. The audience base for news in the 1980s was being challenged by competing media, such as cable TV and independent stations. The growing popularity of remote-control devices meant that already-fickle viewers needed to be engaged and entertained constantly, lest they flip to another station or simply turn off the set. An explosion of state-of-the-art technology meant that information could be transmitted more quickly, further changing television priorities and values. The possibility of a smaller news base and even fiercer competition among rival local news stations battling for viewers meant that the successful newscast of the future would have to place greater emphasis on style, packaging, and technology—with more razzle-dazzle gimmicks, fancier graphics, and faster pacing, all in the form of shorter, bite-size news chunks.

Thistle disdained consultants, the so-called "news doctors," while Rosser paid a great deal of attention to market research, which gave his newscasts something of a bland, generic quality. Where Thistle was not particularly aggressive, Rosser was a brilliant tactician with an obsessive desire to win. Where Thistle was interested in serious news, Rosser was fond of soft features—witness the creation of a slew of weekly segments at Channel 7 such as "Young Times," "Prime Times," and "Ye Olde New England."

Cosmetics—the look, feel, and pace of a newscast—were his obsessions. Often, it was all about the details. Percussion sounds were added to the theme music for the 11 p.m. news, to distinguish it from the one at 6—but how many viewers noticed? At times he carried his pragmatism to extremes—seemingly prone to using just about any gimmick to boost the ratings. In a column ridiculing one such enterprise ("Channel 7 News Goes Shopping for Success"), I coined the term "mallcast" to describe his month-long publicity stunt of staging newscasts from suburban shopping malls during an important ratings "sweeps":

> There, just beyond Friendly's ice cream, is the mind-boggling sight: the Channel 7 news broadcasting live all this week from the Hanover Mall. A shopping center? Yes, you read it right.
>
> It's easy. You just walk through the doors, pass Montilio's bakery (with all those yummy pastries) and the CVS store (with the big Arrid deodorant sign) and make a right by the frozen yogurt shop.[36]

Quickly, he moved to instill discipline and professionalism for the high-visibility jobs—promoting the respected John Dennis to sports anchor (who previously had been jerked around by Bill Applegate and briefly fired); replacing the frothy Janet Langhart with the more serious Angela Rippon, hired from the BBC as entertainment reporter; and dumping sports-clown Zip Rzeppa in favor of Gary Gillis, a Harvard graduate whose father, Don Gillis, had been a sports legend at the old Channel 5. And by the end of 1986, Tom Ellis, who had managed to hold on to his anchor job throughout the stormy period, was finally let go. For whatever reasons, the man who had previously led Channel 4, then Channel 5 to the top of the news ratings had not been able to work his magic at Channel 7.

Frank Shorr, a former Channel 7 executive sports producer (and eight-time Emmy winner) who now directs Boston University's Sports Institute in the College of Communication, recalls attending Rosser's often tense post-mortem meetings after each newscast. "Producers, writers, editors, and ENG people would have to gather in Jeff's small office. Jeff was a perfectionist and would go over every mistake, every wrong camera angle and missed story. The meetings were tortuous and demeaning."[37] On the other hand, Rosser did have his supporters. Phyllis Eliasberg, a Channel 7 consumer reporter, had nothing but praise. "I adored Jeff," she said. "He was a terrific manager. I remember once doing a story on McDonalds, which threatened to withdraw its advertising. Jeff said, 'Let 'em.' I admired his stand."[38]

Rosser's track record on talent (at both Channel 4 and Channel 7) was uneven. Over the years he made some first-rate hires: Liz Walker, the town's first African American woman on a nightly newscast, who turned out to be a huge success (Channel 4); Joyce Kulhawik, a former Brookline English teacher, who became the town's hardest-working and best TV arts and entertainment reporter (Channel 4); and, over at Channel 7, R. D. Sahl, the most cerebral and credible newsman ever to occupy the anchor desk at a Boston TV station. But alas, where Thistle placed great importance on his reporters' news background or experience, Rosser was more addicted to the "pretty people syndrome," favoring personalities who were youthful, physically attractive, but often terribly shallow. In her hilarious book *And So It Goes*, about her life in television, Linda Ellerbee used the word "Twinkies" to describe them: "We call them Twinkies. You've seen them on television acting the news, modeling and fracturing the news while you wonder whether they've read the news—or if they've blown dried their brains, too."[39]

Rosser's hiring of Elizabeth Stern as his "lifestyle specialist" at Channel 7 serves as a good example. A pretty young thing (and yes, she was blonde), Stern was best known as Patty Williams on *The Young and the Restless* soap opera. But without any real qualifications and in a town with a vibrant cultural scene, she was obviously ill equipped for the job. When Channels 4 and 5's arts/entertainment reporters were sent to cover opening night of the Boston Symphony Orchestra, Stern was nowhere in sight. But several nights later, she gave a rave review to *Men in Motion*, a group of male strippers performing at a local joint called the Golden Banana. Stern lasted all of six months.

On the other hand, Rosser's finest achievement may have been his creation of a groundbreaking news-sharing consortium during his Channel 7 tenure. Called the New England News Exchange, the consortium partnered Channel 7's news operation with four regional newspapers outside of Boston—the *Patriot Ledger* (South Shore), the *Middlesex News* (now *MetroWest*), the *Lawrence Eagle-Tribune* (North Shore), and the *Worcester Telegram & Evening Gazette*—as well as five radio stations and six television stations spread over Connecticut, Rhode Island, Maine, New Hampshire, and elsewhere in Massachusetts. The elaborate setup involved stationing three teams of reporters at the papers and constructing three new microwave towers to transmit their signals back to Boston.

It was a remarkable mix of journalism and technology, which additionally offered promotional benefits for the station. "Local news," which had been Boston-centric, was being redefined as "regional news," and expanded to other parts of the state and beyond. Channel 7's rivals were left flatfooted and had to figure out how to expand their own news base. Tellingly, Channel 5 no longer touted itself as *NewsCenter 5*, but as *New England's NewsCenter*. The copycat effect became so pronounced, I found myself writing in one column, "When Channel 7 sneezes, Channel 5 invariably blows its nose." (By the way, after Jeff Rosser read my column he had handkerchiefs made up with the quote for his staff.)

With a steady stream of stories pouring out from areas beyond

Route 128, Channel 7 was starting to play a leadership role in reporting news of a more regional nature. The *New York Times*, in a story about Channel 7, praised it as "a pioneering arrangement."[40] Dick Molinari, a Channel 5 assignment editor was more forthright: "Journalistically, the whole thing is a little hazy. But dammit. I'm jealous. I wish we had thought of it first."[41]

Most of all, Rosser provided strong, stable leadership. As the months went by, Channel 7 scored a number of news coups:

Howie Carr, a good, gritty political reporter, broke two big stories—one about public funds being used for Boston mayor Kevin White's trip to Europe; the other, that the U.S. Attorney's Office was launching a corruption probe in Somerville.

The day Bishop Bernard Law was announced as the successor to Cardinal Humberto Medeiros, Channel 7's Amalia Barreda outhustled Boston's other TV reporters—interviewing Law "live" from his living room in Springfield, Missouri, for the 6 o'clock news.

When it came to sports coverage in a sports-crazed town, Channel 4's Bob Lobel and his crackerjack backup team owned the TV scene. But Channel 7 was starting to come into its own. John Dennis would never have Lobel's charisma, but he brought an intelligent, brisk style to the anchor desk and won points as a tough, aggressive interviewer.

In the TV exclusive *A Conversation with Paul Tsongas* (1984 special), the Massachusetts senator disclosed he had non-Hodgkin lymphoma, a disease from which he would later die. The dramatic news was edited down into an exquisite half-hour special, with virtually no narration and no commercials.

Not that Channel 7 had yet achieved parity with its news rivals. A successful evening anchor team had yet to be put in place, and the ratings, though improved, showed Channel 7 still trailing the other stations. Furthermore, both Channels 4 and 5 had stronger anchor desks, a stronger complement of reporters, and vastly superior political units. Still, thanks to Rosser's leadership, Channel 7's news operation was beginning to jell. Although most of the local press remained leery, others were beginning to notice. In 1984, citing a better news product and ratings trending up, the *New York Times* ran a story headlined "Boston CBS Station Posts Needed Gains."[42]

By 1986, rival news directors had come down with a serious case of heartburn when Channel 7 became the first station ever to win Boston/New England Emmys for best newscast *three* years in a row, as well as the first station to win the AP, UPI, and an Emmy in one year. When Channel 7 won its third Emmy, the other news directors blamed the voting process. Somewhat paradoxically, Jim Thistle and Jeff Rosser would each make a significant contribution that helped define and enrich Boston's Golden Age of local news.[43]

Channel 7 would also make its mark in programming. By 1986, Sy Yanoff had the smarts to hire veteran producer Bruce Marson, who became the station's vice president of programming. A local native, Marson came with an impressive resume, which included his previous job at WCVB, where he produced *Good Day!* and later was the prime mover behind *Summer Solstice*. Among Marson's notable achievements at Channel 7 were *Studio 7*, a superb quarterly arts show hosted by the late Phyllis Curtin, the well-known opera singer, and dean of Boston University's College of Fine Arts; and *Our Times*, a classy news magazine show hosted by Paula Childs that aired on Saturday nights. It was an astute program decision, given the dearth of quality programming on at that time. As evidence of Channel 7's improving fortunes, this is what the *Globe*'s Ed Siegel had to say about *Studio 7*:

What's so impressive about *Studio 7* is you see a portrait of local artist Robert Freeman that makes modern art so nonthreatening that you want to go gallery hopping. You see how local inventor Roy Kurzweil improved the sound of synthesizers and hear Hiro Iida perform on one of his digital instruments and you want to hear more synthesizer music. You see what went into the planning of Rowe's Wharf and you want to drive over and look around.

Studio 7 isn't television that helps you pass the time, but television that helps you decide how to spend your time. If television's promise was to give us a window on the world, this series certainly gives us a window on Boston.[44]

At long last, Channel 7 was coming into its own. The longstanding rumor that the beleaguered station had been built on an ancient Indian burial ground had finally been put to rest. The headline on the Ed Siegel column summed it up nicely: "Channel 7 on the Upswing."

To be sure, there was some irony in all of this. It was not simply that Boston, for the second time in a decade, had a locally owned station that was seriously committed to local programming. Rather, out of the wreckage and chaos of the brutal "war" between the stations, Channel 7, under new ownership and later a more competent management team, had become a legitimate player in the market. The period, to be forever remembered as "This is War!," in combination with the emergence of Channel 7, spurred still more spirited competition among all the stations and ushered in still another phase of Boston's Golden Age of television in the 1980s. For proof, check out the first three chapters of this book and note how many program initiatives and projects took place in the 1980s.

The contest wasn't only about ratings and revenue, though, obviously, both were very important. It was also about high ambition, standards of excellence, critical acceptance, including national recognition, and awards. Lots of them—duPonts, Peabodys, Murrows, Gabriels, not to mention hundreds of regional Emmys in the 1980s. Ramsey Clark, the former activist and United States Attorney General during the riotous 1960s, understood the dynamics full well: "Turbulence is life force," he famously stated. "It is opportunity. Let's love turbulence and use it for change."[45]

Channel 4's *Evening Magazine* cohosts Barry Nolan and Sara Edwards. "*Evening Magazine* is at the root of much of the success of local programming," said Channel 5's Paul LaCamera. Image courtesy Barry Nolan.

Evening Magazine cohosts Sara Edwards and Barry Nolan ham it up with Ronald McDonald. Image courtesy Barry Nolan.

Channel 4 general manager Sy Yanoff looks on as his news director Jeff Rosser speaks at a South Shore event. Image courtesy *Patriot Ledger*.

Channel 4's popular Liz Walker broke a racial barrier when she became Boston's first person of color to anchor the nightly news. Image courtesy Channel 4, WBZ-TV.

"Why can't we get players like that?" Bob Lobel, Channel 4's popular sports anchor, used to ask when the Red Sox were beaten by a player the team used to own. Image courtesy Channel 4, WBZ-TV.

Linda Harris, Jack Chase, and weatherman Don Kent comprised
Channel 4's early morning news team. Image courtesy Linda Harris.

"Would you rather have your kid learn about condoms, or would you rather that
your kid was infected with the AIDS virus?" Channel 4's medical reporter Jeanne Blake
asked when Boston's general managers initially refused to carry condom commercials
during the AIDS epidemic. Image courtesy Jeanne Blake. Photo by Loel Poor.

Nancy Merrill hosted *People Are Talking*, Channel 4's popular talk show. Image courtesy Channel 4, WBZ-TV.

When TV critic Terry Ann Knopf pinch-hit for Nancy Merrill (on *People Are Talking*), Merrill reviewed Knopf's performance and gave it a big thumbs down. Image courtesy *Patriot Ledger*.

Boston Broadcasters, Inc., investors were the driving force in getting an FCC license for WCVB-TV. Featured left to right: Bob Bennett, Judge Matthew Brown, BBI president and CEO Leo Beranek, Richard Burdick (seated), and Tom Maney. Image courtesy Channel 5, WCVB-TV.

Chet Curtis and Natalie Jacobson, Channel 5's enormously popular anchor team, were husband and wife in real life, and dubbed "Mr. and Mrs. News." Image courtesy Channel 5, WCVB-TV.

Channel 5's legendary news director Jim Thistle. "Like Bird or Orr, he lifts the level of play," said Clark Booth, his friend and colleague. Image courtesy Channel 5, WCVB-TV.

Phil Balboni succeeded Jim Thistle as Channel 5 news director in 1982. Ten years later, he cofounded New England Cable News, a regional network that is still on the air, and in 2009 he cofounded the *GlobalPost*, an ambitious online international news company. Image courtesy Channel 5, WCVB-TV.

Peter Mehegan and Mary Richardson were a congenial hosting team at Channel 5's long-running *Chronicle*, now in its 35th year on the air. Image courtesy Channel 5, WCVB-TV.

Media critic Edwin Diamond, *Patriot Ledger* TV critic Terry Ann Knopf, and Channel 5's critic-at-large Chuck Kraemer discuss television on *Sunday Open House*, the station's public affairs show. Image courtesy *Patriot Ledger*.

Channel 5's evening anchor Chet Curtis, morning anchor Anne McGrath, and *Good Day!* cohost John Willis enjoy themselves at a station barbecue. Image courtesy Channel 5, WCVB-TV.

Arnie Reisman, writer/producer for Channel 5's *Chronicle*, celebrates his Emmy with his wife Paula Lyons, who was also the station's consumer reporter. Each won two Emmys apiece over time. Image courtesy Channel 5, WCVB-TV.

Channel 5 meteorologists Dick Albert and Bob Copeland. Image courtesy Channel 5, WCVB-TV.

Anchor Tom Ellis worked his magic at both Channels 4 and 5. But in 1982, amid great fanfare and an astronomical salary offer, Tom Ellis jumped to Channel 7. Image courtesy Channel 5, WCVB-TV.

Robin Young, one half of Channel 7's "Dream Team" with
Tom Ellis, speaks to the students at Marshfield High about the
dangers of drinking and driving. Image courtesy *Patriot Ledger*.

A dejected Tom Ellis leaves Channel 7 in 1986 after learning he had been let go. Image courtesy *Patriot Ledger*

WE WANT TOM ELLIS BACK

Arlene Ellis, Tom's wife, shown rounding up signatures for her petition at a South Shore shopping mall, in hopes Channel 7 might rescind its decision. Image courtesy *Patriot Ledger*.

The new coanchor team of R. D. Sahl and Margie Reedy brought credibility to the Channel 7 anchor desk, but it wasn't enough to move the station's news ratings. Image courtesy R. D. Sahl.

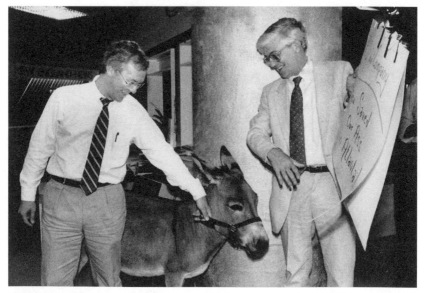

When Channel 7 anchor R. D. Sahl returned from covering the 1988 Democratic Convention in Atlanta, news director Jim Thistle had a surprise for him—a real live donkey. (Good thing it wasn't the Republican Convention.) Image courtesy R. D. Sahl.

Terry Ann Knopf and Raymond Burr (*Perry Mason*) glare at one another during a contentious interview. Image courtesy *Patriot Ledger*.

NBC News anchor Tom Brokaw and Terry Ann Knopf enjoy a laugh after their interview. Photo from Mark Selig of FayFoto. Image courtesy of the author.

"We're gutless, we're spineless," said CBS anchor Dan Rather, speaking about the media at a Boston business luncheon. "The creed used to be 'pull no punches, play no favorites.' It's changed." (Shown here with Terry Ann Knopf.) Photo from Mark Selig of FayFoto. Image courtesy of the author.

"No journalist requires one or two or three million dollars a year. That's for superstars in showbiz: the Redfords, the Streisands, the Newmans," former CBS News president Fred Friendly told Terry Ann Knopf during their interview. Image courtesy *Patriot Ledger*.

: PART TWO :
LOCAL TELEVISION AND BOSTON'S CULTURE

THE LIFE OF A TV CRITIC

Wars can be nasty affairs. So, with the battle lines drawn among Boston's TV stations, what was it like for the local TV critic to be on the front lines? To what degree did the critic get caught in the line of fire? And were there any injuries sustained, beyond that of the critic's wounded ego? To answer these questions, let me begin with a story.

One night, after a long day at work, I was at home watching an episode of *Seinfeld*. My phone suddenly rang while "Jerry" and "Elaine" were in the middle of a hilarious argument. When I picked it up to answer, an unidentified caller asked: "Is this Terry?" When I told him it was—mistake!—he followed up with, "I'M COMING OVER TO KILL YOU!!" Click. It definitely got my attention. A teenage prank? A mischievous threat by an angry general manager or some disgruntled TV personality? While I never found out who the caller was, I did take the precaution of getting an unlisted number.

Still, the fact that I even entertained the possibility that the call might have come from someone who didn't like what I had written underscores the uneasy, often prickly connection between the TV critic and the people she covers. On one hand, this relationship is symbiotic. Each of us needs the other—the local TV stations need the critic to get the word out about a new show or personality, while a basic function of the critic is to inform her readers. Think of it as a pas de deux—in this case, two parties moving in step together and in harmony.

Beyond some shared aims, however, the interests of the two are often in conflict because each has a different agenda. The station invariably wants to publicize its positive news, get glowing feedback on its efforts, or, in the face of controversy, put the best light on a bad situation. Image, reputations, and those all-important ratings points by which the stations lived or died are always at risk. Where the station is motivated by self-interest, though, the critic is motivated by "disinterestedness"—the word used by Matthew Arnold, the nineteenth-century British poet and cultural critic, in his classic essay "The Function of Criticism at the Present Time."[1] He viewed the critic as more impartial, more detached and less influenced by personal advantage or gain than those who were the objects of critical evaluation. To a large extent this was true. Still, we should also acknowledge that all criticism, by definition, is subjective; the critic, being only human, is not always detached or without bias.

During the Golden Age, the relationship between the TV critics and the TV stations was especially complicated. In earlier days, only the largest newspapers, the *Boston Globe* and the *Boston Herald*, had TV critics. But because so much television news was being generated in the Boston market, other newspapers followed suit, hiring their own TV critics. Joining the fray were the *Patriot Ledger*, the *Middlesex News* (later called the *MetroWest Daily News*), and the *Worcester Telegram & Gazette*, as well as continuing coverage by *Boston* (magazine) and the *Boston Phoenix*, the feisty alternative weekly. The *Phoenix* media critics—first Dave O'Brien, then Mark Jurkowitz, and later Dan Kennedy—even kept tabs on the local TV critics.[2]

And then there was the indomitable Norma Nathan, the *Boston Herald*'s colorful, often outrageous gossip columnist, who broke many a story about the local TV and radio stations and their TV stars. Even TV critics were not spared her vitriol. God love her—Norma was sort of the Harry Truman of "gosso-journalists"—she gave us *all* hell. Because there were so many more critics, so much more scrutiny of the stations, so much breaking news, and so much competition among the stations (and yes, among the TV critics themselves), it meant the critics mattered more at that time. In this sense, during Boston's Golden Age, the local TV critics were just another player in the unfolding media drama. For example, the relentless criticism Channel 7 received from the critics during its "This is War!" period was at least one of several factors that led to the early demise of general manager Win Baker and his news director Bill Applegate. And later on, when Channel 7 news director Jeff Rosser hired Elizabeth Stern, a pretty but vacuous soap opera star, to cover Boston's cultural scene, she got thumbs down from the critics. Alas, she was gone quicker than you could say *The Young and the Restless*.

Sparks would additionally fly between the critics and the stations because of their close physical proximity. It was one thing for a Boston TV critic to knock a television executive based in Los Angeles, but quite another for the same critic to write negatively about a local general manager. In Boston, we were all part of a tight-knit media community, and at times it was like being a member of a dysfunctional family. Curse words. Nasty letters and emails. Public reprimands. Intimidation. Screaming matches. This was the kind of blowback a local TV critic could receive during the market's Golden Age. This is not a complaint; it was simply part of the job. Unfortunately, in the heat of battle, cooler heads often didn't always prevail; blood (metaphorically) could be spilled, with verbal shots and wounded egos all around.

WAR STORIES: THE TV CRITIC AS COMBATANT

I'm sure every critic—television or otherwise—has a lengthy list of war stories. Here are a few of my own.

First, a tête-à-tête with Mike Barnicle. At the time (1986), Mike was doing double duty as a *Boston Globe* columnist and on-air commentator for Channel 5's news magazine *Chronicle*. One part charmer, one part con man, Mike was, in short, the kind of challenging subject I loved to write about. And so I did, with a profile in *Boston* magazine called "The Bad Boy of Boston Television."[3] On one hand, I found him to be colorful, quotable, irreverent, and funny—a big lug of a guy. But he could also be foul-mouthed and had a slightly menacing, don't-mess-with-me air about him. Indeed, throughout his *Globe* and television career, he had gotten away with much, thumbing his nose at authority and dogged by charges of plagiarism and fabrication in his columns. (His journalistic lapses eventually caught up with him in 1998 when he was finally, belatedly, forced to resign from the *Globe*.)

For all his charms, I would learn firsthand that he was something of a fraud. Shortly before my article went to press, a *Boston* magazine fact-checker called Barnicle to verify some dates and facts, which was standard practice for reputable magazines. I subsequently got a call from him angrily complaining about being fact-checked. The conversation was short, with an abrupt ending—when he shouted, at full blast, into my ear: "FUCK YOU! You . . . deserve . . . to be working . . . at the QUINCY . . . Patriot . . . Ledger." Whereupon he slammed down the phone. The emphasis on the word "Quincy" was deliberate and intended to make me feel small, even though the South Shore paper was well respected and had long ago dropped the word "Quincy" from its masthead; Bill Ketter, the Ledger's top editor, was even president of the American Society of Newspaper Editors. But what really made the incident so bizarre was that Barnicle's anger surfaced before the article had even been published. I confess I was shaken. There was something so thuggish and disrespectful about his outburst; it was a reminder that behind every bully is a scared little kid.

Then there was the "Peril of Merrill" saga. One day I pinch-hit for Nancy Merrill, the flashy host of People Are Talking, Channel 4's popular daily talk show. It began with a delightful dare. Barry Schulman, the station's program director, invited me to host People Are Talking for a day. I quickly accepted the challenge. For Schulman, it was a chance to put a crabby critic in her place and demonstrate that hosting a television talk show was harder than it looked. For me, it was an adventure—a chance to have some fun, probably at my own expense, and also get some good column material. Jon Lehman, my long-suffering Ledger editor, did me one better; he invited Nancy Merrill to write a review of my performance—which she, too, accepted. Indeed, in the interests of full disclosure, Nancy and I had a rocky relationship owing to a number of critical columns I'd written about her. (I don't think she liked being referred to as "the Rhinestone Cowgirl.") But this was an opportunity for both of us to put down our weapons and have some good-natured fun—wasn't it?

Even before making my "debut," I was learning the pitfalls of being a novice. Instead of boning up on my briefing materials—the subject was health care—I became obsessed with technical details and minutiae. Should I wear my cobalt-blue dress or something more tailored? Would they make me hold up a book to the camera when my nails were such a mess? Why was my hair so unmanageable? I mean, if I couldn't control my own hair, how would I be able to control the show? I worried about mixing up the names and whether to call the guests by their first or last names. And I was strangely anxious about handling viewer phone calls. Uttering the simple talk-show line, "Go ahead, you're on the air," seemed like a major task.

The show's staff could not have been more courteous or supportive. On Monday, I lunched with the show's producer, Alan Schroeder. Despite his gentle, reassuring manner, I barely picked at my chicken salad platter. At one point I found myself slicing my food with a ball-point pen.

The next day, it was showtime. I arrived at the station at 9:30 in the morning wearing my cobalt-blue dress. By now, I was no longer scared—just numb. For openers, I had left an author's book at home. Jean Carney, the makeup artist, was given the formidable task of making me look presentable. I tried not to grimace when someone hooked up a cold, bulky wireless mike under my dress. (At least, we were in the dressing room.) While I was changing a dirty contact lens, I was unexpectedly summoned to do a live promo at 10:28 a.m. At about 11 o'clock, Alan took me onto the set to run through a short introduction that had been written on a Teleprompter—the only problem was that my eyes had difficulty keeping up with the copy. I was told how to use a hand mike, to be used for wading into the studio audience. Then I had to take time out to greet my four guests— trying to make them feel less nervous while hiding my own stage fright.

Before I knew it, we were on the air. Live! In color! From Boston! The opening, which I read from the Teleprompter, went fairly smoothly. But, oh, the mistakes. I made choppy segues to commercial breaks. I spoke in overly long or incomplete sentences, often stumbling over words. I had difficulty making the guests come to life. I was easily distracted by time cues and messages, giving me a shifty-eyed look on camera. Only toward the end, when I went into the studio audience, did I begin to relax and have a good time. For one brief moment, I was "Phyllis" Donahue, with the audience in the palm of my hand. However, when the show was over and my wireless mike was removed, I was still emotionally wired. After thanking the staff for their more than generous support, I left the station and walked to my car. But all I could think of was "Thank God, it's over."

This brings me to Nancy Merrill's review, which appeared a couple of days later in the *Ledger*. Nancy did not mince words:

> Dear Terry Ann,
>
> There are two kinds of critics—constructive ones and destructive ones. The bad news is that you, Terry, and Monica Collins, your feline friend at the *Herald*, are of the former penchant. The good news is that your unprofessional personal attacks on me over the past three and a half years have had no negative effect on my career.
>
> You've said that this is my chance at "revenge." But I'm not given to such time-wasting, negative behavior. In any case, "living well" is the best revenge, and indeed I am living well as the host of New England's number one talk show, *People Are Talking*, and soon in my new job in Chicago, the nation's third-largest TV market. . . . I do have a problem, however, Terry, in this role reversal, because I just saw the tape of you hosting my show. I'm appalled at your language—describing welfare bureaucrats as "dumbos" is tasteless and using the word "besmirched" is a pompous attempt to impress the viewers.
>
> But let me stop here in this critique, as I recall something my mother always said: "If you can't say something nice about somebody, say nothing at all."
>
> NOTHING AT ALL.
>
> Best Regards,
> Nancy[4]

This section could be titled "Love Letters from Needham." Every critic understands that in doing her job, feathers will ruffle. After all, who enjoys being criticized? Like other critics, I received my fair share from the stations. Channel 7's Phyllis Eliasberg told me her boss Jeff Rosser wanted to "behead" me—and this was before ISIS. And Bill O'Reilly, of all people, once charged me with "character assassination."

However, of all the stations, Channel 5 turned out to be my biggest nemesis. Over the years, I found the higher-ups there to be unusually thin-skinned, defensive, and self-righteous. For whatever reason(s), they seemed to feel they were above criticism; at times, I felt as though I were filing my copy from a war zone. Our dealings were continually marked by conflict, interrupted by occasional periods of peace, ending with a return to our respective barricades. There were angry phone calls and letters responding to this column or that and bouts of public dressing down. When I gave the nod to Channel 4 over Channel 5 for its New Hampshire presidential primary news coverage in 1988 ("Channel 4 the Winner, Channel 5 the Loser"), Jim Coppersmith, Channel 5's general manager—a bright man who had a way with words—responded with a pointed letter to me, ccing Bill Ketter, the *Ledger*'s top editor. In it he asserted that I was biased, splashing "gallons of venom" on his station over the years. And he capped it off with the following zinger: "As I've told you before, and Winston Churchill told Adolf Hitler . . . 'You do your worst and we will do our best.'"

And this from news director Phil Balboni, except he charged that I was in bed with a different station—Channel 7 (WNEV-TV):

It never ceases to amaze me how you can so blatantly show your by now well-established bias for your colleagues at WNEV. You make excuses when they do poorly, and seldom miss an opportunity to boost their fortunes, such as with the patently fawning expression "Keep an eye on the kid wearing No 7." This is journalism?

On one occasion, the hostilities threatened to get out of control, when coanchor Chet Curtis unleashed his simmering anger toward me during a live televised event at his station celebrating its fifteenth anniversary. I was there to cover the event for the *Ledger*. Norma Nathan, in her widely read "Eye" column at the *Boston Herald*, headlined "Chet Bashes Critic at Birthday Bash"—well, I'll let Norma tell it—it was her story:

On screen, there was sugar and spice and everything nice at WCVB-TV's 15th birthday bash. Off-screen, there was critic bashing and tooth-knashing [sic] from Channel 5 anchor, normally the chipper chief of bland chitchat.

(Chet) Curtis's wrath was directed at Terry Ann Knopf, TV writer for the *Patriot Ledger.* A steaming Curtis reamed Knopf for her rat-a-tat of raps against the station that pens his paycheck. And he did it before open-mouth onlookers watching wide-eyed with shock, at the party after the bash. "You don't get your facts straight," Chet chaffed. "You knock us every time you can."

Chet said Terry showed favoritism for WNEV-TV because her paper is part of Channel 7's New England News Exchange, and that she incorrectly credited Channel 7 for news bits like the weather-watchers and high school sports awards. (He said both features were 5's first.)

Twice Terry tried to answer, but the star anchor and motor-mouth wouldn't let her get a word in. Chet sputtered until Vice President Paul LaCamera arrived on the scene, and gently led the anchor away.[5]

To his credit, Chet called me to apologize two days later.

Looking back and keeping things in perspective, I'm reminded of the time I went to a terrific baseball art exhibit at the old Institute of Contemporary Art on Boylston Street in Boston. My favorite painting, a real charmer, showed an umpire lying flat on his back, motionless, stretched out over the third-base line. It was called "Kill the Umpire." I imagine a similar painting—this one shows a poor, haggard television critic, slumped over her computer keyboard—lifeless, with blood splattered all over her desk, along with an empty gun cartridge the assailant left behind. This one is called "Kill the Critic!"

THE TV CRITIC AS GOSSO-JOURNALIST

One of the interesting things about Boston television during the Golden Age was its place in the celebrity culture. Hollywood had its stars; Washington, D.C., its politicians; and New York, its bankers and financiers. Boston, aside from the Kennedys, had its local TV personalities, especially the anchors, who were often the subject of profiles and at-home stories or written up in the gossip columns. When Channel 4's Liz Walker went through her controversial pregnancy, it was not only local news; it became a national—actually, an international—story that dragged on for months. And in 1981, when Channel 5 news anchor Natalie Jacobson, who was married to her on-air partner Chet Curtis, gave birth to a baby girl named Lindsay Dawn, it was the lead story on *NewsCenter 5* that night. The *Boston Herald American* slapped the news on page 1 the next day, with TV critic Monica Collins describing the event as "the most famous pregnancy in Boston television history."[6] The couple reportedly received some 5,000 congratulatory cards from their fans. Jane Fonda may have had her exercise video, but our Natalie may have been the country's only news anchor to have her own video called "Natalie's Kitchen."

Such was their celebrity that when "Chet and Natalie," as they were affectionately known, got a divorce in 2001, it was big news, with Chet Curtis leaving Channel 5 and joining New England Cable News. And, when Curtis died of pancreatic cancer in 2014, his passing received not only extensive coverage locally, but was also noted in some national newspapers, including the *New York Times*.[7]

Boston also benefited from its status as a major market (ranked sixth); it was only a forty-five-minute air-shuttle flight away from New York City, where the major news networks and some nationally syndicated talk shows were based. As a result, there was a constant flow of news and showbiz celebrities coming in and out of Boston. Phil Donahue one day, Sally Jessy Raphael the next.

Network newspeople always seemed to be coming to town—either to pick up lucrative lecture fees from the hundreds of Boston-area colleges and universities, or to receive or hand out awards. NBC's John Chancellor came to Boston University to receive a lifetime achievement award in connection with Boston University's Dennis Kauff Memorial Scholarship Fund, named for a Channel 4 reporter killed in a drunk driving accident. Charles Kuralt and Diane Sawyer each made trips to Boston to promote their pairing on CBS's early morning news show. Mike Wallace spoke at the Harvard Law Forum.

And, of course, many a Hollywood movie star and TV celebrity flew to Boston to promote their shows and films. For both the stations and the critics it was a showbiz bonanza that included stars such as Valerie Harper, Tyne Daly (trying to save *Cagney & Lacey* from cancellation), Angela Lansbury, Shirley MacLaine, Jane Fonda, Warren Beatty, Richard Simmons, and dozens of others. Sometimes, entire New York–based network shows, such as NBC's *Today* and ABC's *Good Morning America*, would do on-location shows from Boston.

Like it or not, the popularity of celebrity interviews and profiles added excitement and glamour to a television market that some considered staid and overly serious. Indeed, the town went nuts when the cast of *Cheers*, which was based on a Boston bar, came to town to celebrate its 200th episode. With Boston's City Hall Plaza the setting for a giant rally, most of the stars were on hand, soaking up the adulation: Ted Danson ("Sam Malone"), wearing glasses, along with an adorable bald spot; chubby George Wendt ("Norm"), performing aerobic exercises; Rhea Perlman (the wisecracking "Carla"), cavorting with several Boston Bruins players; and finally, Kirstie Alley ("Rebecca," Sam's sweetheart), shouting with joy when a fan presented her with a street sign called "Kirstie's Alley."

Depending on who the celebrity was, the interview could elicit juicy quotes. Geraldo Rivera, who earlier worked at ABC News, took a swipe at ABC News star anchor Peter Jennings—not very nice, but it made for good copy: "I saw Peter Jennings right after the Hagler-Leonard fight. We were both in San Francisco. Neither one of us acknowledged the other. Putting himself on Mt. Olympus, he has to walk around with a tank filled with oxygen."[8]

Other interviews were pure, unadulterated fun. When the *Today* show's Willard Scott, who was not a meteorologist but really a weatherclown, came to town with the *Today* show, I asked him how he checked out the weather for himself: "I simply open the window and stick my finger outside," he replied. Mary Hart, the perky host of *Entertainment Tonight*, defended her show at a time when it was veering away from entertainment news in favor of more puffery and gossip, with items like "celebrity birthdays." "We're not doing the evening news," she explained. "We're not talking about the bombing in Cambodia or Moammar Khadafy's terrorist tactics. We're talking about Cheryl Tiegs having a baby or Tom Cruise starring in his latest feature film." And I have fond memories of the time when *General Hospital*'s Tony Geary of "Luke and Laura" fame spoke at a "soap seminar" at Harvard's Kirkland House in the early 1980s, when soap operas were all the rage, especially among young people. Decked out in purple pants, purple socks, and running shoes and with his hair in its usual frizzy state, "Luke" joked and jive-talked for more than an hour before 175 delirious female students. At one point, when he asked if he could borrow somebody's pencil, the room dissolved into ear-shattering squeals.[9]

Most of the interviews I conducted with network newspeople were on the serious side. Ted Koppel from ABC's *Nightline* talked about his historic weeklong series of interviews from South Africa in 1985, when the country was in crisis over its apartheid policies. Tom Brokaw provided insights on the Iran-Contra scandal. The legendary CBS newsman Fred Friendly, in town to deliver the keynote address at an ethics conference, railed against the superstar salaries of network newspeople such as Barbara Walters. "No journalist requires one or two or three million dollars a year. That's for superstars in showbiz: the Redfords, the Streisands, the Newmans," he intoned in a loud, thunderous voice.

Every once in a while an interview would make national news. Larry Grossman, a former NBC News president (and former head of PBS), once came to Brandeis for a speaking engagement. But during his somewhat bland remarks he casually mentioned that GE, which owned NBC at the time, had pressured him to tone down the *Nightly News* during the 1987 stock market crash—a very serious charge, because network news divisions are supposed to be free of interference from their corporate owners. Sitting in the audience, I sensed there was a much bigger story to be told. After his speech, I approached him and arranged a phone interview with him upon his return to New York. This resulted in several stories I filed for *Electronic Media*, the industry weekly for which I freelanced. One piece, which ran on page 1, was headlined "Grossman vs. GE: Did NBC Owner Try to Sway the News?" The story had Grossman elaborating on his charges, along with quotes from various heavyweights strongly denying the accusations, including NBC News anchor Tom Brokaw ("We didn't shade the news or buckle") and a representative for GE chairman Jack Welch.[10]

On the other hand, as the values of the celebrity media culture continued to creep into print journalism, I sometimes felt compelled to spice up an otherwise serious, issue-oriented interview. My encounter with Mike Wallace, of *60 Minutes* fame, demonstrates the awkwardness of being a TV critic during that time. Many of the topics we covered were appropriate—his growing up in Brookline, his alleged Republican affiliation, his pioneering role in "ambush journalism," and his ordeal in connection with the $120 million libel suit filed by General William Westmoreland against CBS for its controversial 1982 documentary, "The Uncounted Enemy: A Vietnam Deception." Wallace was the on-camera reporter for the documentary and a key player in the CBS defense. The trial came to an abrupt end when Westmoreland withdrew his suit in February 1985. I asked Wallace about the toll the case had taken on him, both personally and professionally, to the point where he had to be hospitalized: "It was diagnosed as nervous exhaustion. I was just drained emotionally and physically," he said, adding: "And, of all things, the Westmorelands sent me flowers." Okay. But was it necessary to pepper him with other questions such as these: Was he a good father? Why was he separated from his third wife after thirty years? What about the death of his son, a Yale sophomore, in a mountain-climbing accident in Greece? And finally, the pièce de résistance—did he dye his hair?

> "Ah, the old hair question. Come here. Take a look at it," he said, bouncing out of his chair and sticking his head under a lamp. "See, you see a lot of gray. It doesn't show on camera. It looks black because it looks shiny. I have never touched my hair. And, it's so amusing to me. (Johnny) Carson kids me about it; Barbara (Walters) also asked the question."[11]

In hindsight, I suspect I was trying to show the old master that I could be just as tough and intrusive as he was in his interviews. But I also realize I was playing to the crowd—readers who apparently couldn't get enough of this stuff. One time, I even got Dick Cavett, one of my personal heroes, to talk about his midlife crisis and emotional breakdown. He was in town to plug his memoir, though that was something he had omitted from his book. That story went national, and I received a feature-writing award from the New England Press Association. But it was all so odd. Eventually, I began to wonder: Had I myself—the moralistic one—become a small cog in an elaborate media apparatus insanely obsessed with celebrities? Did all of us journalists spend too much time digging up dirt and poking around the private lives of public people? Had we all become chroniclers of the celebrity culture that we had long decried? In the final analysis, had we all become cultural voyeurs? Regrettably, the truth was the public craved it, the editors expected it, the culture demanded it, and many of us simply went along with it.

THE TV CRITIC AS MEDIA ANALYST

As television evolved, so did the role of the critic. Initially, the critic simply functioned as a reviewer of new shows. But as television became increasingly widespread during the 1970s, the critic often acted as a reporter. (The largest papers divided the beat into two separate positions; the smaller papers simply had their critics do double duty.) As the medium continued to expand in the late 1970s and 1980s, many of us additionally performed the role of media analyst. Now, in the same way a political columnist covered politics, at both the local and the network levels, we not only covered televised events but also critiqued and interpreted them. (Tom Shales, the *Washington Post*'s Pulitzer Prize–winning TV critic, was probably the best in this regard.)[12]

Indeed, one of the most meaningful experiences I had as a TV critic came on the day of the 1986 *Challenger* shuttle disaster, which was largely played out on live television. On the morning of January 28, my day at the *Ledger* began uneventfully enough. In between sips of lousy newspaper coffee in the features department, I casually sorted through a stack of press releases, trying to decide on my next day's column. But about 11:45 a.m., sensing a commotion in the newsroom, I joined a group of reporters who had quickly gathered around several large TV monitors. This is how we learned the *Challenger* had exploded shortly after takeoff, witnessed by thousands of horrified spectators at the scene. There we were in our newsroom, our own little world—a bunch of hard-nosed, cynical reporters—now grim-faced, fighting back tears and milling around in a state of shock. As the day wore on, thousands of Bostonians and millions of others throughout the country were similarly glued to their TV sets—at work or in their homes—learning about the tragic accident that had taken the lives of seven gallant astronauts.[13]

More often than not, television is perceived as the Great Divider—polarizing the country on issues like the Vietnam War and the civil rights and women's movements. But paradoxically, in terms of crisis events—such as a presidential assassination and the 9/11 terrorist attacks—television functions as the Great Unifier. And nowhere was this more evident than in television's role in covering the space disaster. During that day of national crisis, Boston's local TV stations and the broadcast and cable networks provided us with information, however fragmented, and also served as an emotional cushion, offering comfort and reassurance. Only Ted Turner's Cable News Network (CNN) carried the 11:38 a.m. liftoff live. But within minutes of the fiery explosion, all three commercial networks were on the air. NBC broke in first at 11:42 a.m., ABC came on at 11:43, with CBS following at 11:45.

Given the unusually great interest in Christa McAuliffe, the "teacher in space" from New Hampshire, Boston's TV stations made extra-special efforts. (Indeed, McAuliffe had been selected from more than 11,000 applicants, according to *Education Week*.) Channels 4, 5, and 7 already had reporters stationed at Cape Canaveral, Florida, mindful of the New England connection, but moved swiftly to dispatch reporters to Washington, D.C., as well. Channel 4 devoted most of its 5:30 p.m. newscast to the tragedy, while Channel 7 preempted *Wheel of Fortune* for a half-hour news special at the same time. Channel 5, which hyped itself as the station providing more national coverage, surprisingly carried *All in the Family* as usual. In addition to their regular newscasts, all three stations had specials at 7:30 p.m. The programs at Channels 4 and 7 were mostly rehashes of the 6 p.m. news; only Channel 5's *Chronicle* managed to provide some fresh insights, with a historical look at NASA's problems.

But the real story was the nonstop live coverage provided by the networks throughout the day. (ABC, CBS, and NBC also presented specials at 10 p.m.) Pointedly, shortly after noon, when reporters pressed Larry Speakes, President Reagan's acting press secretary, for details, he acknowledged the White House was getting its information from television.

Given the ad hoc nature of live events coverage, particularly in the early stages, the network reporting was necessarily unwieldy, chaotic, and repetitious at times. Operating in an information vacuum, there was considerable speculation by the anchors and correspondents ("I'm guessing here," "There is a report circulating"). There was also a great deal of padding. "I'm vamping for time," conceded CBS's Dan Rather at one point. There was more than a little confusion and misinformation, such as the initial report that someone looking like a parachute jumper might have been a survivor. And there were some notable goofs. A tired Dan Rather announced: "As we wait for President Nixon—I mean President Reagan—to address the nation." At 4:30 p.m., the network cameras switched live to the Johnson Space Center in Houston, with Director Jesse Moore giving out the first official word from NASA. But ABC temporarily lost its sound. An angry Peter Jennings seemed exasperated. "Will someone *please* find the audio?" he said.

On the local level, there were self-serving ploys, such as Channel 5's preempting chunks of ABC's afternoon coverage in favor of showcasing anchors Maryanne Kane and Jim Boyd and reporter Shirley McNerney. And too often, especially with Channel 7, the coverage was heavily focused on tear-jerking interviews with relatives, neighbors, and friends of Christa McAuliffe—all of which conjured up George Will's memorable phrase about "the pornography of grief."

But for all its imperfections, television had kept its cool. It provided responsible coverage under the most trying circumstances. It gave us a front-row seat to an agonizing historic event. And finally, it took what could have been an impersonal disaster story and transformed it into a human drama that touched us deeply. The dramatic pictures of the explosion were shown over and over again. Oddly, it was a beautiful sight at first, with white puffs of smoke set against a deep blue sky. But then came that dreadful moment when the shuttle disintegrated into a grotesque fireball. Some would later charge network overkill, what with instant replays and slow motion shots like a televised football game. But we should also remember that many viewers were tuning in at different times throughout the day. Then there was President Reagan, scrapping his State of the Union speech in favor of brief, simple, low-key remarks to the American public. There were also some touching, spontaneous moments, such as the exchange between ABC's anchor Peter Jennings and Senator Jake Garn of Utah, a former shuttle crew member, who tearfully compared the explosion to the time he lost his first wife in a car accident.

Finally, the heartbreaking scenes of Christa McAuliffe. An unusually warm, appealing person, Christa had become the darling of the media. What irony in all those unforgettable TV images before us. We saw replays of Christa and her colleagues, so full of life, walking to the van earlier in the morning. We saw McAuliffe's husband, Steven, and their two children, on the nearby rooftop of Mission Control headquarters, beside themselves with pride. Two miles away in the VIP grandstand we saw McAuliffe's parents and friends getting ready to recite the countdown chant. Seconds later they would recoil in horror when they saw the monstrous blast in the sky. And then, shots of Christa's excited high school students back in Concord, New Hampshire, assembled in the auditorium. One moment, they were wearing party hats and blowing noisemakers. Suddenly, they saw the shuttle, carrying their teacher, explode before their eyes on national television. The party was over.

Typically, in the aftermath of tragedy, the media are accused of excessive coverage, shallow reporting, and sensationalism. But the real point regarding the *Challenger* calamity was how television, at both the national and the local level here in Boston, had bound us together in our hour of national need.

"BANNED IN BOSTON"

PURITANISM

Traditionally, Massachusetts has been regarded as a socially progressive and politically liberal state—from its early activism against slavery before the Civil War, to its distinction as the only state to give its electoral votes to the losing Democratic senator George McGovern running for president in 1972, to its historic role as this country's first state to issue marriage licenses to same-sex couples.

But one of the things that gives Massachusetts its unique and complex character is the set of contradictory forces at work: the peculiarities of New England's Puritan heritage, the conservatism of the state's powerful Roman Catholic Church, and the strong streak of parochialism that has sometimes put a brake on the culture's more liberal impulses.

The phrase "Banned in Boston" was first used in the late nineteenth century through the mid-twentieth century to refer to a book, song, or film prohibited from being circulated or exhibited by local officials. But the roots of such severe restrictions date from colonial times, when the religious group known as the Puritans, as every schoolchild knows, sailed from England and founded the Massachusetts Bay Colony. Despite the Puritans' apparent love of freedom, their religious principles were extremely limiting and permitted little deviation from their strict moral code. Idleness was a sin. A man could not kiss his wife in public, lest he face hours in the pillory. As of 1656, women were forbidden to wear short-sleeved dresses, "whereby the nakedness of the arm may be discovered." The practice of drinking toasts was outlawed in 1639, and upon getting complaints Boston closed down a dance school. As early as 1651, censorship was imposed when William Pynchon, a colonial fur trader and the man who founded Springfield, Massachusetts, wrote a book critical of Puritanism. Not only was the book banned and reportedly burned, but also the author was pressured to return to England the next year.

By the end of the seventeenth century, the Puritan political influence had largely faded away, but remnants of its rigid code and harsh disciplinary practices would persist for many years. In the mid- to late nineteenth century, the Boston Brahmins—the wealthy, Protestant elite—felt their power and social standing were starting to erode. Their distress found expression in 1878 in the creation of a group called the New England Society for the Suppression of Vice. The group, later renamed the Watch and Ward Society, had as its mission "to watch and ward off evildoers." The Watch and Ward Society did not have formal ties to the Boston Archdiocese, owing to theological differences and longstanding antagonisms. But both were strong endorsers of censorship. Indeed, the society often worked with Catholic police chiefs and district attorneys to implement obscenity laws.

And so, a powerful anti-vice movement took hold in Boston. Burlesque shows were run out of town, and books containing sexually explicit scenes or foul language were banned, along with theatrical posters deemed too suggestive. By today's standards, much of the censorship would be considered ludicrous, as noted by Neil Miller in his book *Banned in Boston*: "One of the great controversies of the 1890s revolved around sculptor Frederick MacMonnies' statue of the nude Bacchante (a female devotee of Bacchus), which was removed from the courtyard of the Boston Public Library and shipped to the Metropolitan Museum of Art in New York in 1897 after a huge public outcry."[1]

In 1929, some sixty books were banned, including ones by Hemingway (*A Farewell to Arms*) and D. H. Lawrence (*Lady Chatterley's Lover*). That same year, theatergoers wishing to see *Strange Interlude*, Eugene O'Neill's Pulitzer Prize–winning play, had to travel to Quincy. And then there was the Everly Brothers' 1957 innocent little ditty "Wake Up Little Susie," which was about a young couple who fell asleep at the drive-in. Though this was the duo's first number one hit, the record still managed to get banned on some Boston radio stations.

Book banning was not halted in Boston until the 1950s. By the 1970s, as public tastes changed and court decisions became more liberal, the Watch and Ward Society began to decline. The group changed its name to the New England Citizens Crime Commission and focused on drugs and gambling. Indeed, by this time, the sobriquet "Banned in Boston" had actually become a useful marketing tool. When Richard Sinnott, chief of the Boston mayor's licensing division (the city's censor), died in 2003, it more or less marked the end of an era (years earlier, Sinnott had prevailed on Edward Albee to delete sixty lines from *Who's Afraid of Virginia Woolf?*, causing the playwright to vow never to return to Boston again).[2]

PAROCHIALISM: IN TV, NO FOREIGNERS NEED APPLY

The word is "parochial"—as in provincial, narrow-minded, defensive, unsophisticated, suspicious of outsiders, and resistant to change. Yes, "parochial," as in our fair city of Boston. And, oh the grudges against enemies in the neighborhood, real or imagined.

Some would deny or at least qualify the charge. James Carroll, the prominent writer and author, calls it a "clichéd perception of Boston parochialism."[3] Former Massachusetts governor Mike Dukakis claims that Boston is finally changing, becoming more cosmopolitan, more inclusive, and less turf-conscious: "That's ridiculous! Absolutely ridiculous! There's nothing parochial about Boston these days,"[4] he says.

But while Boston may be transforming itself with innovative projects, like the Seaport District development underway, a strong strain of parochialism remains embedded in its history. In his book *Liberty's Chosen Home*, Alan Lupo, the late *Boston Globe* columnist who knew the city well, wrote: "And that is the story of this city. It is, and always has been, a city torn apart by the extremes, a city both liberal and conservative, enlightened and parochial and stifling. At times in history, it has been very hard to be an Irishman in Boston, or an Italian, or a Jew, or a black, or lately, a Yankee."[5]

As we have seen, part of Boston's parochialism dates from colonial times, when the Puritans, seeking to "purify" the Church of England from its Catholic influences, came to New England and established the Massachusetts Bay Colony. But in their belief that they were doing

God's work they were often highly intolerant of others. Part of the city's parochialism can be traced to class and ethnic divisions going back to the waves of Irish Catholic immigrants who came to Boston in the nineteenth century. The wealthy, educated Beacon Hill Brahmins felt threatened, resulting in discrimination and social ostracism of the new arrivals. The infamous employment ads and signs indicating "No Irish Need Apply" were one reminder of Boston's bigotry. As James Carroll writes:

> In other places, Irish immigrants and their descendants moved rather smoothly into positions of economic, social and political power, but in Boston they were confronted by a Yankee establishment that did not want them. The stain of that rejection marked the soul of the city. Despite all appearances of patrician high-mindedness, Boston's initial hatred of the Irish remains its Original Sin. *Thus, the Irish presence has been known from the start for a spirit of xenophobic defensiveness that is still evident* [my italics].[6]

For the aggrieved group, politics was seen as the means to upward mobility, which, in the words of William V. Shannon, the late journalist and ambassador to Ireland during the Carter Administration, became "an Irish family affair," characterized by "inbreeding and a complacent parochialism."[7]

Along with longstanding resentments, ethnic rivalries, and the defense of neighborhood turf, racism was also factored into the city's parochialism. In the 1970s, under federal court-ordered supervision aimed at desegregating Boston's schools, white students were bused to black neighborhoods such as Roxbury, with black students bused to white enclaves such as South Boston and Charlestown. The result was a series of ugly, often violent clashes and white student boycotts, which tore the city and its political leaders apart.

In the end, despite its noble intentions, the experiment turned out to be deeply flawed because it pitted the poor and disadvantaged against one another while leaving the white suburban towns out of the equation. Recently, Jean McGuire, who had been a bus monitor forty years earlier, recalled the turmoil: "I remember riding the buses to protect the kids going up to South Boston High School. And the bricks through the window. Signs hanging out those buildings, 'Nigger Go Home.' Pictures of monkeys. The words. The spit. People just felt it was all right to attack children."[8]

Finally, Boston's parochialism was related to the dominance of the Roman Catholic Church, whose strict teachings on mandatory celibacy, the role of women in the church, sex and sexual orientation, abortion, evolution and climate change, and so many other issues, have continued to be viewed by its critics, within and outside the church, as narrow-minded, exclusionary, and hostile to change. As Lupo observed: "The Catholic Church was as fine an inheritor to Puritan rigidity as could be found."[9]

Even if we take into account Boston's changing demographics and greater inclusiveness in recent years, the town's parochialism has remained strong. In 2004, Massachusetts became the to first state in the country to allow same-sex marriage. But it wasn't until 2015 that gays and lesbians were allowed to march in Boston's annual St. Patrick's Day parade. Not for nothing has Boston had trouble living down its national reputation in this area. Jokes and putdowns outside of Boston are still quite common. In 2015, when the United Sates Olympic Committee chose Boston over Los Angeles to be the sole bidder for the 2024 Summer Olympics, Bill Plaschke, a *Los Angeles Times* sports columnist, harrumphed: "Huh? How on Earth does Los Angeles lose the Olympic bid to Boston? How does the only American city to host both an Olympics (twice) and a World Cup final lose a chance to bid on the planet's biggest sports competition to a parochial burg that's never even hosted a Super Bowl or Final Four?"[10]

"A parochial burg"? Thus, given its history and national reputation, we should not be surprised to find that Boston's parochialism was very much in evidence when it came to local television during its Golden Age. In a way, the phrase "No Irish Need Apply" was effectively replaced by "No Foreigners Need Apply." Not only were the locals notably disinclined to hire on-air people from outside the United States, but also ethnic names were considered "un-American." Nobody in Boston had ever heard of a Channel 5 anchor team named "Chester Kubicwicz" of Polish descent and "Natalie Salatich," the daughter of a proud Serbian family. But of course, everybody knew and loved Chet Curtis and Natalie Jacobson, both of whom changed their last names and reigned as "Mr. and Mrs. News" for years. (Jacobson once told me she regretted changing her name.) At the time, Tsongas (as in the late U.S. senator Paul Tsongas), Dershowitz (as in the famed Harvard law professor Alan Dershowitz), and Yastrzemski (as in the Red Sox Hall of Famer Carl Yastrzemski) were all superstars in their fields. But they would have had a tough time making it on Boston television had they insisted on keeping their real surnames.

The pattern at the national level was mixed. Before Christiane Amanpour, British-born, raised in Teheran, took a job at CNN, a friend had encouraged her: "You know, this is a great opportunity for somebody like yourself who's foreign, who has a foreign accent. We hear foreign accents on CNN. It's crazy, it's wild, who knows, maybe they'll take you because you certainly don't fit in, in the American spectrum of news."[11]

Hired by CNN in 1983, Amanpour went on to become one of the world's best-known and most respected foreign affairs correspondents—an international superstar and the winner of countless journalism awards. But in 2010, she decided to leave CNN and join ABC News to anchor *This Week*. Unfortunately, the ratings for her show fell precipitously, with Amanpour returning to CNN the next year (though ABC News retained her as a global affairs anchor). A few Canadians have been allowed through the doors—notably Peter Jennings, who held down the coveted anchor position at ABC's *World News Tonight* for nearly a quarter of a century. On the other hand, Dave Wright, a likable, folksy Canadian anchor hired by Channel 7's Jeff Rosser, lasted but two years in Boston.

Nowhere were the hazards of going international better demonstrated than in the hiring of Angela Rippon, a BBC television star, as Channel 7's arts and entertainment reporter. It was one of Jeff Rosser's more unorthodox and most intriguing moves—and something of a coup. Rippon was the first woman ever dubbed "Newsreader of the Year" and was also known as "the Barbara Walters of British television." She had authored numerous books and was an award-winning documentary filmmaker. And, though most of her seventeen years in British television were spent in news, her interests included modern dance, ballet, and acting. By every measure, her on-camera experience, and her reputation and popularity in England, all suggested she was more than qualified to cover the arts and entertainment scene in Boston. A *Boston Herald American* writer called her "a blue-chip import custom-built for broadcasting and sure to boost the ratings."[12] Indeed, in a trans-Atlantic telephone interview I had with the broadcast editor of the *London Times*, Peter Davalle offered high praise. "I think you're very lucky. You are getting the best of our women personalities. There isn't another Angela Rippon in England."[13] Interest and excitement were running high in the Boston market. But the real question was whether the Brit would fit in in this rather parochial town. At the time, *Globe* TV critic Jack Thomas skillfully laid out the doubts about her:

> The first is the notion that Boston viewers are too provincial to tolerate criticism in a foreign accent by a woman, no matter how charming, animated, clever, confident or impeccably dressed.
>
> The second is that, because of the differences between British and American entertainment, and especially humor, she might miss nuances that would be obvious to her audience.
>
> The third is that she might seem too aristocratic to be taken seriously by television viewers like those at, say, the Eire Pub in Dorchester, where Watney's Ale is about as popular as tea and scones.[14]

Given its excessive hype during its "This is War!" period, Channel 7 was understandably cautious in its marketing. The idea was to ease her into the viewers' consciousness, slowly—though even before Rippon's plane had arrived at Logan Airport the viewers were treated to footage of her at home in Devon, England. Making her debut on January 30, 1984, she garnered quite favorable early reviews, with words like "intelligent," "sharp," "well researched," and "professional" used to describe her work.

Four months after her debut, she agreed to sign a three-year contract, though it contained an opt-out clause by either side. Rosser was clearly delighted. By November, Rippon and her British husband, businessman Christopher Dare, started house hunting in the Boston area. "There is no doubt in any of our minds that Angela's dedicated efforts have contributed greatly to the overall growth of Ch. 7's news," Rosser later told the *Globe*.[15] She even proved a good sport when it came to the more frivolous aspects of the job, such as taping a promo with her dog and riding an elephant when the circus came to town.

But in a development that caught nearly everyone by surprise, on January 5, 1985, Channel 7 announced that Angela Rippon was returning to England, despite the fact that she hadn't lined up another job there. The *Boston Herald American*, appreciating a juicy story, splashed the news on page one the next day ("Angela Rippon to Quit TV Job"). It was all very mysterious. Only a month earlier she had been showcased in a holiday special—her second of the season, with more reportedly planned. Was she pushed or did she jump? Was she homesick for her husband, who had been commuting to Boston? Is it possible Americans still hadn't forgiven King George III? Reluctantly agreeing to an interview with the *Ledger*, she was tightlipped, merely citing "a complex set of circumstances on both sides."

None of it was clear, though a few things were. Throughout Rippon's brief stay in Boston, the public, the press, and even her own station were forever fixated on her "British-ness." A *Globe* headline on the day of Rippon's debut read: "Channel 7 Acquires a British Accent." Similarly, a facetious *Ledger* headline called her "An Arts Reporter with 'True Brit'" (yup, my headline).

Rival executives continued to jab away. "I was amused that the announcement [of her hiring] was made over tea and scones," said Channel 5's general manager Jim Coppersmith. "I wouldn't go out of the country for an arts and entertainment reporter," said a bemused Tom Goodgame, his Channel 4 counterpart. "It's a spectacular move, like fireworks on the Fourth of July, but once they go off, all you've got is a spent cartridge."[16] And I'm sorry to report that I was just as patronizing, taking note of her Briticisms: "Rippon reached for some 'smarties' (M&M chocolates), mentioned her friend 'Frosty' (David Frost) and spoke of life in the English countryside and 'its farmers who live in Wellies' (Wellington rubber boots), you see."[17]

In a Q&A with Rippon a week before her Boston debut, Jim Baker, the *Boston Herald*'s TV critic, felt compelled to ask about her British accent:

Q—Do you see a British accent as a problem in drawing viewers here and communicating with them?
A—If you start looking for problems you'll find them and they will magnify. There are so many British TV productions and so

many accents here anyway. . . . What would be a problem is if I tried a phony Boston accent.[18]

The day after her debut, Baker was still obsessing about her accent: "Rippon earned an 'A' in speech with a highly polished British delivery, but it's one that will require adjustment time for Boston viewers," he wrote. He also reported some ominous feedback from his readers:

Even before appearing on air, Rippon and WNEV-TV drew criticism from several writers and callers who had never seen her. Some questioned why the station would go outside the country to hire a reporter. And there was one caller who asked ever so loudly: "Hey, who's this Angela babe? If Ch. 7 wants viewers, they went too far. They should've stopped in Ireland. All they need is a young lass named Kathleen O'Malley! Put her on the air and let the good times roll."[19]

Even Rippon's bosses may have erred when, seeking to capitalize on her British lineage, she was sent to London for two weeks to promote New England tourism. ("Come back," she told her countrymen, "all is forgiven.") The station also may have tried too hard to "Americanize" her by having her do a five-part series on Elvis Presley.

Everything seemed to come down to her accent. There were titters in some quarters when she pronounced *Dynasty*, the ABC soap opera, as "*Din-isty*." Some found her promotional spots condescending, as when she said she wasn't fond of Picasso. In the end, there may have been more than one reason that caused Angela Rippon to take her leave. Still, it's hard not to conclude that the Brit didn't fit and that Bostonians felt simply she wasn't their cup of tea.

SEX

In addition to grappling with Boston's overly rigid and moralistic heritage, the stations were perpetually fearful of turning off their viewers, offending their advertisers, and having to contend with powerful constituencies, including the Boston Roman Catholic Archdiocese. Local sensitivities were only heightened during Ronald Reagan's conservative presidency and the attendant "culture wars" debate that raged between traditionalists and progressives on "hot-button" issues, such as abortion, homosexuality, and censorship. The excesses included the Jerry Falwells on one side versus the Jerry Springers on the other. On all too many occasions the local general managers or station owners found it easier to bend to pressure groups rather than risk their wrath. This was especially true when it came to program matters involving sex or morality. The squeamishness of Boston's TV stations over Robert Mapplethorpe's sexually explicit photographs at the Institute of Contemporary Art in 1990 has already been cited, as has the case of the nude female statue resting peacefully in the courtyard of the Boston Public Library a century earlier that had to be shipped to New York's Metropolitan Museum of Art because of public complaint.

And then there was the local uproar about sexual content involving a CBS special that was banned in Boston. The 1988 special, called *Inside the Sexes*, was an intelligent, serious exploration of human sexuality—quite literally an inside look at the human reproductive system. The topics ranged widely from sex education and treatments for impotence, to scientific advances in surgery, to the mechanics of the AIDS virus. Narrated by the actor Roy Scheider, the program also featured an award-winning team of producers. Alfred R. Kelman, the executive producer, earlier had received a Directors Guild, an Emmy, and a Peabody for his work on the acclaimed series *Body Human* for CBS.

The reviews from critics around the country were positive. In the *New York Times*, Walter Goodman cited the "adventurous" camera work, such as the budding of nipples and penis in the fetus, hastening to add: "You don't have to be a voyeur to be fascinated by these intimate views." In her *Los Angeles Times* review, Lynne Heffley called it a "wondrous hour" and "a jaw-dropping journey into the workings of sex." But out of CBS's 200 affiliated stations around the country, only *three* decided not to air the show—Salt Lake City, Louisville—and yes, Boston.[20]

In a written statement, Sy Yanoff, Channel 7's general manager (backed by his board chairman David Mugar), contended the program was "inappropriate for us to air" and described the show as "extremely explicit." He told the *Boston Globe*'s Bruce McCabe that the show's first ten minutes were especially offensive to him, "talking about lovemaking, multiple orgasms and ejaculation."[21] (Oh my, Sy.) In my own column, I took strong exception, writing: "It is essentially a science program on the order of PBS's *Nova*, not a titillating peep show about sex. It is about as much of a turn-on as looking at an amoeba under a microscope."[22]

Yanoff's objections to the show's first ten minutes were utterly mystifying. To show the physical differences between male and female bodies, there was a brief, shadowy drawing of a male body showing the barest outline of a penis. The visual was about as shocking as an anatomical chart we might see in a doctor's office. (In my own column, I mused: "Sy, you want suggestive? Check out Jim Palmer's ads for Jockey shorts.") After showing two lovers in a tender embrace (from the neck up, by the way), a high-technology microscopic camera showed the physical changes that occur in the male and female bodies upon sexual arousal. Viewers saw a radioactive image of a man's beating heart responding to nerve and muscular tension. They also saw the walls of a vagina. In matter-of-fact fashion, narrator Roy Scheider noted that orgasm occurs when "nerve impulses flutter sexual muscles at precisely 8/10 of a second intervals in both man and woman." There were also some "historic pictures" of a living human fetus, about the size of a button; and footage, using time-lapse techniques, of how a speck of tissue evolves into a male or female sex organ by the fifteenth week.

It was all so clinical. So how to explain Channel 7's prudishness? Part of it was easily traceable to Boston's Puritanism regarding anything to do with sex. Part of it likely stemmed from the station's fear of the Boston Archdiocese, located in Brighton, only a mile or two from the Channel 7 studios in Boston. And part of it was reflective of the juvenile, locker-room mentality that many middle-aged, male television executives had about sex in those days, which rendered supposedly grown men unable to differentiate between erotica and education.

What was additionally disturbing about Yanoff's ban was the double standard at work. It was difficult to reconcile how a general manager of a major station would censor a pretty tame exploration of human sexuality, while at the same time air a never-ending stream of trashy TV movies that exploited sex and violence. To wit, on July 24, 1988, Channel 7 carried the CBS movie *Sin of Innocence*, which was about a high school senior who becomes romantically involved with his stepsister. On September 13, 1988, it aired *Mistress* (a repeat, no less), and four days later served up *Mayflower Madam* (still another repeat). One wondered whether the station management had any qualms about *Internal Affairs*, a two-part CBS movie with the racy double-entendre title, which aired just in time for the November sweeps. This was a film about a psycho who gets his jollies from tying up women and then murdering them. Was this "appropriate," to use the general manager's own word, for the viewers?

THE CONDOM CONUNDRUM

Interestingly enough, one of the segments in the banned CBS special dealt with AIDS. For it was at this time the incidence of this lethal disease had "increased rapidly through the 1980s," peaking in the early 1990s, according to the Centers for Disease Control.[23] The epidemic coincided with a key moment when educators and health officials were pleading for more public awareness about sexual matters, emphasizing the media's special responsibility to provide more, not less, information.

By the mid-1980s, AIDS, the fatal disease that could be transmitted sexually or through the reuse of hypodermic syringes, was out in full force. Faced with this national crisis, right around January 1987 three of the country's local TV stations—KRON-TV in San Francisco, WRTV-TV in Indianapolis, and WXYZ-TV in Detroit—each made a courageous decision to accept condom commercials as a health prevention device. In each case, the decision was made in response to the growing body of scientific and medical evidence that the AIDS epidemic, once largely confined to male homosexuals, was now making its way into the heterosexual community. The U.S. Surgeon General's office estimated that by 1991, 270,000 people would have AIDS, with 6,000 alone in Massachusetts.

However, the news that several of the country's TV stations would accept condom commercials unleashed a firestorm of protest. After all, anything having to do with the word "s-e-x" (shoosh!) made people uncomfortable, and besides, the public, by and large, had extremely negative attitudes toward homosexuals, the group most closely identified with AIDS. Conservative groups such as Morality in

Media and the Roman Catholic Church argued that such advertising would usher in a new era of permissiveness.

A deep split emerged between the broadcasting community and various interest groups on one side, and the scientific, medical, and public health community on the other. Doctors and other experts were largely supportive of allowing condoms to be advertised on television, viewing it as a practical way of promoting safer sex. But resistance in the television industry remained strong. At the time, all three major networks and nearly all the local TV stations across the country were steadfast in their refusal to air condom commercials on the grounds that viewers would find them offensive.

In Boston, station officials at Channels 4 and 5 said they opposed airing such commercials, while Channels 7 and 56 indicated that they hadn't yet made up their minds. A pivotal moment came on January 21, 1987, when Channel 5's general manager Jim Coppersmith was invited to appear on ABC's *Nightline* to discuss the condom controversy. An intelligent man with strong opinions, Coppersmith seemed to speak for the broadcasting community as a whole. Unfortunately, on this national platform, he also came across as one of those self-righteous, self-appointed guardians of public morality and good taste. While saying he favored more programming and public service announcements about AIDS, he drew the line against TV stations running condom ads. "One of the things that a general manager of a television station gets paid to do is to judge what the market he serves will stand for," he said. Then, taking his argument one step further, he contended that condom manufacturers were simply looking to the make money. "We're not for rent for anyone that comes along with a can of quarters," he said.[24]

Jeanne Blake, Channel 4's medical reporter, did not hold a medical degree but had done extensive reporting on AIDS and was among the town's most outspoken critics of Coppersmith's position. "I want to see a poll. If Jim Coppersmith can say he's measuring the pulse of New England, I want to see it in writing. There should be two questions: 'Would you rather have your kid learn about condoms? or Would you rather that your kid was infected with the AIDS virus?'"

Blake added she was "disappointed" by the policy of her own station's corporate owner, Westinghouse Broadcasting Co., which prohibited its five stations, including her own, from accepting condom commercials. "I will continue to do everything I can personally. I feel it's my responsibility," she said. Four days after the *Nightline* show, *Boston Globe* columnist David Nyhan, calling local and network broadcast executives "bozos," issued a stinging rebuke:

> The bozos who run television would rather have kids play with cars and beer than with contraceptives. Which tells you something about the values of television executives. This has nothing to do with money, this one. The condom makers would pay good money for their airtime, just like every other advertiser. . . .
>
> But the network execs and the local general managers would have to take heat from all those people who refuse to accept that half of all teenage girls lose their virginity by age 17. Unused to standing on principle, out of their element in a decision where money is not involved, the TV boys are in concrete. Their attitude is: better sorry than safe. For the want of the odd condom ad, a lot of kids are going to get AIDS, and a lot of girls are going to get pregnant. It's not right.[25]

A *Patriot Ledger* survey of Boston's own TV physicians and medical specialists released on January 26, 1987, also found that *all* took strong exception to the broadcast industry's position and to Coppersmith's remarks, including Dr. Tim Johnson, his own resident doctor at Channel 5. All agreed that abstinence was an ideal, but unrealistic, goal in preventing AIDS. They said that condoms, while not foolproof, offered protection for sexually active people. And they advised TV stations to accept condom advertisements as a health measure. Dr. Johnson, who also was a medical consultant to ABC, said: "If the effect of condom commercials is to prevent the threat of AIDS, I'd see it as a positive end. I see it as a preventive device, not just for its own sake." All sounded a note of urgency. "It has the potential to become the most serious issue since the plague if the numbers continue unchecked," counseled Dr. Johnson. Dr. Murray Feingold, Channel 4's resident doctor, also added that Coppersmith's remarks about condom manufacturers making money off their product by advertising were irrelevant. "The penicillin people advertise in our medical journals all the time. It still saves lives."

All of those interviewed said that television needed to become more directly involved. "We're talking about a deadly disease," Dr. Feingold warned. "We have a responsibility in television. We don't need little pistols; we need an A-bomb. If our general managers knew how rapidly the disease was spreading, maybe they would say we have to take this extra step." All were in agreement that ignorance, prejudice, and fear of offending segments of the public—especially the Catholic Church—were factors in the Boston stations' reluctance to accept condom commercials. Asked if stations were afraid of alienating the Roman Catholic Archdiocese of Boston, Dr. Johnson replied: "I'm a fifteen-year native of Boston. I presume that's true. All of the TV stations, consciously or unconsciously, are sensitive to the issue."

But suddenly, without any apparent warning, something quite extraordinary happened. In little more than a month, more than twenty-five stations in eleven markets nationwide said they were ready to air condom commercials, not for birth control but as a form of personal health protection. In the Boston area, one by one the stations began to fall into line. On January 27, Channel 56 (WLVI-TV) became Boston's first station to announce it would accept condom ads; the next day it was Channel 27 (WHLL-TV) in Worcester. On February 13, Channel 7 (WNEV-TV) became the first of Boston's three major stations to announce an ambitious AIDS campaign, which included the acceptance of condom commercials. And that week, Channel 25, the Fox Broadcasting–owned station, disclosed it too would accept such ads.[26]

Even the networks, which had publicly espoused a hardline position, were now modifying their stance. A week earlier, ABC became the first network to accept a public service announcement about AIDS, citing condoms as a potential preventive measure to the fatal disease. On the same day, NBC and CBS informed their owned-and-operated stations that they were free to decide whether to accept public service announcements or commercials mentioning condoms. (Immediately, WCBS-TV and WNBC in New York and KCBS in Los Angeles, all network-owned stations, said they would accept condom commercials that mentioned AIDS prevention.)

Obviously, Coppersmith and, indeed, the vast majority of the nation's broadcasters, had failed to appreciate the crisis proportions of the AIDS epidemic as well as the public's changing attitudes toward sexual activity. It was a time of great uncertainty. Ideological, philosophical, political, financial, and religious considerations had been swept away by more pragmatic concerns. In the absence of a cure for AIDS, many people regarded condoms, although not foolproof, as one important means for stopping the spread of sexually transmitted diseases such as AIDS. Surgeon General C. Everett Koop had become a critical figure in the debate. A political conservative who was the darling of antiabortionists, Koop had emerged as the most outspoken federal official in favor of condom advertising. His advocacy and high public profile helped legitimize the issue.

Television itself was now playing a role in raising public consciousness. Although the word "condom" was once taboo, shows that year such as *Cagney & Lacey* and *Valerie* had episodes dealing with teenage boys who got ahold of condoms. The *Nightline* show dealing with the condom commercial controversy had served to crystallize as well as amplify the issue, with NBC *Nightly News* and ABC's *World News Tonight* doing follow-up reports, citing statistics about more and more stations reversing their original positions. Broadcasters who had been sitting uncomfortably on the fence no longer felt quite so isolated. It was as if the collective broadcast community had suddenly realized that "little pistols" wouldn't do—what was really needed was "an A-bomb."

LESBIAN NUNS

Then there was the "lesbian nun" controversy, which began as a local issue but turned into a national story. It started with a *Boston Globe* feature on March 17, 1985, headlined "Nuns Speak Out on Love, Sex in Forthcoming Book."[27] The book, edited by two former nuns, was a collection of personal stories by fifty-one Roman Catholic women who had sought to devote their lives to God, but wound up coming to grips with their lesbianism. The *Globe* piece contained a brief mention that the editors Rosemary Curb and Nancy Manahan would appear on Channel 4's *People Are Talking* the next month. The Rev. Peter Conley, secretary for community relations for the Catholic Archdiocese of Boston, then promptly fired off a letter to Tom Goodgame, Channel 4's general manager, expressing the church's opposition to the booking on the grounds that it was "insensitive to Catholics" and seemed to confirm "a growing suspicion that anti-Catholicism is an acceptable bias."[28] Conley reportedly contacted twenty-five Catholic parishes, urging them to object to the show's airing. The station received about eighty letters and two petition letters, one with 150 signatures and one with fifteen signatures.

To be sure, the Catholic Church in Boston and elsewhere perceived itself under siege. The hit play in Boston, *Sister Mary Ignatius Explains It All for You*, a biting satire about Catholic education, had earlier drawn criticism from some Catholics. And on Easter Sunday CBS's *60 Minutes* featured a provocative report called "Equal Before God," in which various nuns argued that women should have the right to be ordained.

But there were also larger issues at stake. As I wrote in a column: "The issue here is not the right of the Catholic Church to express its views—or to be treated fairly. We live in a free country, after all. What is at issue is a TV station's obligation to maintain its independence and to make decisions based on reasonable judgments that serve the larger interests of the community, regardless of pressure from outside groups."

Nevertheless, Goodgame canceled the segment, then issued a written statement the next day to explain his position. In it, he spoke in hazy generalities about "the sensitivity of a significant portion of our audience" and subject matter that might be "offensive to a large part of our audience." Yet, in a telephone interview with me, Goodgame made the startling admission that he had not seen the book before making his decision. Since I had gone out and purchased a copy, I felt it was clear that, whatever one's views on lesbianism or the Catholic Church, the book was sensitive, serious, and revealing. Those looking for cheap thrills had better look elsewhere. Goodgame all but admitted he was playing to a powerful constituency. "Was I sensitive to the Catholic Church? Yes, I was. But I didn't yield to the 'pressure' of the church." Indeed, he dismissed the cancellation as much ado about nothing—a "nonissue," he called it, adding: "It's the proverbial tempest in a teapot. We change our bookings all the time."

One of the troubling aspects of Channel 4's position was the sense that a double standard was being applied. Goodgame stressed the need for a TV station to be responsible in selecting subjects. "I think discretion on our part is important. I think we owe it to ourselves not to be exploitive to any group. We have a right to discuss anything meaningful to the people we serve. Would we air *Deep Throat*? No." Words like "discretion" and not being "exploitive" to any group had a lofty ring—were it not for the fact that his *People Are Talking* show had a long history of seeking out sensational, sometimes sleazy, subjects. One wondered how female viewers felt about some of the show's previous guests, including Seka the Porno Queen; Helene the Voodoo Queen; and the world-famous Princess Cheyenne, the socialite turned stripper presently performing at the Two O'Clock Lounge in Boston's seedy Combat Zone. What did it mean for women— never mind the Catholic Church—when the talk show booked an exmadam who was once sentenced to thirty days in a nunnery? And how about the infamous booking of Kellie Everts, the former Miss Nude Universe who now stripped for God? Did the interview with the ex–Miss Nude Universe have more social redeeming value than a canceled segment with the lesbian nuns, both of whom, by the way, had been college professors?

There was no question that the subject of lesbian nuns was an explosive one, bound to stir up bitter controversy. For Channel 4, however, the problem with the segment seems to have been less with the word "lesbian" than the word "nun." The station was simply living by the 11th Commandment in television—Thou Shalt Not Offend— especially when it involved an influential religious group such as the Catholic Church. WJZ-TV in Baltimore, site of the country's oldest archdiocese, also canceled the two women. Both WBZ (Channel 4) and WJZ were owned by Group W (Westinghouse).

Other TV critics blamed the church for mishandling the situation. In a *Boston Herald* column, Greg Dawson took the Archdiocese to task for having made "a Mickey-Mouse" decision:

> As the sorcerer's apprentice in Walt Disney's *Fantasia*, Mickey is bedeviled by a mischievous broomstick that keeps fetching pails of unwanted water. Seeking to stem the tide, Mickey chops the broomstick in half—and gets *two* broomsticks. . . . Soon he has a real mess on his hands. Like Mickey, Father Peter Conley should

have quit while he was behind. Like Mickey, he took a trickle and turned it into a tidal wave.[29]

The plot continued to thicken. Around the time that Channel 4 banned the two women, they had been scheduled to appear on the nationally syndicated show *Donahue*. The coincidence proved embarrassing on two fronts. First, Channel 4 was already getting hammered in the press for its decision on the grounds of being narrow-minded, hypocritical, and, in some quarters, antigay. And second, here were Rosemary Curb and Nancy Manahan, the same canceled guests—well spoken, calm, and reasonable—appearing locally on rival Channel 5, which carried *Donahue*. Adding insult to injury, there was Rosemary Curb announcing on national television that she and her colleague had been banned in Boston by Channel 4. What was too hot for Boston was apparently not for *Donahue*, which aired in more than 200 cities around the country.

There was still more fallout. *Hour Magazine*, hosted by Gary Collins, was a nationally syndicated show produced by Westinghouse Broadcasting and Cable, Inc., which also owned WBZ in Boston. Once again, Curb and Manahan were booked for this show, which aired on 155 stations, including Channel 4. But when Larry Fraiberg, president of the TV Station Group for Westinghouse, learned about that booking he ordered all five Group W stations not to air that particular show—which meant the two editors effectively had the distinction of being banned twice on Channel 4. Explaining his decision to the *Ledger*, Fraiberg said: "We are not opposed to controversial issues. But I am not interested in the issue of freaks unless it can be enlightening. There is no point in exploring anomalies," he said, adding: "It's a question of taste. There is nothing positive about this kind of exploration of lesbian nuns. If someone wanted to discuss rabbis who have three heads, I would also say, 'What's the value?'"[30]

Freaks? Three-headed rabbis? Today, Fraiberg's remarks probably would have cost him his job. Just ask Donald Sterling, the former owner of the Los Angeles Clippers basketball team. In 2014, his racist rant about blacks caused him to be banned by the NBA for life and fined $2.5 million by the league.

Ironically, Rosemary Curb and Nancy Manahan seem to have had the last laugh. The whole Boston controversy and its ripple effects were quickly picked up by the wire services and became a national story, which included the *New York Times*. Under the headline "Book on Lesbian Nuns Upsets Boston, Delighting Publisher," this was how the story began: "Once again being 'banned in Boston' is having an effect in the literary world, and, partly as a result, an extraordinary new book about homosexuality among nuns is gaining national attention."[31]

The article went on to say that the book's publisher, Naiad Press, had printed 125,000 copies of the book, 10,000 of them hardcover. And with all the publicity, Warner Books purchased the mass-distribution paperback rights for a six-figure sum. "A book like this will go into supermarkets and drugstores and terminals all over the country," said Mark Greenberg, president of the Warner in-house advertising agency. "We are not counting on controversy with the church, but if it's there, it's there. And it's going to sell books."[32]

REPORT NO EVIL: THE CLERICAL SEX ABUSE SCANDAL

One of the best things about *Spotlight*, Tom McCarthy's acclaimed film about the *Boston Globe*'s investigation of the city's clerical sex abuse scandal, was its integrity.[33] The film, which won two Oscars in 2016, one for Best Film, the other for Best Screenplay, chronicled the *Globe*'s crucial role in bringing the issue of abuse to light and exposing Cardinal Bernard Law's part in the cover-up. The film also pointed the finger at the *Globe* itself for having been so late in coming to the scandal. More than once in the film a question is posed to the reporters: "What took you so long?"

But what about the other media outlets during Boston's Golden Age of local television? Where were Boston's crackerjack TV stations—especially the two dominant ones, Channel 4 (WBZ-TV) and Channel 5 (WCVB-TV), which, for many years, were regarded as the two finest in the country? Where were all the TV news reporters? Dan Rea, a former Channel 4 reporter who covered the church, was among the town's most versatile and tenacious reporters during his thirty-one-year career. Referring to the sex abuse scandal, he candidly acknowledged: "In retrospect, we did not take action. We (reporters) circled the wagons."[34]

But it wasn't only the television newsrooms that were skittish; the stations' program and public affairs departments were, too. As an example, in 1985 Channel 2 (WGBH-TV), Boston's prestigious public television station, decided to produce a nighttime special about Bernard Law. He had arrived in Boston six months earlier, and it seemed an appropriate time to introduce him to Boston-area viewers. The fact that Channel 2 was a noncommercial station not beholden to sponsor pressures would seem to have made this an ideal forum. Unfortunately, the special, tellingly titled "Pray for Me: A Portrait of Bernard Cardinal Law," was a disappointment. Pure puffery. A cop-out. No reporter or host was on hand to ask pointed questions, which gave Law a free platform to speak directly to the camera. And oh my, the visuals: clips of the cardinal at St. Leo's Church in Dorchester, playfully putting his red cap on a young boy's head, and shots of him at a retirement home for nuns, where a frail, elderly nun burst into prayer for her special visitor. And, when he was in Rome for his elevation to Cardinal, the camera caught him sweetly asking if anyone had seen his mother. Law himself emerged in the program as an intelligent, thoughtful man who obviously relished ideas. Yet no attempt was made to explore his views, particularly on sensitive or controversial subjects. The viewers were left to wonder: How did the cardinal feel about a recent Channel 4 poll showing that 85 percent of Catholic women questioned found abortion acceptable? How did he reconcile his strong belief in racial equality with his stated views that women should not be allowed to become priests? And how did he feel about the explosive segment on priests and celibacy when Phil Donahue recently came to town? My own review ended with a question: "It is one thing to humanize Cardinal Bernard Law, but isn't it a little premature to sanctify him?"[35]

Part of the problem was cultural. Sexual abuse was among the taboos people rarely talked about, in Boston or anywhere. The idea that a man of God would violate an innocent child was beyond belief. For the victims and their families, denial was often the only way of coping. Simple numbers were another factor. Catholics were the state's largest religious group—53 percent in 1980. And, while falling to 44.9 percent as of 2010 (the last time a religious census was taken), Catholics are still the majority religion in the state. Many were descendants of Irish immigrants who had fled from the mother country during the Great Famine of the 1840s, and in a later immigration wave, settled in port cities such as New York, Philadelphia, and Boston. Life then was extremely harsh, with many forced to live in tenements, facing poverty and discrimination, while the upper-crusty elite known as Boston Brahmins treated them as outcasts. As time went on, some of the new arrivals discovered politics as a way to move up the social and economic ladder. By the mid-point of the twentieth century, Catholic politicians in Massachusetts, with family names like Kennedy and O'Neill, had become thoroughly entrenched in power. In effect, they had become an essential part of the establishment, with strong ties to the Catholic Church.

Then there was the Bernard Law factor. Arriving in Boston in 1984 to replace the late Cardinal Humberto Medeiros, Law proved a more dynamic and ambitious figure than his predecessor. He was not only a religious leader but also an influential member of the political establishment—for instance, dining regularly with Billy Bulger, the powerful Massachusetts Senate president. Nor was Law shy about inserting himself in personal matters. When Massachusetts Congressman "Joe" Moakley was dying of leukemia, he asked his friend Representative Jim McGovern to deliver the eulogy at his funeral. Though the congressman agreed, Cardinal Law, apparently put off by McGovern's liberal views on abortion and gay rights, intervened and prevented him from speaking.[36] Further injecting himself in political matters, Law waged an unsuccessful campaign against Margaret Marshall's nomination to the state Supreme Court in 1996.[37] Marshall was eventually appointed chief justice, and in 2003 wrote the historic decision that allowed same-sex marriage in Massachusetts.

But Law's ties went far beyond state politics. As WBUR-FM reporter David Boeri, who has covered the Catholic Church for years, said: "Here was a cardinal in Boston who had Karl Rove on his speed dial. He was really wired to Washington."[38] Cardinal Law also built bridges to Boston's power brokers in the business and finance community, a large number of whom were Irish Catholic. Many graduated from Catholic colleges and universities, sat on Catholic boards, and were active in raising and donating millions of dollars to various organizations and charities, including the Catholic Church. For example,

Peter Lynch, a Boston College graduate who managed the Fidelity Magellan Fund, was president of the Catholic Schools Foundation. Jack Connors, a Boston College graduate and cofounder of the Boston advertising firm Hill, Holliday, Connors, Cosmopulos, Inc., was a close advisor to Law over the years, also raising and donating millions to the church. The late Thomas Flatley, who built a New England real estate empire estimated at $1.3 billion, was another who gave generously to the church, and advised Cardinal Bernard Law on business matters.

Some of Boston's best-known media executives, who happened to be Catholic, also enjoyed cordial relations with the Catholic Church. Paul LaCamera, a longtime, civic-minded Channel 5 executive and later WBUR-FM's general manager, once served as vice chairman of the board of Catholic Charities, the social services arm of the archdiocese. Jim Thistle, the legendary TV news director who worked at four Boston TV stations, was on the board of directors of the Boston Catholic Television Center and was chairman of the Boston Catholic Archdiocese Synod Subcommittee on Communications. On the print side, for many years Matt Storin, the *Boston Globe*'s top editor from 1992 to 2001, carried water for the church;[39] and when the daughter of Pat Purcell, the publisher/owner of the *Boston Herald*, got married, a priest named John Geoghan officiated—the very same priest who was later found guilty of sexually molesting more than 130 boys.[40]

The bonds between Boston's movers and shakers was also evident in the annual garden party held at the cardinal's residence to raise money for Catholic Charities, the largest private provider of social services in Massachusetts. In what the *New York Times* called "the social event of the year,"[41] hundreds of Boston's politicians, corporate bigwigs, and community leaders would attend, including the local media executives. The TV stations alone would purchase blocks of tickets, some paying as much as $10,000 for the event. And there, Cardinal Law would hold court, sitting under a tent, as Boston's richest and most powerful leaders lined up to have their photographs taken with him.

In this cultural environment, the town's large number of mostly Irish Catholic movers and shakers became a band of brothers—a kind of "interlocking directorate," says Boeri. Extremely loyal and protective of one another, they were bound together by their Catholic faith and professional relationships with the cardinal. Indeed, there is a revealing scene in *Spotlight* between the *Globe*'s Michael Rezendes (played by Mark Ruffalo) and the victims' attorney, Mitchell Garabedian (played by Stanley Tucci). When the reporter learns that incriminating Church documents housed in the Springfield courthouse are missing, he is shocked:

> Rezendes: Mitch, are you telling me that the Catholic Church removed documents from the courthouse?
> Garabedian: Look, I'm not crazy, I'm not paranoid. I'm experienced. Check the docket. You'll see. They control everything.

The real Michael Rezendes, who is still on the *Globe*'s Spotlight team, has told me he regards that scene as the most important in the film. While the Catholic Church may not have controlled "everything," the scene underscores just how powerful the church was during that time.

In the case of clerical sex abuse, no one was better positioned to maintain the culture of secrecy and silence than Cardinal Bernard Law himself. In 1992, when allegations of sex abuse against an ex-priest named James Porter were first made public and other victims began to come forward, Law's instinctive response was to hide behind his imperial robes. Instead of disclosure and an acknowledgment of responsibility, he blamed the media: "The papers like to focus on the faults of a few. . . . We deplore that," he said, in remarks made at St. Patrick's Church in Roxbury. Then he added what sounded like an ominous warning: "The good and dedicated people who serve the church deserve better than what they have been getting day in and day out in the media. By all means we call down God's power on the media, particularly the *Globe*."[42]

Think of the cardinal's response as a form of "institutional denial," but one open to alternative interpretations as well. A psychosocial approach suggests that the church hierarchy, along with the sex abuse victims and their families, used it as an unconscious defense mechanism to avoid the feelings and facts that were so intolerable as to make them unable to speak out publicly. The situation also can be viewed from an ethnocultural perspective. Monica McGold-rick, a family therapist and an Irish American, writes perceptively about the sociocultural factors involved in families, including those who are Irish American: "Their history is full of rebels and fighters, and yet they tend to be compliant and accepting of authoritarian structures. They place great stock in loyalty to their own, and yet they often cut off relationships totally. They have a great sense of respon-sibility for what goes wrong, and yet they characteristically deny or project blame outward."[43] In terms of the relationship of Irish Ameri-cans to the Catholic Church, McGoldrick adds: "For generations the parish, rather than the neighborhood, defined the family's context. The Church demanded absolute obedience to its rules and no right-thinking Irish Catholic dared to question its decisions nor those of its representatives, the local priests."[44]

With specific reference to the media, one other explanation de-serves mention. Elisabeth Noelle-Neumann, an influential German political scientist, devised a theory known as "the spiral of silence," to explain how perceived public opinion affects a person's own opin-ions and actions.[45] The closer an individual's opinions are to the majority-held opinion, she argued, the more likely the individual is to express it in public discourse. But when someone has a different opinion from the majority, fearing isolation or reprisal, that person is more likely to remain silent. And if fear continued to escalate within the minority opinion holder, it would result in a downward spiral in which the minority opinion was never expressed.

Furthermore, because of their agenda-setting function, the mass media played an important role in this process, especially in dictat-ing the majority opinion, Noelle-Neumann asserted. She thought this was especially true for television, given its ubiquity, repetition, and immediacy. As applied to the Catholic Church's sexual abuse scandal, it suggests that individuals who might otherwise have spoken out in-stead felt helpless in the face of a powerful media that were largely silent. Underscoring her point, she called attention to the media's "articulation function": "The media provide people with the words and phrases they can use to defend a point of view. If people find no current, frequently repeated expressions for their point of view, they lapse into silence; they become effectively mute."[46]

Call it what you will—"institutional denial" or a "spiral of silence." In the end, the result was the same. Though hundreds of heinous crimes over the years were being committed against innocent children, people wouldn't talk, the church wouldn't act, and the media were nowhere to be found. All of which was taking place in a town that was a little too small, too inbred, and too incestuous for its own good.

With the lack of urgency operating at so many levels, it wasn't until May 7, 1992, that Joe Bergantino, head of Channel 4's (WBZ's) investigative unit, became the first TV reporter to expose an ex-priest named James Porter, who had long since moved to Minnesota. Bergantino's exposé and follow-up reporting became Boston's first pedophile priest legal case, the first of many, with Porter sentenced to eighteen to twenty years in a maximum-security prison. In his I-Team report, Porter, who had been interviewed by phone by Bergantino, was heard in his own voice admitting to some shocking criminal acts. In a blog recently posted on the *Huffington Post*, Bergantino recalled an extraordinary conversation with him: "In a recorded phone interview, I asked him how many children he had molested. His answer, without a trace of remorse or emotion: 'fifty or sixty, I guess.'" Porter didn't know that the statute of limitations was frozen the moment he left Massachusetts more than twenty years earlier. In 1993, Porter pleaded guilty to molesting twenty-eight children and spent the rest of his life behind bars.[47]

Bergantino was not new to a sharp, incisive approach in covering the Catholic Church. Despite having been born, raised, and schooled as a Catholic, he strongly believed in the watchdog function of the media, which meant the church should be covered as an institution, not just as a religion. In the 1980s, for example, he did a three-part series called "Power of the Cloth," which demonstrated how the archdiocese was failing to provide its nuns with adequate wages and benefits. "Those stories immediately made me persona non grata in the eyes of the Archdiocese," he says, "and that continued until my last day on the job at WBZ in May 2008."[48]

In 2009, Bergantino and his Boston University colleague Maggie Mulvihill cofounded the nonprofit New England Center for Investigative Reporting affiliated with Boston University, which focused on local and regional issues. Retiring as executive director in 2016, he recently reflected on the media's attitude of "see no evil, hear no evil" and, above all, "report no evil" during Boston's Golden Age: "The church was covered, in both print and television, the way we covered a sports team. When Rose Kennedy died, we brought in a priest to do the play-by-play at her Mass. The church wasn't covered the way we would cover the government. . . . And, because the church was not transparent at the time, it was like covering the Kremlin."[49]

Bergantino's choice of the words "sports team" is telling because it highlights the media's cheerleading, "root-for-the-home-team" mindset so pervasive at the time. Bergantino's dogged reporting opened the door to reporters at other TV stations covering the clerical sex abuse, though by the late 1990s stories of pedophile priests greatly declined. As he acknowledged in his *Huffington Post* piece, it was "because, many of us—including reporters at the *Boston Globe*—believed there wasn't much more to report." Tragically, it wasn't until years later that the full dimensions of the scandal would be revealed.

But what about the other TV reporters covering the Catholic Church back then? Nearly all those reporters were Catholic; many had gone to Catholic schools and colleges. The question is whether their backgrounds and religious affiliation affected their journalistic responsibilities, especially in relation to the clerical sex abuse scandal. In interviews I conducted with former TV reporters who had covered the church then, many expressed outrage toward the pedophile priests. "Monsters" was the word used by Clark Booth, formerly Channel 5's highly respected "special correspondent." But did Booth, a Holy Cross graduate, and other TV reporters, steeped in the Catholic tradition and its mystique, have divided loyalties? Was their relationship with the church a little too tight? Or, putting it in a larger context, was there a double standard for reporters when it came to covering the church as opposed to covering government, business, and other institutions?

Dan Rea acknowledged he covered the church "a little more respectfully" and mostly did "friendly stories." Rea, who now hosts *NightSide*, a nightly talk show on WBZ radio, said, "Once it became apparent that some of the priests were perverts, Cardinal Law should've gone to their offices and ripped their collars off their necks."[50]

David Boeri, a thirty-year reporting veteran who has worked at WGBH-TV, WCVB-TV, and now WBUR-FM, has reported on the Catholic Church for years. He remains highly critical of Boston's overall TV coverage. "Junkets" was what he called many of the trips when local TV reporters traveled abroad with the cardinal. "It was all part of the ratings," he said. "When (WCVB anchor) Chet (Curtis), who was of Polish descent, went with the cardinal to Poland, that was a huge deal for the station and became a news series. When they went to the concentration camps, it took on significance as a 'Great TV Event.' Remember, it's a Catholic audience. Visiting the Dalai Lama wouldn't cut it."[51] Declining to mention specific reporters, Boeri added: "There was something troubling about those reporters who would kiss the ring and genuflect."

"Times were a lot different," countered Clark Booth. "There was a little more reverence for the church. We (reporters) were more ceremonial, more ecclesiastical—it was the big event—it was about the music, the color, and the incense. We never got into issues." When asked if TV reporters covering the scandal were too soft on the church, he replied, "Was the *Boston Globe* too soft? Was the *New York Times* too soft? Was the *Guardian* too soft? In retrospect, we all should not have gone so softly."[52]

Years would pass before another media outlet would seriously advance the sex abuse story. Though never given the credit she deserved, Kristen Lombardi, a superb reporter for the *Boston Phoenix*, broke new ground in "Cardinal Sin," her massive, 7,200-word story in 2001 exposing Father John J. Geoghan as a notorious sexual predator.

The *Globe* may not have been first on the story, but armed with the financial resources and clout of a big-city newspaper, it struck the decisive blow. By most accounts, the 2001 hiring of Marty Baron to replace Matt Storin as editor proved crucial. Not only was he Jewish, but he was also an outsider. A Florida native, Baron worked at the *Los Angeles Times* and the *New York Times* before coming to the *Globe* from the *Miami Herald*. (In 2012, Baron left to become editor of the *Washington Post*.) Under his leadership, the *Globe*'s Spotlight Team launched a five-month investigation.

The smoking gun came when the reporters gained access to previously sealed court records on Father Geoghan who, over a thirty-year period, was accused of molesting more than 130 children. Confidential documents revealed that in the face of such allegations, the church simply shuffled Geoghan around from one parish after another, and that Cardinal Law himself was involved in the cover-up. For its explosive two-part series on January 6 and 7, 2002, and relentless follow-up reporting, the paper would claim the Pulitzer Prize the next year.

The *Globe* revelations proved the ultimate wake-up call for the culture. One by one, the walls of silence came tumbling down. In January, Jack Connors—the millionaire businessman, philanthropist, and once close advisor to Cardinal Law—broke ranks with him. Sickened by the *Globe* revelations, he went on to withhold a $300 million contribution to the archdiocese's capital campaign. "I don't have problems with my faith. I have problems with the leaders of my faith," he told the *Washington Post*.[53]

On March 5, Paul LaCamera, WCVB's general manager, aired a station editorial saying Law had lost his moral authority and should consider resigning. Other power brokers stepped up as well. On March 13, a *Boston Herald* editorial, personally approved by its publisher/owner Pat Purcell, called for Law's resignation. Finally, on December 13, 2002, four days after fifty-eight Boston-area priests sent a hand-delivered letter to the cardinal's residence calling on Law to step down, the disgraced cardinal announced his resignation.

Looking back, the scandal underscored the need for continued soul searching and vigilance by Boston's TV stations, as well as the print media. For too many years, they wore blinders when covering the Catholic Church. And in the face of a church that was notoriously secretive and lacking in transparency, there were far too many "friendly stories" and too many reporters "who would kiss the ring and genuflect." As David Boeri put it, "It took a long time for the church mice to get brave."[54]

ISMS & SCHISMS: RACE, GENDER, AND SEXUAL ORIENTATION

Television has long been an easy mark for its critics. In 1961, FCC chairman Newton Minnow famously branded it "a vast wasteland." In her book called *The Plug-in Drug*, Marie Winn argued that television was addictive and served "to blot out the real world." Author and essayist Renata Adler deemed television essentially worthless, "clearly not an art but an appliance," suggesting it was of no more consequence than a kitchen can opener or an electric broom. Small wonder for many years it was called "the boob tube" and the "idiot box."

But without denying its many failings, television is also so much more. By virtue of its immediacy and reach, it plays a variety of roles in our culture. It informs, educates, and entertains us—that much is obvious. It also has important effects on our culture—from the food we eat, to the clothes we buy, to the candidates for whom we vote. Perhaps more fundamentally, it affects our attitudes, beliefs, and values, which, ultimately, transform the culture. As Jason Mittell states in his book *Television and American Culture*: "Television is a mirror of our world offering an often-distorted vision of national identity, as well as shaping our perceptions of various groups of people."[1] As an example, just at the time when women were making strides in the halls of power and Hillary Clinton was toying with a second run for the presidency, Alessandra Stanley, the *New York Times* TV critic, wrote on the eve of the 2014 television season:

For some reason, Mrs. Clinton is embedded in several new fall dramas, most obviously *Madam Secretary*, a new CBS drama with Téa

Leoni playing a take-charge secretary of state. There are also im-prints of Mrs. Clinton on an NBC show *State of Affairs,* in which the president is a woman (Alfre Woodard) and her most trusted ad-viser (Katherine Heigl) is a bold C.I.A. analyst who daily assesses—and almost single-handedly averts—national security threats.[2]

In this sense, television stands as a useful benchmark by which to gauge the culture—where it has been, where it stands, and where it is headed. And, as we shall see, during Boston's Golden Age local television served as an invaluable prism through which to view the culture.

RACE

More than forty years ago, I wrote a piece about soap operas that ran in the *New York Times,* which took note of television's lack of di-versity:

> Blacks and other minority members are still grossly under repre-sented on all the networks. With few exceptions, they merely get peripheral roles not central to a theme. We find out precious little about them as people—their lives, their families, their problems. And most of the parts go to light-skinned, straight-looking and straight-thinking individuals—the kind who are most palatable to white America. Like the late Martin Luther King, I too have a dream: that one day I shall see a very big, very black woman wear-ing a huge afro on, say, CBS's *As the World Turns.*[3]

However, as a result of major political and social changes in the country during the 1960s—the civil rights movement, the race-related riots, and the enactment of historic civil rights legislation—the face of American television, slowly, began to change in the en-suing years. Shows centered around African Americans themes and characters cropped up in the 1970s and 1980s, including *The Auto-biography of Miss Jane Pittman* (1974), *King* (1978), and, of course, the blockbuster *Roots* (1977), which received unprecedented ratings, nine Emmys, and a Peabody Award. It was also a time of groundbreaking sitcoms, thanks largely to the socially conscious producer Norman Lear. His hit shows, often dealing with racially charged themes and characters, included *All in the Family* (1971–1979), which centered around a working-class bigot named Archie Bunker; *Sanford and Son* (1972–1977); *Good Times* (1974–1979); and *The Jeffersons* (1975–1982). Nor should we forget the hugely successful *Cosby Show* (1984–1992), which focused on the Huxtables, an upper-middle-class African American family living in Brooklyn, New York.[4]

But if network television had moved the needle forward on this country's racial progress, what of the state of race relations in Boston during its Golden Age of local television? To what extent did racial diversity come to the local TV stations? To be sure, there were some promising developments. When Channel 7 changed ownership in May 1982, 12 percent of the new stockholders were minorities—the largest of any major station in the country. The various stations occasionally aired local specials concerned with minority issues; a favorite of mine was Channel 4's *Mississippi Summer: The Unfinished Journey*, a poignant 1984 retrospective on the twentieth anniversary of the deaths of the three civil rights workers murdered in Mississippi. All three major stations had weekly shows aimed at minorities (though all were relegated to the "weekend ghettos" and operated on shoestring budgets). And, in 1985, Channel 5 launched *A World of Difference*, an ambitious public service campaign designed to combat prejudice.

But against these praiseworthy initiatives, the stations had a dismal record overall. As noted earlier, in contrast to many other markets, Boston didn't have a single minority weeknight anchor until 1981, when Channel 4's Liz Walker received a promotion. Not one station had an African American general manager, nor did any TV station employ more than five African American reporters. Indeed, in 1982, when I conducted a survey of on-air talent at the major stations, Channel 5—regarded as the class act in town—turned out to have the market's worst record. The news department only had two African Americans and one Hispanic reporter out of eighteen—a figure that didn't include its all-white sports and weather slots.[5]

Minority reporters there were openly disenchanted. "I'm discouraged," Jim Boyd said. "The station's track record speaks for itself. I don't understand it. It's obvious we don't have the Walt Sanders, the Sarah-Ann Shaws, and Linda Harrises (Channel 4 minority reporters) over here. The situation for nonwhites (at Channel 5) who are off-camera writers and producers is even worse." His on-air colleague Pam Cross agreed. "It's frustrating," she said, "when you know there are more qualified minorities out there. The station hasn't been as liberal as our image may appear."

The town's racial sensitivities and conflicts were felt in other ways as well. In 1987, the same year that WGBH produced *Eyes on the Prize*, the landmark, much-acclaimed PBS documentary series[6] that chronicled three decades of the civil rights movement, WGBH's *Frontline* produced another PBS documentary that hit much closer to home. Called *Street Cop*, this documentary had a narrower focus—relations between the police and the black community in Boston. The program, which took ten months to film, followed the day-to-day experiences of Sergeant Stanley Philbin, a twenty-six-year veteran of the Boston Police Department who was in charge of its Anti-Crime Unit. Included in the program were a number of drug arrests and several domestic violence incidents, most of which took place in Roxbury. But almost immediately, when WGBH held an advance press screening before the program aired nationally, it unleashed a heated controversy locally. Among those at the screening was Kirk Johnson, a media researcher, who had recently completed a study at the University of Massachusetts/Boston concerning race and the local media outlets. The next day, in a phone interview with *The Ledger*, Johnson charged that *Street Cop* was "racist":

> The show perpetuates negative stereotypes of blacks and Hispanic people. Watching the program, you would assume that everyone in Roxbury is heavily into drugs and domestic disturbances. Viewers will come away thinking that all black and Hispanic people are drug abusers or pushers, and all blacks and Hispanics are violent.
>
> There is a great deal of community activity going on to get rid of crime and drug abuse. None of this is in the program.[7]

Frontline producer Michael Kirk vigorously defended the show. "I'm disappointed some people are unhappy. The film is about the police and how they interact with the community. Mickey Roache (Boston police commissioner) said he would clean up drugs. We took a look at the problem at the street level. The fact is most of the door-to-door street crime is in Area B (in Roxbury)." Other community leaders, such as Donald Polk, president of the Urban League of Eastern Massachusetts, voiced criticisms. The situation grew more inflamed when Alan Foster, executive producer of *The Ten O'Clock News* (and Kirk's colleague at WGBH), publicly suggested he agreed with the program's critics. "It's racist in the sense that it feeds some strong stereotyping of blacks. Mike (Kirk) says he was just making a cop film. It's a little naive to say it's as simple as that. I've seen the film several times. I was upset to see police with sledgehammers knocking down doors and not finding (any drugs) there. I think that the reaction of the black community is understandable."

But the issue refused to go away. Two months later, the Boston Association of Black Journalists, comprised of employees from various newspapers, radio, and TV stations, fired off an angry letter to David Fanning, *Frontline*'s executive producer. Not only did the group charge that *Street Cop* was "one sided," but also WGBH itself came in for broader criticism for its hiring practices. With one exception, the letter asserted: "*Frontline* has a five-year history of not hiring minority producers."[8] Fanning strongly denied the charges. But a WGBH employee, requesting anonymity, told the *Ledger* that *Street Cop* was a symbol of deep and longstanding tensions within the station. "It (*Street Cop*) has been a way in the door," he said. "It's become a cause célèbre. It's become a political football. The debate is less about the film and more about minorities at 'GBH."

Other kinds of racial tensions also had a way of surfacing in connection with TV movies about Boston's recent past. With Boston such a charming and attractive city, it was not uncommon for production companies to come to town to film scenes and exteriors for TV shows and theatrical films, especially those set in Boston. It was a win-win situation for all—good publicity for the town and gobs of free advertising for the film producers.

But there were some notable exceptions, as when the subject was race, and, above all, it involved painful events from the city's recent past. At such times, strains had a way of surfacing, particularly on the part of turf-conscious residents who resented "outsiders" coming to their neighborhoods. Take the flare-up that involved *Common Ground*, a 1990 docudrama centered on Boston's racial strife during the city's court-ordered busing. The four-hour TV movie, to be shown on CBS, was based on the Pulitzer Prize–winning book by the same name written by J. Anthony Lukas. Like his book, the film focused on three real-life Boston families whose lives were dramatically changed during the turbulent 1970s.

As tensions in Boston mounted in advance of the CBS airdate in late March, Lorimar Television, the production company, decided to sponsor an advance screening of the film at Boston's World Trade Center. The hope was that the event would both diffuse tensions and generate publicity for the film. Along with a large contingent of press and Channel 7 officials on hand were real-life members of the families portrayed in the film; political and community leaders; Lorimar executives, including executive producer Daniel Blatt; and J. Anthony Lukas himself. Former Boston mayor Kevin White, attracting a slew of photographers, basked in the limelight and seemed bemused by the TV movie. He clearly got a kick out of watching actor James Farentino play him on the screen, laughing at the thought of an Italian chosen for the part of an Irishman, and pleased that the producers selected "someone so handsome." (Poor old Louise Day Hicks, the local politician who had become nationally known for her passionate opposition to court-ordered busing, wound up on the cutting room floor.) Ever the colorful character, White told a story about meeting with the publishers of Boston-area papers in an attempt to persuade them to play down the busing story. "The press was outside. And, Mother of God, the publishers had left through the back door."[9]

White's presence at the event was contrasted by the absence of Boston mayor Ray Flynn, who elected not to attend. A former busing foe who was now trying to keep the lid on Boston's escalating violence, Flynn reportedly had a hand in denying the producers permission to re-create anti-busing marches on the streets of Boston. (A good deal of the film was shot in Toronto.) Mel King, a prominent black activist, also declined to attend, suggesting he had little respect for either the Lukas book or the CBS film: "There is a major flaw in the book," he told *The Ledger*. "White people were asked to talk about black people, but black people were not asked to talk about whites. The author sees black people as the problem."

For Kevin White, it was a night to reminisce and tell war stories. But for others in the audience, the movie summoned up bitter memories and high emotion. Lukas took pains to praise Lorimar for hanging tough while CBS reduced the movie from seven hours to four. "This mini-series came within twenty-four hours of not being aired," he said. "CBS is the third-ranked network. They had the pressure of economic profits and they got nervous. There were times when my respect for CBS was strained."

James Kelly, an arch busing foe from South Boston and now a Boston city councilor, was there, defending the good name of his town as if it were still under siege. Elvira ("Pixie") Palladino, one the most strident anti-busing voices, was also on hand, still spewing venom. James Kelly recalled that Channel 7's general manager Sy Yanoff asked him to tape a public service announcement saying, "Safety is the most important thing." Kelly proudly recalled that he refused. Indeed, during the intermission, after executive producer Daniel Blatt was musing about what he thought was an improved racial climate since the 1970s, Kelly unleashed an angry tirade directed at the Lorimar executive. "I'm not sure what your message is. This is not an accurate portrayal of the folks from South Boston. This film makes light of the sacredness of neighborhoods," he said.

But the angriest, most incendiary comments came from Palladino. Interrupting speakers during the discussion, yelling catcalls as though she were at Fenway Park, Palladino was a rude reminder of Boston's ugly past. Dismissing the film as "a fairytale," she asserted: "We're back where we started. This film is being shown at the wrong time. I asked Channel 7 and the mayor of Boston that this picture not be shown at this time. It's very sad for the people of Charlestown. I don't think this film does them justice."

Palladino's comments touched off sparks from both blacks and whites in the audience. A tall black man standing by a microphone looked toward Palladino and asked: "When is the right time to show this film? Closed communities don't work, Pixie Palladino." Lisa McGoff, formerly a Charlestown High student whose mother (played by Jane Curtin) was an anti-busing activist, delivered an angry rebuke to Palladino. (The McGoffs were one of the three families depicted in the film.) "I just wanted to go to school. I just wanted to grow up.

My mother was right alongside of Pixie," she said. When Palladino began interrupting her, Lisa's temper flared. "Nobody talks about my mother like that. I love my town. I still live there," she said. As if to underscore the fragile and elusive nature of Boston's "common ground," one of Lisa's brothers found Palladino's hostile comments too much to take. "You haven't changed in fifteen years," he shouted, storming out of the room.

So much for Boston's improved racial climate.

GENDER AND AGE

In the late 1970s, *All in the Family* had an episode in which dear, sweet Edith Bunker invites an offbeat character—a female impersonator—over for Christmas dinner. Naturally, her husband Archie explodes: "Let me tell you somethin' you're forgettin'. A man's home is his castle. And in dis here castle, I'm the king." To which Edith promptly replies: "And I am the queen." While Archie's bluster was thoroughly in character, the stand taken by America's dearest dingbat may have surprised some viewers. It shouldn't have. For slowly, almost imperceptibly over a period of time, Edith Bunker, symbol of the oppressed housewife, had begun exhibiting signs of growth—a quiet liberation of sorts from the totally dependent creature tied to her husband, her kitchen, and her $1.98 apron trademark. Her growth was more personal than political, more intuitive than intellectual. No copies of *Ms.* magazine were strewn about the Bunker household. Whatever the level of her consciousness, Edith Bunker's frumpishness and naiveté still overshadowed any incipient feminism.

Still, the gradual change in Edith's character was no accident. The show's history, which began in 1970, coincided with the rising women's movement. While Archie's bigotry provided the essential focus for the show initially, other social themes—including women's issues—were later incorporated into the storylines. During my *Miami Herald* days, I had the pleasure of a phone interview with Jean Stapleton, Edith's namesake, who herself was an active feminist. She readily acknowledged having had input into her alter ego character: "I think Edith was touched by the women's movement. I can recall the first time Gloria (her daughter) brought home a friend to prepare for a feminist fair. The whole question of male chauvinism came up, while Archie quoted from the Bible to justify keeping women in their place."[10]

From Betty Friedan, who authored the groundbreaking book *The Feminine Mystique*; to the formation of organizations like the National Organization for Women (NOW) and the National Women's Political Caucus (NWPC); to the ascendance of high-profile activists like Gloria Steinem and Germaine Greer; to the introduction of the Equal Rights Amendment—all were evidence of significant forces at work. Indeed, the impact of these developments reached deep into the popular culture. Helen Reddy's smash hit "I Am Woman" was adopted as the feminist anthem; Phillip Morris introduced a thin cigarette called Virginia Slims in 1968, aimed at young, professional women, with the tagline "You've come a long way, baby"; while advertisers sought to portray women in more independent and assertive ways. One commercial at the time showed a couple chatting while spooning down a cup of Campbell's soup. The husband, sensing his wife was anxious about finishing in an upcoming race, tries to reassure her. "Finishing? I'm worried about winning!" she retorts.

Thus, in the same way that the civil rights movement helped transform the face of television on the subject of race, the effects of the women's movement in the 1960s and 1970s were similarly felt on the small screen. In earlier times, television, as a mirror of society, did not pay much attention to women. Typically, in the 1950s it wasn't the stay-at-home mother who was in charge of the family, but rather her wise, all-knowing husband, as in the aptly named *Father Knows Best*. Women were usually secondary characters, while the heroes of detective, medical, and legal dramas were men. Yes, we all loved Lucy, but she was simply good for laughs—we didn't have to take her very seriously. And, when the networks did venture into new terrain, they were quick to run for cover—all too ready to cancel shows with women as the lead character. In 1975, Lee Grant played a divorced forty-three-year-old legal secretary in *Fay*. Despite good critical notices, the show didn't even last two months.

But given the evolving role of women in society, the dynamics on television changed dramatically in the 1970s and 1980s, when all of a sudden women began to star in their own shows. The 1970s brought us sitcoms such as *Maude* (1972–1978), *Rhoda* (1974–1978), and *Alice* (1976–1985). In the same way, the 1980s included shows such as *Cagney & Lacey* (1982–1988), *Kate & Allie* (1984–1989), and those feisty *Golden Girls* (1985–1992). Clearly, we had come a long way from the days when a cop show starring Rock Hudson and Susan Saint James could be called *McMillan and Wife* (1971–1977).

BOSTON AND THE WOMEN'S MOVEMENT

The culture was undergoing such a major transformation that in 1975, *Time* awarded its "Man of the Year" to "American women." Not surprisingly, the effect of these changes reverberated at the local level in the Boston television market. Feminist issues, such as abortion, gender discrimination, marriage, child care, and sexuality were all grist for the talk-show mills. Working on *Good Day!* in the 1970s, I booked many of the leaders of the women's movement—Gloria Steinem, Bella Abzug, Germaine Greer, Florynce ("Flo") Kennedy, as well as prominent feminist authors such as Susan Brownmiller (*Against Our Will*) and Kate Millet (*Sexual Politics*).

Indeed, as the women's movement gained traction, a bargain of sorts was struck between such guests and our show producers. We would invite well-known "cause" people onto the show to deliver their feminist messages (paying for their hotel and occasionally giving them a $100 honorarium). In return, they would be marketed as headliners and "celebrities" for our show. Warren Beatty may have been an A-list celeb, but in our view, Gloria Steinem was also money in the bank.

Then there was a small but revealing incident when we booked Gloria Steinem for a nighttime special with *Sesame Street*'s Oscar the Grouch, the furry little green creature who lived in a trash can. The skit called for Steinem to be chatting with Oscar about something or other. For the "payoff," she was to squelch the sassy little guy by bopping him over the head with a garbage can cover. "Do I have to do this to Oscar?" she asked plaintively before the show. "It's such a hostile thing to do." Mercifully, Oscar was spared the indignity, while Steinem avoided doing something with which she wasn't comfortable.

There was also the debate I arranged circa 1975 between Betty

Friedan and Phyllis Schlafly. The subject was the controversial Equal Rights Amendment, which had passed both houses of Congress in 1972, but now had to be ratified by the states. On one side, the "mother of the women's rights movement," Betty Friedan; on the other, Phyllis Schlafly, a staunch conservative and leading opponent of the amendment.[11] As expected, the sparks flew—it was great television—as Schlafly, an attorney and a skilled debater, wound up eviscerating Friedan on live television. Ellen Goodman, the *Globe*'s highly respected feminist columnist, had come to the station for the debate, but was appalled by the spectacle. "How could you book Schlafly on the same show as Betty?" she demanded to know, turning her head in my direction. "It wasn't a fair fight. You know, she's *not* a debater." Actually, I didn't, but I kept my mouth shut. After the show, Goodman sat down for a prearranged interview with Schlafly. "Do you mind if I tape our interview?" she asked, turning to Schlafly. "Not at all," Schlafly replied, whipping out her own tape recorder. So there it was— a tense encounter between the two contemporary women with very different worldviews, complete with dueling tape recorders, glaring at one another at a nearby table.

Feminist shows in Boston were all the rage in the 1970s. Channel 2 had an all-women's show, *In Her Own Right*, hosted by Karen Klein, an assistant professor at Brandeis. Displaying the sensibilities of the time, she declined the services of a makeup man or hairdresser.[12] Channel 5 offered up *Your Place and Mine*, produced by Eunice West, an avowed feminist, station stockholder, and editorial board member. Over at Channel 4, Pat Mitchell hosted a five-day-a-week morning show called *Women '74*, which was subsequently moved to 12:30 and called *Women '75*. Not that it was always easy for the station's women. Hamlin recently recalled the time when she was the station's cultural reporter and management approached her about hosting a new talk show.

[I was] asked to host the daily morning show, with a group of men managers explaining it as a "y'know, for dodo birds who stay home—just some recipes, fashion, a star or two." I said, "No, not a chance." I would (rather) stay as the first cultural reporter in the country on the nightly news since that work had meaning and this had none. "But Sonya, you'd be a stah." (Y'know, that Boston accent.)

My husband told me to go back and tell them if they would let me hire an all women's staff and program what I wanted I would do it. And they said yes!! So we became the first such show in the country with a solo woman host and such "radical" intentions.[13]

Boston stations also offered some ambitious special events programming. Earlier I cited *Yes, We Can!*, Channel 4's impressive sixteen-hour televised fair, involving panel discussions of various issues, offering literature and referral information. Channel 5 had a neat programming coup of its own. In June 1986, just six months after the historic summit meeting in Geneva between President Ronald Reagan and Soviet leader Mikhail Gorbachev, Channel 5 engaged in its own form of people-to-people diplomacy. Called *Citizens' Summit II: Women to Women*, it featured some 200 women from the Boston area assembled at the WCVB studios in suburban Needham, while another 200 Soviet women gathered in a Leningrad studio. (An earlier citizens' summit had been held in Seattle.) Through the use of large-screen monitors, and with the aid of moderators Phil Donahue, stationed in Channel 5's Needham studio, and Soviet spokesman Vladimir Pozner (who spoke perfect English) in a Leningrad studio, two groups of women, with very different worldviews, were linked together live by satellite. In this unusual setting, they discussed such hot-button topics as the dangers of nuclear radiation, divorce, abortion, and freedom of information. A small group of protesters gathered outside the Channel 5 station, handing out leaflets urging the American participants to press their Moscow counterparts on the plight of Soviet Jews. But the Soviet audience denied Jews in their country were being persecuted and prevented from emigrating. "Any Jew who wants to emigrate simply has to apply to the government," said one woman. "Only those working on government secret projects cannot leave." The three-hour forum was taped, then edited down to a one-hour special on Channel 5 that aired in prime time the next week. It was a small but timely step in keeping with Gorbachev's new policy of glasnost, or greater openness and transparency in his government.

WOMEN IN TV: "PRIMITIVE CAVEMAN TELEVISION" (STILL?)

In the early days of network news, television women were members of a very small club. When Pauline Frederick first worked for ABC as a freelancer, her assignments centered on "women's stories," such as the shortage of nylon stockings and how to get a husband. Hired by ABC in 1949, she became the first woman to work full time for an American network; by 1953, she had joined NBC as its UN correspondent, a position she held with distinction for the next twenty-one years.[14] In 1960, Nancy Dickerson became CBS's first female correspondent; later, she worked at NBC from 1963 to 1970, where she became the first woman correspondent on the floor of a political convention. And Aline Saarinen was named a correspondent in 1964, and later became NBC's Paris bureau chief.

But these women were the exceptions. From the start, television was a male-dominated business with a great deal of prejudice against women. As NBC's John Chancellor once mused about 1950s television. "It was sort of a primitive caveman television that we were putting out at that time."[15] Yes, and because "the cavemen" were in charge, it wasn't until the 1960s and 1970s that women really began to make their way in front of the camera. Barbara Walters, Lesley Stahl, Marlene Sanders, Judy Woodruff, and Jane Pauley represented a new generation of network women who, in turn, paved the way for others.

Yet women were still a long way from gender parity. The actual number of on-camera women remained relatively low. According to a 1985 article by Judy Flander in the *Washington Journalism Review*, there were 52 female correspondents out of 259 reporters (or 20 percent) at the three major commercial networks—ABC, NBC, and CBS.[16] Moreover, as of that time, there were no female anchors on the networks' prestigious weeknight newscasts—a fact that prompted a famous *TV Guide* cover story in 1983 called "Why There Are Still No Female Dan Rathers."[17] (Lesley Stahl, flanked by Judy Woodruff and Anne Garrels, adorned the cover.)

In some respects, the Boston market was ahead of the networks. As of the mid-1980s, all three of the major news stations—Channels 4, 5, and 7—had male-female anchor teams on their weeknight newscasts. The 10 o'clock newscasts on Channels 2 and 56 also paired men and women at the anchor desk. And Boston appears to have been unique in having a video matriarchy, as Channel 5's Natalie Jacobson and Channel 4's Liz Walker were by far the dominant anchors of their time.[18] On the other hand, contrary to popular belief, the percentage of local female reporters, although higher than that of the networks, was still nothing to write home about. In 1986, out of the seventy-nine reporters and anchors employed by the three major stations, only twenty-seven (or 34 percent) were women—still a long way from parity.[19]

As with racism, the other "isms" in our society never really die; progress tends to be incremental—two steps forward, one step backward. This was certainly true in Boston where two other "isms"— sexism and ageism—were fully operational at the time. To begin with, on-air women faced a double whammy. Not only did they have to fight harder than men to get hired, but they also had to worry more about holding on to their jobs as they got older. The pressure was always on to "prove" themselves. As Pat Mitchell, Channel 4's entertainment reporter and coanchor for one of its newscasts, told the *Globe* in 1976: "I was working 18 hours a day my first year here (in 1972) and I still am."[20] Marilyn Salenger, a Washington-based reporter for Channel 7, recalled: "When I came here four years ago, I was the only woman besides the secretary of the news director."[21]

In what has become (and remains) a familiar story, when it came to looks and appearance for on-camera women, there was also a double standard. In the 1970s and 1980s, a network man could be pudgy (Willard Scott), bald (Charles Kuralt), long-nosed (Marvin Kalb), bespectacled (John Chancellor), silver-haired (Harry Reasoner), or, by television standards, just plain old (Irving R. Levine, whose career at NBC News spanned forty-five years until his retirement in 1995 at the age of seventy-three). The same values held true for the Boston market, where the male on-air talent could be gray-haired (John Henning), double-chinned (Arch MacDonald), or portly (Don Kent).

Similarly, at both the national level and in markets like Boston, a female reporter usually had to be young, pretty, and trim. No glasses, no bulging midriff, no double chin, and no crow's feet, thank you. Indeed, in all my years as a TV critic, the only full, well-rounded women on camera I can recall—bless them—were legendary anchor Ann Bishop, who worked at WPLG-TV in Miami in the 1970s, and consumer reporter Phyllis Eliasberg, who was at WHDH-TV in Boston in the 1980s.

When the aging process would set in, a man was considered distinguished, while a woman was more likely to get demoted or shown the door. As veteran newsman John Henning mused in 1986, "(Television is) a youth-oriented business. Gray hair and lines give a man the look of sagacity; people look at women differently."[22] Ten years after Henning's observation, and one month after her sixtieth birthday, Shelby Scott, Henning's dependable colleague—famous for her fearless snowstorm coverage—was out the door at Channel 4, relegated to mere freelancing.[23]

If Barbara Walters was a symbol of how far women had come nationally in the 1970s, Christine Craft, a Kansas City, Missouri, anchor at KMBC-TV in the 1980s was a symbol of how far women had yet to go in local television. In 1981 Craft was demoted at the age of thirty-seven after a focus group deemed her "too old, too unattractive, and wouldn't defer to men."[24] Later, she filed suit against Metromedia, the station owner, and initially won $500,000 in damages in a federal court. But Metromedia appealed the case all the way to the U.S. Supreme Court, which in 1986 declined to hear it.

But what about management women in Boston? Let's begin with a scene from *L.A. Law* in the late 1980s that shows Ann Kelsey, the pretty attorney and partner in the firm of McKenzie, Brackman, Chaney & Kuzak, in her baby's nursery. The lights are dim as she speaks in soft, loving tones to her child: "Know what? I ruined a whole deposition yesterday because of you. Probably lost a client. Cost the firm a lot of money. Know what else? I don't care."

Cut to a real-life scene around the same time at Channel 4. It was 8 o'clock on an April evening, and Francine Achbar, executive producer and acting program director, was minding the store. On this day, she had negotiated with syndicators, resolved a backstage crisis at *People Are Talking*, and even zipped up to Rockport, where a locally produced TV movie starring June Allyson was being filmed. Achbar had also received word that program director Barry Schulman, who had taken a six-month leave from the station, had decided to return to his old position, dashing Achbar's hopes for a promotion. Know what else? At forty-two, having paid her dues, she did care about not getting her long-awaited promotion.

Forget Ann Kelsey. Francine Achbar was one of a growing number of women in the 1980s who, having entered the workforce in the 1970s, had risen to mid-level management positions. In the Boston market, they were now news and talk-show producers, research and marketing directors, and heads of public relations departments. But at this point, they had reached the proverbial glass ceiling. At Boston's three major stations, there was not—and had never been—a female general manager, news director, or program director. (Two independent stations did have female program directors: Leslie Savage at Channel 38, and Candace Fisher at Channel 25.) Thus, in the 1980s, women had become something of a force in TV management, but greater progress would come later. For now, they were simply ladies in waiting.[25]

MEN, WOMEN, AND POWER

The 1970s and 1980s were a fascinating vantage point from which to view the culture. Thanks largely to the feminist movement, women were beginning to gain power in the workplace. But it also meant confronting the men in charge, many of whom felt under siege. Television, as with many male-dominated industries and institutions, had long been a bastion of blatant sexism—whether it involved hiring, pay scales, promotions, or simply treating women with respect.[26]

Of course, the roots of the sexism were, and still are, terribly complex, involving historical, psychological, and sociological factors. But what was striking in the Boston market was how much the tone was set by the general managers, who usually came from the sales division (as opposed to news or programming). Because the stations' financial stakes were so high, this division had a highly competitive, locker-room, mine-is-bigger-than-yours sensibility. And such a coarse, roughhouse environment could be quite inhospitable to women. Derogatory and disrespectful putdowns, sexual innuendo, and sexist jokes aimed at the women were not uncommon; guys talked about "boobs" and "getting laid." A friend of mine who once worked in sales at Channel 56 tells a story about a conversation she had with a newly hired weatherman. When he mentioned he had a girlfriend, my friend asked how she liked Boston. "She's still in Washington, but my cock is in Boston," he said, leering at her.

One result of the women's movement was the passage of new laws and regulations, as well as the adoption of in-house policies, prohibiting sex discrimination and sexual harassment in the workplace. In 1980 the U.S. Equal Employment Opportunity Commission wrote "sexual harassment" into its regulations; in 1986, the U.S. Supreme Court declared sexual harassment to be sex discrimination. Thus, in 1990, when a Channel 7 program executive was found guilty of verbal and psychological harassment, as well as physical abuse in the form of forced hugging of one of the station's female employees, the man was forced to resign.

Unfortunately, not every person guilty of harassment was exposed or held accountable—either because the victim (usually a woman), fearing for her job, didn't report it, or the press didn't know about it. What follows is an account of one such ugly episode in the early 1980s—reported here for the first time—that involved a senior-level executive at Channel 4 and one of the station's on-air news personalities. Be forewarned, the details of the incident are graphic.

It began with a simple lunch engagement on a nice, sunny day in 1983. The two were colleagues at Channel 4. She was "talent," as in on-air personality, he was management. An intelligent, attractive African American woman in her early forties, Linda Harris had been with the station since 1975 and had held a variety of on-air positions, including consumer reporter and coanchor of the early morning and noon news. Well respected and popular among her colleagues, she was considered one of the more grounded people working in the often crazy business of television.

He was a senior-level executive at the station. After a pleasant, uneventful lunch at an upscale restaurant in Boston's financial district, the two got into his car and proceeded to drive back to their station on Soldier's Field Road.

Suddenly and without warning, while he was driving and she was looking out the window, she found herself being sexually assaulted in his car. Even after all these years she remembers the exact spot where it took place—some things in life you never forget:

The assault happened on the Mass. Pike section that runs through downtown Boston long before you get out to the Brighton/Allston exit. I remember being aware of the tall downtown buildings when he took hold of my left hand, grabbed it, and tried to yank it to his erect penis. I yelled, "What are you doing?!" He seemed to have been prepared for what he wanted to do because he had already taken out a handkerchief. We struggled; he ejaculated on his pants and, looking at his semen, said, "Look what you made me do!"[27]

Look at what *she* made *him* do! The ordeal left Harris alternately teary-eyed, traumatized, and embarrassed; it wasn't until several weeks later that she told one of her colleagues about the incident. After listening to the sordid details, I asked Harris why she didn't report the man or take legal action. "I am a black woman; he was a white man. I didn't know if anyone would believe me. Besides, I liked my job and didn't want to lose it," she said.

Ironically, some months after the man had left the station, he called Harris and asked her to dinner at the Hampshire House—a safe, neutral place near the Boston State House. There he explained he had been drinking that awful day and wanted to make amends by apologizing. In one of our interviews, I asked Harris if she had forgiven him. "No! Why would I forgive him?" she replied, her voice rising in anger. "This sort of thing still goes on—in the military and at college campuses. Men still call the shots. For God's sake! This was a man who worked at the station that signed my fucking paycheck! This is what women still have to face in the workplace."

SEXUAL ORIENTATION

In 2011, characters Arizona and Callie from *Grey's Anatomy* became "wife and wife" (though by 2015 their marriage was on the rocks). In 2014, when Cameron and Mitchell from *Modern Family* got married in a two-parter during the May "sweeps," the show's ratings went through the roof. During the same year, Showtime unveiled *Transparent*, its critically acclaimed show built around a family in which the father, a retired college professor, turns out to be transgender. (Not only that but Sarah, the oldest sibling, leaves her husband and their two children for another woman.)

Such developments on television reflect a sea change in more tolerant attitudes by the public toward the LGBT community. But they didn't take place in a vacuum. Rather, they stemmed from a series of milestone events and forces over the years, which included the Stonewall Rebellion, the Greenwich Village riot that occurred when police officers raided a popular gay bar in 1969; the rise of the gay liberation movement in the 1970s; the vote by the American Psychiatric Association in 1973 to remove homosexuality from its list of mental illnesses; and significant changes in positions and policies by our political leaders. Another turning point came in 2012, when Vice President Joe Biden was on NBC's *Meet the Press*. In response to a question, Biden declared his support for same-sex marriage (followed by President Barack Obama's own (belated) public endorsement on national television several days later). The vice president also seemed to acknowledge the important role of television in "normalizing" homosexuality. "I think *Will & Grace* probably did more to educate the American public than almost anything anybody's ever done so far," he declared.[28] All of these things set the stage for the Supreme Court's historic decision in 2015, by a 5 to 4 vote, declaring same-sex marriage legal in all fifty states. Speaking at the White House, President Obama praised the Supreme Court's ruling, saying it arrived "like a thunderbolt"—though, in reality, it had taken a series of thunderbolts over the years.

It wasn't always that way. In the early days of television, the subject of homosexuality was simply ignored. Later, gay characters began to appear sporadically. In 1971, *All in the Family* had its first gay character (for one episode) in the form of a friend of Archie's named Steve, a macho ex-football player. ABC's soap opera spoof called *Soap* (1977–1981) featured a gay character named Jodie Dallas (played by Billy Crystal)—though he was presented as a stereotypically effeminate man given to having "Froot Loops" for breakfast.[29] Still, in 1972, *That Certain Summer*, starring Hal Holbrook and Martin Sheen as lovers, proved a breakthrough TV movie—the first to present gays in a sympathetic manner. This trend gained momentum in the 1980s with TV films such as *Consenting Adult* (1985), about a young man coming out to his parents, and *Second Serve* (1986), starring Vanessa Redgrave as the transsexual tennis player Renee Richards—a movie that was far ahead of its time.

But the situation grew a lot more complicated when, in the early 1980s, the Centers for Disease Control reported the first cases of AIDS in the United States. Widely believed to have originated in west-central Africa, and perhaps in Haiti as well, AIDS is a clinical condition that results from infection with the human immunodeficiency virus (HIV), which progressively damages the body's ability to protect itself from disease organisms. At that time, the disease was invariably fatal. HIV could affect anyone regardless of sexual orientation, race, ethnicity, gender, or age. But in the United States and in other Western countries, gay and bisexual men were more severely affected by HIV than any other group.

Suddenly, alarm bells went off in the culture. At a time when religious and social conservatives had become politically powerful, would the prejudice against homosexuals and homosexuality increase? Already, some religious conservatives had taken to calling the disease "the gay plague," claiming it was God's wrath against homosexuals. Would AIDS threaten to undo a generation of progress regarding gay rights? Would television, such an important vehicle for transforming attitudes and educating the public, now shy away from dealing with AIDS? Would the positive portrayals of gays, lesbians, and transgendered people on television become a thing of the past? And, finally, how would local markets, such as Boston, respond to the issue of homosexuality and the AIDS epidemic?

Ironically, the answer was something of a paradox—the angry rhetoric, discrimination, and incidence of antigay violence against homosexuals intensified in some places, but so did the power and efficacy of leaders and supporters in the gay rights movement. Activists were now clamoring for new laws to protect gays and lesbians and a national policy to deal with the AIDS crisis, including government funding to find a cure. Pressure was additionally placed on the networks and local stations "to do" something. As Dennis Altman, an Australian academic and gay rights activist, notes: "It is difficult to speak of the impact of AIDS without speaking of the changing perceptions of homosexuals, so intertwined are the two in the public imagination. AIDS seems to have heightened both the stigma and the respectability of homosexuals; in unraveling this apparent contradiction, we can come to terms with certain crucial social changes."[30]

Initially, all three major networks and the vast majority of the country's local TV stations declined to accept condom commercials, which public officials advocated as an effective and practical way to reduce the risks of AIDS. (See "The Condom Conundrum" in chapter 6.) But between 1981 and 1987, the CDC reported more than 50,000 people had contracted AIDS, 95.5 percent of whom had died.[31]

Television, never mind the public, could no longer look away. At the networks, regular weekly series began to include AIDS in their storylines. In 1983, on NBC's *St. Elsewhere*, the doctors at St. Eligius, a fictitious Boston hospital, treated a family man who had contracted AIDS through a homosexual liaison; while in 1986, on the same series, Dr. Bobby Caldwell (played by Mark Harmon) contracted AIDS and had to leave the hospital.[32] In 1985, PBS's *Nova* presented "AIDS: Chapter One," which looked at what modern science had learned about the disease. And, in 1985, NBC aired *An Early Frost*, a long-awaited TV movie about a gay attorney (played by Aiden Quinn) who learns he has AIDS. It was an important breakthrough—the first TV movie to deal with AIDS. Watched by more than 34 million people, the film was nominated for fourteen Emmys (winning three) and later won a coveted Peabody Award. Equally important, it set the stage for subsequent TV and theatrical films dealing with AIDS, including *The Littlest Victims* and *The Ryan White Story* (both 1989), *Longtime Companion* (1990), and *Philadelphia* (1993).

Whether the subject was AIDS or just homosexuality, such efforts were not without controversy. When *An Early Frost* aired, NBC lost $500,00 in advertising revenues from sponsors who were skittish about being identified with the film. It was not without precedent. In 1989, ABC's *thirtysomething* featured a scene showing two gay men in bed (*after* having sex)—believed to be a first for primetime television; but that scene cost ABC $1.5 million in advertising. The network received roughly 400 calls after the show, of which about 90 percent were negative.

Meanwhile, *P.O.V.*, an award-winning PBS series known for its cutting-edge documentaries, was continually under fire. In 1991, 174 out of 284 *P.O.V.* stations declined to air *Tongues Untied*, an explicit and intensely personal exploration of black gay male identity. (WGBH in Boston did air the program.) Not long after, PBS itself pulled the plug on *Stop the Church*, another *P.O.V.* film, which chronicled a protest in 1989 by a group of AIDS activists at New York's St. Patrick Cathedral. (Two PBS outlets—KCET-TV in Los Angeles and KQED-TV in San Francisco—decided to show it anyway.)

The local TV stations, including those in Boston, were slower to respond. By and large, it wasn't until the mid-1980s that they finally dealt with the issue. Talk shows, news series, and public service campaigns in Boston became a part of the local response. To be sure, some reporters were not always responsible or sensitive in covering the story. As Dr. Jerome Groopman, chief of hematology and oncology at New England Deaconess Hospital and a leading AIDS researcher, told the *Boston Globe*: "When someone like Delores Handy from Channel 7 gets off an elevator and sticks a microphone in somebody's face and says, 'You're an AIDS victim. How does it feel?' Well, she hasn't spent the time (with AIDS patients). That's like saying to a guy who's been run over by a dump truck, how's your stomach feeling? You don't do that to someone you're sensitive to."[33]

Of all the Boston stations, Channel 4 (WBZ) led the way. Initially, WBZ, in accordance with the policy of its owner, Westinghouse Broadcasting (Group W), declined to accept condom commercials. But apparently moved by the gravity of the situation, Group W announced in 1987 that it would produce five one-hour-long educational programs on AIDS for its five owned stations and additionally make them available to others around the country. The ambitious project was designed to generate as much as $1 million in contributions for AIDS organizations. Public service announcements, news items and educational videotapes would be offered as well. Moreover, Channel 4 medical reporter Jeanne Blake, in particular, played a very important role in educating the public, with numerous news series and specials on AIDS, including her superb *AIDS: The Paul Cronan Story*, which profiled a young telephone repairman who contracted AIDS. Denied his job after taking a medical leave, Cronan filed a $1.5 million lawsuit against New England Telephone. An out-of-court settlement was reached, which reinstated him. A year and a half later, he died, at age thirty-two, of an AIDS-related illness.

But AIDS really hit home in the Boston market in 1985 when WBZ, the station doing the most to educate the public, was confronted with a problem from its own employees. Some of the station photographers, fearing they might contract AIDS, either through a victim's saliva accidentally touching microphones or through casual contact, did not want to go out on AIDS-related assignments. It was a perfect metaphor for the near hysteria gripping the Boston area and many communities throughout the country. Ironically, Jeanne Blake had been working on a three-part news series, *AIDS: Killer Without a Cure*. One of the messages was that health and science experts were assuring the public that AIDS could not be spread through casual contact; it could only be transmitted by intimate sexual contact, contaminated needles, blood transfusions, and exposure through open wounds. But now, four photographers were refusing to go with Blake on a story for her series.

A frustrated Blake placed an urgent call to her news director, Stan Hopkins, who was in Tennessee attending a news directors conference. It was a sticky situation. Channel 4's policy was that no employee would be forced to go out on an AIDS-related assignment. Hopkins later told me, "I am regarding this situation as similar to any other hazardous assignment. We do not require a photographer to fly or go scuba diving against his will. We simply provide the right to refuse an assignment."[34]

Nevertheless, he called the Channel 4 newsroom to try to talk to one of the frightened cameramen who had refused the assignment, but he simply reiterated his position. Three other photographers also declined forcing Hopkins to cancel the shoot that day. Hopkins understood the terrible dilemma for the media, telling the *Ledger*, which broke the story, "Obviously, we are dealing with a great deal of fear and ignorance, which is making it harder for us to communicate the AIDS story."

The situation was not unique to Boston. A week earlier, NBC's *Today* show had a five-part series on AIDS dealing with medical myths and facts, and discrimination against those with AIDS. However, on one particular show featuring an AIDS patient and his mother, the two were put in a separate room from the show's other guest. Kathleen Graham, a *Today* spokesperson, explained, "Scott Goldstein (the producer) made the decision several days earlier. He felt that the guests were nervous enough going on television and didn't want any added nerves."

But even with better public education, there were occasional lapses by the local media that created near panic. In 1991, for example, Dr. Earl Gelman, a Brockton gynecologist, was arrested for having had sex with a prostitute who may or may not have been infected with the AIDS virus. Although there was no proof that he was infected with HIV, his arrest resulted in a page one story in the *Patriot Ledger*, with follow-up stories the day after in the *Boston Herald* and on all three of Boston's major TV stations. The *Herald* branded the gynecologist the "Sex Doc." (In the absence of corroboration, the *Globe* chose not to do a story.) "The media right now are on a feeding frenzy on AIDS," declared George Annas, professor of health law at Boston University Medical School.[35]

Many of us working in the Boston media were affected by the AIDS crisis in a very personal way. Three of our own would contract the dreaded disease—one, a quirky TV weatherman; another, a promising young TV critic; and finally, the town's most popular radio talk-show host.

Stuart Soroka was the zany meteorologist for the old Channel 7 between 1973 and 1977 and also had radio stints with several local radio stations. In a wry piece in 1982 about her own TV dream team, Diane White, the *Boston Globe* columnist, voted Stuart Soroka her favorite weatherman. "Other weathermen may give us news of pollution counts, acid rainfall and high-pressure fronts over Western Canada," she once wrote. "Only Soroka ever forecast the best days for hanging out laundry."[36] In 1974, in its annual Best of Boston awards, *Boston* magazine voted him the town's best weatherman. ("Accurate and crazy. Absolutely crazy," was the magazine's description.)

Sadly, on Easter Sunday in 1990, the *Globe* reported that at the age of forty-five, Stu Soroka had died at a Florida hospital, reportedly of pneumonia.[37] That was a discreet, if misleading touch on the part of the obit writer, for Soroka had died of AIDS. His former colleagues had nothing but kind things to say about him. Charles Laquidara, the WBCN disc jockey where Soroka once filed weather reports, called him "a great flake and a very gentle guy."

Above all else, Stu Soroka was an original. He was Boston's first weatherclown—a TV personality whose offbeat, unpredictable style set a standard of sorts for later meteorologists. By some quirk of nature, he had a knack for doing crazy things that made people laugh. The stories about his on- and off-the-air antics had become legendary. One former colleague recalled that at KDKA-TV in Pittsburgh, he once caught his tie in the fax machine. Bob Gamere, another Channel 7 alumnus, laughed recalling the time Soroka got his finger stuck between some weather maps in Pittsburgh. Ted O'Brien, a former Channel 7 anchor, chuckled recalling the famous "water bucket" incident. Before weather became computerized, the maps were marked up with chalk and had to be cleaned off with soap and water. "We had a huge sponge to clean off the chalk. One night, Stu stuck his foot in the water bucket and stomped around during his weather report with the bucket. The water came up to his ankle." What made the incident even funnier was that the camera never showed Stu's foot. And so, while Stu struggled to deliver his weather report, the rest of the anchor people were doubled up with laughter, much to the befuddlement of the viewers.

If Soroka had a need to test limits in his professional life, he was similarly bold, and occasionally self-destructive, in his personal life. At times he seemed to court danger. During the '70s, when many gay men preferred the security of the closet, Stu was open about his homosexuality. He even put the names of his lovers on the Channel 7 bulletin board. From 1982 to 1983, Soroka worked at CNN in Atlanta and continued to find himself in trouble. A clip showing him falling into the weather map and pinned against the wall somehow made its way onto Dick Clark's *TV's Bloopers and Practical Jokes* show. Accident or not, the CNN management wasn't amused.

After he left CNN, Soroka found his career and personal life on the skids. The end was sad. Relocating to Florida, Soroka contracted AIDS and wound up living in a quasi-religious compound next door to a crack house. "He didn't go anywhere," recalled Ron Gasbarro, one of his few friends. "He just watched his ten or twelve cockatiels flying around the room."[38] At the time of his death, Stuart Soroka, Boston's original weatherclown, was penniless and an AIDS patient, living on welfare.

And then there was Ron Doyle. Despite all that I'd written about AIDS, I was unprepared for the phone call I received one night while watching the local news. A reporter for *The Middlesex News* in Framingham called to tell me that Ron Doyle, that paper's TV critic who once won a *Boston* magazine award for best TV critic, had just died of AIDS. For the paper's obituary, did I have a comment? I was devastated; it took me several minutes to compose myself. I had known that Ron was sick, but I didn't know why. I hadn't seen him at TV functions of late but didn't make anything of it. Now AIDS had hit home in a terribly personal way. Someone I had known, liked, and respected—a colleague—had succumbed to AIDS. (My feelings may well have been intensified because an old boyfriend of mine had died of AIDS five years earlier.)

Two years earlier, Ron had quietly informed Ken Hartnett, the editor of the *Middlesex News*, that he had AIDS. His ordeal was long and painful. "He never whined about life being unkind," said Hartnett. "He continued to do his job and do it well until riding down the Mass. Turnpike (to and from work) became too much."[39] A month earlier, Connie Paige, an investigative reporter, and a few of her colleagues visited Ron at Brigham and Women's Hospital, where he was getting a blood transfusion. "Four of us went together. We were cowards," she said. "It was really, really sad. He was very weak and emaciated. He couldn't sit up; he could barely talk. But he started talking, making jokes, and making us feel comfortable." When the end was near, Hartnett visited Ron one more time. "He still recognized me," he said. "We had a conversation, but he was obviously suffering. At one point, he told me he had to get to work. I think he was hallucinating." At 3 a.m. on a Tuesday, Ron died in his sleep at his South End home. He was all of thirty-three years of age.

Finally, David Brudnoy—a unique media presence. During his nearly three-decade-long career in Boston, he provided film reviews and commentary for several local TV stations; he served for many years as a movie reviewer for the Community Newspapers chain in the Boston area; he freelanced for such publications as the *National*

Review and *Boston* magazine; and he was a founder of the Boston Society of Film Critics and the Boston Theater Critics Circle. The most cerebral of Boston's radio talk-show hosts, he held several degrees—a BA from Yale, a master's in Far Eastern studies from Harvard, and a PhD in American civilization from Brandeis University. Somehow, he found the time to teach part time at Boston University's College of Communication and numerous other colleges and universities in the area.

But most of all, Brudnoy will be remembered as Boston's most beloved and respected radio talk-show host—variously working at WHDH, WRKO, and WBZ, as well as having had stints at Channels 7 and 4 doing reviews. In a business too often associated with mindless blather and shouting, Brudnoy was known for his intelligence, wit, and civility. And, though Massachusetts was largely a liberal, Democratic state, listeners had long since accepted his libertarian views and conservative politics. They even forgave him for what one *Globe* writer called his "penchant for polysyllables" and for the occasional times when his iconoclastic views lapsed into racial insensitivity. David was always David.

Despite his popularity, in 1990, WBZ management, looking for cheaper syndicated programming, tried to get rid of him. But the community uproar was so loud—aided by public support from the *Boston Globe* and a couple of media-savvy friends who knew how to work the media—the red-faced station was forced to reinstate him.

One other thing. David Brudnoy was gay, and in 1988 was diagnosed with HIV/AIDS. This too, is part of his story. While in media circles it was widely known that he was gay, Brudnoy preferred to keep his private life private. And, for a time, because he was asymptomatic, he managed his busy schedule as usual—that is, until one day in 1994 when he collapsed in the lobby of his Commonwealth Avenue apartment building. Hospitalized because of viral pneumonia and an enlarged heart, he remained in a coma for nine days and nearly died. But upon his recovery, and with more than a little trepidation, he decided to come out publicly, announcing it on his radio show. He went on to become a forceful advocate for AIDS research, establishing the David Brudnoy Fund for AIDS Research at Massachusetts General Hospital, and wrote a candid memoir, *Life Is Not a Rehearsal.*

In 2003, Brudnoy learned he had Merkel cell carcinoma, a rare and deadly form of skin cancer. Taking a leave of absence from his show, he returned several months later—now broadcasting from his home because of his weakened condition. On December 9, 2004, Brudnoy died at the age of sixty-four. A month earlier, he bet Boston mayor Tom Menino a steak dinner that the city could not get a pothole fixed in twenty-four hours. Menino won the bet. But in typical fashion, Brudnoy, knowing the end was near, arranged for a friend to take the mayor to dinner after his death.

The late 1980s and early 1990s were characterized by greater public education; the development of multiple antiretroviral drugs, known as the AIDS "cocktail," to better manage the disease; and continued acceptance of gays, lesbians, and transgendered people by the larger community. Along with these changes came a growing number of public figures, such as Massachusetts congressman Barney Frank (1987) and Ellen DeGeneres (1997), who decided to disclose their homosexuality.[40]

The same was true for people working in television news. In 1993, Randy Price, a popular Channel 4 anchor in Boston (now at Channel 5), became the first major market news anchor—and possibly the only local anchor in the country—to publicly disclose his homosexuality. The reaction in the larger community and in his own newsroom was muted. "It's mostly joking, like 'You'll do anything for publicity,'" said Price.[41] David Bartlett, president of the Radio and Television News Directors Association (RTNDA), put the situation in perspective: "It's reflective of a trend in society in which there is less and less stigma to being gay in any kind of work, least of all, TV news."[42]

DUKE RUNS FOR PRESIDENT IN 1988: THE LOCALS GO NATIONAL

By the dictates of good journalism, the media are supposed to be skeptical and nonpartisan; they are sworn not to take sides. Yet, when it comes to politics, they have been known to let their guard down—sometimes falling in love with the candidates they cover. It was true in 1960 when the media fell madly in love with Jack Kennedy, the handsome and charismatic Democratic candidate running for president. It was true in 2004, when Barack Obama successfully ran to become the first African American elected president.[1] And it was true in 2016, when the media couldn't get enough of Donald Trump during the Republican primaries, vying to become the party's nominee for president, so mesmerized were they by his flamboyance and colorful persona.[2] Earlier, it was also true when Michael Dukakis, the popular three-term Massachusetts governor, in 1987 announced he was running to become the Democratic nominee for president. This time, it was the Boston TV stations that fell in love.

"Good morning, everyone," said Channel 5's affable anchor Susan Wornick on March 16, 1987, as her station cut into ABC's soap opera *Ryan's Hope.* "Here's what's coming up on *NewsCenter 5 at Midday.* The speculation is over. *NewsCenter 5* has learned that Governor Dukakis will, in fact, run for president of the United States. His people tell us that he will hold a press conference at 2:30 this afternoon, at which time he will be more explicit about his plans. We will have two live reports from the State House coming up on *NewsCenter 5 at Midday.*"[3]

Although the Dukakis announcement was hardly unexpected, it touched off a frenzied but exciting day for the Boston media, especially the local television stations. All three major stations covered the governor's afternoon news conference live. Fifteen cameras were on hand for the event. That night the newscasts were filled with interviews with the governor; his wife, Kitty; and his eighty-three-year-old mother, Euterpe. In addition, there were man-on-the-street reactions, background pieces, special reports, and live satellite interviews from Washington. The smaller stations also got into the act. For instance, *The Ten O'Clock News*, on Channel 2, put its own distinctive spin on the story, sampling reaction from some breathless joggers running along the Charles River, with the "Chariots of Fire" theme playing triumphantly in the background.

Those favored local TV reporters assigned to the presidential campaign over the next year and a half would have the time of their lives. So many war stories for their grandchildren as they covered the primary season; later, the Democratic Convention in Atlanta in July 1988, anointing Dukakis as the party's candidate; and finally, the presidential race between Dukakis and Vice President George H. W. Bush, which his Republican rival would ultimately win, and by a substantial margin. The campaign trail was often a relentless pressure cooker for the reporters: traveling on the road for long stretches at a time; enduring endless wake-up calls in anonymous hotels; gulping burgers on the run; rushing to meet deadlines; poring over the dreary position papers churned out by the campaigns; listening to the candidates give the same speech over and over, four, five, six times a day; bickering with rival reporters over inconsequential tidbits; putting up with screaming producers and their news director because the station was scooped on a story; and getting midnight calls from a mournful spouse wondering if the reporter was ever coming home.[4]

The tenor and quality of the coverage would be set even before his announcement when the governor began wading into presiden tial politics. Indeed, the amount of local TV coverage surrounding the governor's presidential bid would become nothing short of mind-boggling. On one trip to Iowa in February, when Dukakis was merely testing the political waters, he was followed by no fewer than forty local reporters and camera people. (The Iowa caucuses on February 15, 1988, represented the candidates' first official test of strength.)

When Dukakis and rival candidate Missouri representative Richard Gephardt squared off in a debate at Drake University, in Iowa, on August 8, reporters from four Boston TV stations (including Uma Pemmaraju from Channel 56) were on hand. Both Channels 4 and 7 televised the debate live at noon (remember, this was on a *Saturday!*), and Channel 5, making a more sensible decision, aired it on a taped delay basis at 7:30 that night. In St. Louis, which was Gephardt country, not one TV station bothered to carry the debate, much less send a single reporter. "We've been amazed at the Boston media," said Michael Reynolds, managing editor for KCCI-TV in Des Moines. "What is Dukakis back there—God?"[5] Similarly, a *Washington Post* story by Eleanor Randolph on August 9, taking note of the Boston media's saturation coverage of the debate, noted:

> The front page of the *Boston Herald* today shouted "Head to Head," in big bold letters, trumpeting what seemed like the sporting match of the decade.
>
> But the photos were of Massachusetts Governor Michael S. Dukakis (D) and Rep. Richard S. Gephardt (D-Mo.), whose debate drew so little excitement elsewhere that even in Iowa, where it was held, the local television stations were opting for cartoons, football and a discussion of Oriental art.
>
> Not so the Hub, as Boston's tabloids once enjoyed calling the city. Here the Dukakis-Gephardt debate generated more excitement in the news media than many Celtic games.[6]

But was it possible to have too much of a good thing? The reasons for Duke fever were not difficult to fathom. To begin with, the Dukakis candidacy was a local story with national implications. It wasn't every day that a hometown kid had a shot at becoming the next president of the United States. And because Dukakis had assumed informal favorite-son status for the crucial New Hampshire primary the following February, the local coverage of his candidacy became a national issue. In the ferociously competitive Boston television market, there were also built-in pressures not to be left behind on stories relating to a Dukakis's candidacy.

Eight months before the New Hampshire primary, both Channels 5 and 7 aired promos hyping their political units. This being the Golden Age of local television, each of the TV stations had the money and resources to go all out. All three major stations had formal political units and did their own polling. All were Duke-ing it out, trying to outflank their rivals for the upcoming Iowa caucuses and New Hampshire primary. Each one searched for a technological or logistical advantage. In November, Channel 4 set up bureaus in New Hampshire and Iowa. Channel 4 political consultant Gerry Chervinsky recalled, "In 1984 we had people in New Hampshire ten days before the primary, and in Iowa four days before the caucuses. This year we're starting in November. We're treating both New Hampshire and Iowa as local events." Channel 5 one-upped its competitors when it bought a second satellite van. Both vans were to be deployed in New Hampshire.

The biggest challenge was for the local TV stations to use their resources wisely. This was all the more important because of the peculiar dynamics of the first-in-the-nation New Hampshire primary. The New Hampshire numbers, coupled with the results of the Iowa caucuses, which would take place just eight days earlier, had come to play an unbelievably powerful role in the selection of presidential candidates. As part of a study, William C. Adams, a political scientist at George Washington University and an expert on the presidential primaries, drew up a map of the United States in which New Hampshire was sixty times as big as Alaska, Iowa dwarfed Texas, and the Western states, except for California, scarcely existed at all. His purpose was to demonstrate a political reality: the states were drawn in proportion to the news coverage their primaries and caucuses received in 1984.[7] And, for better or worse, since 1952 no one had been elected president without first winning the New Hampshire primary. Equally important, the vast majority of people in the Granite State got their television news from Boston's stations. Thus the voters' feelings and perceptions about the various candidates would be greatly influenced by the Boston media, especially Boston's TV stations, which transmitted such powerful images and impressions.

Every Boston station claimed to be providing fair and balanced coverage. Said Channel 7 news director Jeff Rosser: "We're covering Dukakis as a candidate for president and as the governor of the state. We're trying to throw hardballs, not softballs, which he can hit over the fence." On the other hand, Chervinsky accused Channel 7 of falling all over Dukakis. "If you look at Channel 7, you'll see all the hype in the way the anchors 'intro' the pieces, in the tone of the reporters' scripts. (Coanchor) Kate Sullivan says, '*Our* governor is a candidate. Gee whiz.' They show Dukakis on a tractor. (Political reporter) Joe Day stands live with Dukakis and that's it. It's totally Dukakis-oriented. No one watches Channel 7 anyway. They don't know any better."

But a closer look at the coverage suggested that *all* the Boston's TV stations had gone gaga over the guv. They continued to over-cover him while giving short shrift to his rivals. They propped up his candidacy by elevating him to front-runner status too early in the game. They all but gave him a free platform on which to speak in glittering generalities, rarely pressing him for specifics. And they largely failed to provide critical analysis or perspective on important issues. As played out on our nightly newscasts, the presidential campaign largely became a sappy melodrama called *The Mike Dukakis Story*.

A kind of mindless boosterism took hold. The Duke was treated as a hometown hero about to win the World Series (even before he had made the playoffs), and the stations had become his personal rooting section, cheering him on to victory—on at least one occasion, literally. On February 4, after a long day of watching Dukakis politicking, many Boston reporters settled in at an Osceola, Iowa, restaurant to watch how the local television stations covered Dukakis. According to the *Boston Globe*, "When one station led the news with footage of Dukakis, a small but unmistakable cheer went up from the supposedly objective press group. Several reporters said later that they were surprised at the reaction."[8]

In Eleanor Randolph's August 9th piece in the *Washington Post*, Jim Coppersmith, Channel 5's general manager, made a candid, if not startling admission. Owning up to "a big rooting activity here," Coppersmith said: "He's a great guy and he's a great governor, and our experience with President Kennedy tells us that if you get a local man who becomes president, wonderful, new, tall government buildings suddenly start springing up around here."[9]

No less startling was the Channel 7 promo that literally designated the station's own political reporters as Dukakis's "running mates." An off-camera voice said: "Monday, March 16. Governor Michael Dukakis announces his candidacy for president. On the same day, *The New England News* assigns Joe Day, R. D. Sahl, Marty Sender, and Rehema Ellis to be his running mates. Their assignment: stick with Dukakis throughout the campaign." The camera then switched to Joe Day walking and talking with the candidate. New meaning was given to the station's slogan, "We're All on the Same Team."

In his book about the 1984 presidential campaign, *The Great American Video Game*, Martin Schram, a respected political writer and author, had some harsh words about the shallow coverage by the Boston TV stations, noting: "The candidates know that going bowling and singing barbershop is just a trick to get the TV stations to put them on the air; and the stations know that too, but they do it just the same."[10] Their coverage of the 1988 presidential campaign suggests that the locals hadn't learned very much. On March 24, the day Alexander Haig declared his candidacy for the Republican nomination, the cameras caught him in the dramatic act of eating an ice cream cone. Channel 4 reporter Shelby Scott asked him about the flavor. "White Russian," quipped Haig. "It's capitalistic ice cream."

But the lion's share of photo ops was given to the Duke. Boston TV viewers got to see Dukakis eating tomato-and-macaroni soup and a tuna-fish sandwich at Martha's Sweet Shoppe, in Nashua; riding a tractor, schmoozing with farmers, and playing basketball with some kids in Iowa; posing with Boston Celtics' star Kevin McHale at the Minnesota State Fair; and reading to a group of second graders at the Longfellow Elementary School, in Cambridge, one day before a candidates' debate in North Carolina on the subject of education. The local news anchors played an important role. A knowing glance, a warm smile, an inflection of the voice were often dead giveaways about which team they were on.

Too often, they were the stage setters for favorable stories, engaging in boosterish byplay with reporters and serving up fluff-ball questions in live interviews. During Dukakis's trip to Iowa in February, Channel 4 reporter Andy Hiller, in a live interview with the undeclared candidate, had the camera pan the hordes of reporters surrounding him. "They are just all good friends," the Duke said knowingly. (Too true, too true.) Back in the studio, Channel 4 anchor Liz Walker chimed in, "I think the governor's going to have a lot of friends with him." (Too true, too true.)

On March 16, when the Duke announced that he would seek the presidency, Channel 5 anchor Jay Schadler (later an ABC News correspondent) obligingly lapsed into the role of apologist concerning the candidate's lack of credentials in the area of foreign policy. "Though Governor Dukakis does lack foreign-policy experience," Schadler said, "that criticism can also be leveled at several other presidential hopefuls this year, including former governors Bruce Babbitt and Pete du Pont. What's more, the experience of Jimmy Carter and Ronald Reagan suggests that foreign-policy inexperience isn't fatal to a candidate." And on April 29, the day Dukakis delivered a more formal announcement for the presidency, Channel 5 anchor Natalie Jacobson was singing the praises of his "strong platform" on AIDS. Here's what the Duke actually said: "I believe our children have a right to live in a country that is caring and compassionate and concerned about all of its citizens. A country where AIDS is recognized for what it is—the single most important threat to the public health in our lifetime, and a disease that must be conquered." How was that for a comprehensive blueprint for action?

On September 3, Channel 7 was on the ball, so to speak, going live to Minnesota for an on-camera endorsement by Boston Celtics player Kevin McHale at the Minnesota State Fair. Blue-and-white "Dukakis for President" signs were carefully placed in the background. When anchor R. D. Sahl noted that people had begun wondering about the candidate's lack of specifics on the farm problem, the Duke dodged the question by talking about a biotech revolution afoot, and how all the farmers were listening to what he had to say. This mumbo jumbo was followed by coanchor Kate Sullivan cheerfully asking McHale what he was bringing to the Dukakis campaign. The basketball star told her he comes from a depressed area in Minnesota, adding, "I do know a good man and a good person when I see him." (End of slam-dunk interview.)

A refreshing change of pace from this flag-waving journalism occasionally came from Christopher Lydon, who coanchored Channel 2's *Ten O'Clock News*. Traveling with Dukakis in Iowa in February,

Lydon injected some much-needed skepticism into the campaign, referring to "this picture of the yuppie in the cornfields, the high-tech governor in the cornfields, presuming to tell the depressed farmers in the heartland that they might ease off the corn and the soybeans and think of growing some of the table food that Americans have been importing lately—endive, berries, apples, or mushrooms." In a rare display of pointed criticism, Lydon concluded, "It's as if he were telling General Motors to get out of making cars and start making fern baskets."

Channel 56's Uma Pemmaraju provided some of the most naive reporting. Following the candidate around in New York City on April 2, she proved to be a public relations person's dream. "That's Dukakis on the campaign trail speaking Spanish to the Hispanic residents of the South Bronx," she gushed. (Shots of dilapidated buildings, old cars, and garbage.) "The candidates come here to gain perspective on the problems that plague the residents," she added earnestly. Next, shots of babies peering out of windows and gruff-looking hardhats followed by a sound bite of Dukakis saying that he was committed to decent, affordable housing. Pemmaraju continued: "And on this initial trip, Dukakis is getting a good reception from the folks who asked him to come here." Cut to a South Bronx resident who says: "He's done it in Massachusetts. His record is well known in Massachusetts. It's well known that he's particularly committed to local groups that have worked with government." Back in the studio, Pemmaraju gushed: "And this footnote. Dukakis is big news in Athens, Greece. A TV crew from Athens has followed the governor around all day because Greeks are proud to have one of their own running for president." (The Dukakis team should have sent her a complimentary plate of moussaka.)

Public-opinion polls, especially those conducted in the early stages of a political campaign, are essentially meaningless, serving only as an indication of name recognition at a time when the voting public has yet to size up the candidates. They also have the negative effect of encouraging reporters to tailor their stories to the poll results. In part, the polls arise out of the media's compulsion to attach a front-runner label to a candidate.

They have also become useful tools, enabling a station to promote and advertise itself as having "exclusive" results. In Schram's *Great American Video Game*, Channel 4 news director Stan Hopkins is quoted as having serious doubts about the polling process, especially in advance of an election or primary. "I don't think the viewing public understands a lot about polling," he said, adding: "What is the value of doing it? I'm not sure there is any great value."[11] Despite Hopkins's reservations, in the 1987/1988 political season, Channel 4 stood as the most poll-happy station of the bunch. From January through Labor Day, Channel 4, working with the *Boston Herald*, conducted no fewer than nine polls, compared with one for Channel 5 and none for Channel 7. On March 16, the day Dukakis initially announced his intention to run, a WBZ-TV4/*Boston Herald* telephone poll was conducted in time for the 11 o'clock news. The poll turned up the earth-shaking conclusion that Massachusetts voters favored the Duke over former Colorado senator Gary Hart 55 to 14 percent.

On Monday, August 10, two days after the Richard Gephardt–Mike Dukakis debate in Iowa, Channel 4 anchor Jack Williams led the 6 o'clock news as follows: "An exclusive WBZ-TV4/*Boston Herald* poll shows that Michael Dukakis is topping the list of potential voters in the Iowa Democratic caucuses, but barely." And what did his lead consist of? It turns out that Dukakis had 15 percent compared with Gephardt, who had 13, followed by Illinois senator Paul Simon, with 12. The fact that 39 percent of the potential voters were undecided was played down in the report. (The front-page story in the *Herald* the next day was even more biased, headlined: "Poll: Duke Is Decking Rivals.") But while Channel 4 and the *Herald* were jumping up and down, giving Dukakis front-runner status, many in the national media were more cautious. In a *New York Times* piece that ran on August 23, veteran political reporter R. W. Apple Jr. wrote that "several recent polls have shown 40 to 50 percent of the party's supporters undecided—the largest percentage at this stage of a campaign since World War II." The headline accompanying the piece read: "In Democratic Field, No One Is Nearing the Winner's Circle."

Indeed, Boston's TV stations showed a pronounced tendency to filter polls, debates, and other events relating to the presidential campaign through a local prism in which Dukakis was the center of the political universe. In August, when a former campaign adviser to Gary Hart suggested that the ex-candidate might reenter the Democratic race,[12] the Boston stations tended to play the story in terms of what it would mean for the Duke. For instance, Channel 4 reporter Bill Shields whipped out a two-week-old poll showing the matchup results between Hart and Dukakis in New Hampshire. By contrast, the three major networks sampled reactions from various candidates (Richard Gephardt, Al Gore, Pat Schroeder, and Jesse Jackson, among others) and political observers. ABC News went one step further, tracking down another campaign aide, Bill Shore, who had spoken with Hart in Dublin that day. Shore said his former boss categorically denied plans for a new campaign. Not a peep about Dukakis on the network news that night.

In debate situations, our local stations invariably placed a local spin on the story—with a heavy dose of pictures before the debate centering on the Duke (inspecting the hall, testing the sound, for example). The post-debate analysis usually focused on the question of how "our guy" did. When all seven Democratic candidates met for a two-hour debate at the Iowa State Fair, on August 23, the emphasis was on Senator Albert Gore Jr. attacking, if not ganging up on, "our guy." Channel 5 anchor Jack Harper teased the story by saying, "Gore goes after the Duke." Channel 4 reporter Mike Macklin was protective: "But Dukakis, the acknowledged front-runner, didn't let Gore's criticism bother him." Channel 7 trotted out Republican political consultant Todd Domke, who proclaimed Dukakis the winner because Gore's strategy was "too transparent, too calculated." That night, the CBS Evening News devoted fifteen seconds to the debate and placed it in a larger context. Referring to the candidates, anchor Charles Osgood declared, "Mostly they attacked President Reagan." (The New York Times story the next day on page 16 was headlined, "Democrats, in Iowa Debate, Make Reagan Their Target.")

Given all the media attention lavished on Dukakis, it is noteworthy how little criticism he received at the time—both as a governor and as a presidential candidate. Said one veteran TV reporter: "Mike Dukakis the governor never would have signed the legislative pay raise, then run away for a three-day holiday. He signed it on a Friday before the Memorial Day weekend. There was no emergency to have a pay-raise bill. But no cameras were allowed and no one questioned him about it over the weekend. The guy is getting away with murder."

Other observers were also dismayed. "Breathless" was the word used by Lisa Myers, an NBC correspondent based in Boston. "It's not even a close call. In general, it's nothing short of adoring. To some extent, that's expected. But when do the Boston stations start covering him less as a favorite son and more as one of seven Democratic presidential candidates? I had expected that by now the excitement over his candidacy would have been tempered." Joe Bergantino, now an ABC correspondent based in Boston and formerly a Channel 4 investigative reporter, cried overkill. "Clearly, it was overkill in the beginning. Watching Boston TV, one would believe Dukakis was the front-runner and the man most likely to be president," he says.

Political consultant Michael Goldman called the boosterism effect "huge," arguing that the TV stations had a stake in the Dukakis candidacy. "It would be ridiculous to assume TV stations have no vested interest in Michael Dukakis. They have file footage; they know him. This can be important when the national media ask for help." Goldman also thought that some Boston television reporters, consciously or not, believed they would benefit personally from a Dukakis victory. "Lou Cannon covered Reagan for the *Los Angeles Times*. Right after Reagan became president, he was grabbed up by the *Washington Post*," he said.

The romance between the Duke and the Boston TV stations ended, however briefly, on September 30, when Dukakis's well-oiled political machine was rocked by the revelation that campaign manager John Sasso—despite vigorous and repeated initial denials—had in fact prepared and distributed an "attack video" that helped destroy the presidential campaign of Senator Joseph Biden Jr., who withdrew from the race. The attack video showed a Biden speech that used, without attribution, the language and theme of a campaign speech by British Labor Party leader Neil Kinnock.[13] Later in the day, Sasso resigned. The stations were all over the story with live coverage, interviews, reaction, and file footage. Channel 4 devoted twenty-five minutes to the story at 6 p.m. and followed it with an additional half-hour wrap-up at 7:30 p.m. Other stations were nearly as aggressive.

In any case, the relationship was interrupted not because the stations had woken up, but because the campaign had been caught in an indiscretion so flagrant that not even the governor's live-shot suitors could ignore it. Until September 30, Boston's stations had covered the campaign with their arms around—rather than at arm's length from—Dukakis. Until the Sasso fiasco, Mike Dukakis had nothing but smooth sailing. He was articulate in debates. He was respected for his intelligence, honesty, and managerial skills, and he had a record of genuine accomplishment. He garnered some favorable national press early on. (Nor did *Playgirl*'s designation of Dukakis as one of America's ten sexiest men hurt in the publicity and image department.) And he demonstrated an impressive ability to raise money.

Still, it was one thing for the media to affectionately dub him "the Duke," but quite another to crown him "King of the Candidates" so early in the game. Around the time of the Iowa caucus in February, an obscure TV reporter from Iowa shrewdly grasped the madness that had seized the Boston media. Reporting on a visit by Dukakis, Mike Day of KCCI-TV, in Des Moines, sounded bemused. "During his visit to Iowa last week," he said, "the Reverend Jesse Jackson (another candidate) took time to milk a cow. Massachusetts governor Mike Dukakis, on the other hand, milked the press for coverage."

EPILOGUE:
FADE TO BLACK

In her exhaustive biography of William S. Paley, the broadcast pioneer and legendary founder of CBS, Sally Bedell Smith makes reference to his huge ego and ferocious love of life. Paley died in his Manhattan apartment in 1990, at the age of eighty-nine. But toward the end, when he was in failing health, the man who built the Columbia Broadcasting System kept asking a longtime friend: "Why do I have to die?"[1]

Of course, nothing is forever; all things must pass. Empires come and go. Economic booms eventually go bust. Even the New York Yankees couldn't go on winning forever. And so it was with Boston's Golden Age of local television. Suddenly, almost without warning—at least that's how it felt—a serious economic recession in the early 1990s, coupled with dramatic changes in the television landscape, would spell its doom.

THE NEW ENGLAND RECESSION

The 1990 to 1991 recession in the United States, which officially lasted eight months, saw unemployment rise to 7.8 percent nationally. But its impact on the workforce, especially in Massachusetts, was "quite severe," according to one labor economist: "The labor market continued to deteriorate long after other indicators began to improve, and the official ending date of the recession date was selected. . . . White-collar workers in general and workers in the finance, insurance and real estate industry were at greater risk of losing their jobs in the early 1990s than at any time in the past."[2]

The causes included the collapse of the real estate market, stock market turmoil, loan failures, rising taxes, the Gulf War in the Middle East, and a spike in oil prices.[3] New England itself was especially hard hit, with slumping high technology, defense cutbacks, higher taxes, and a near depression in construction. By the middle of 1990, auto sales were falling, housing starts were at their lowest level since

1982, retail sales and industrial production were flat, and inflation remained persistently high. All this, and bad real estate loans were bringing some banks to the brink of disaster.[4]

But it wasn't only the economy that affected Boston's TV scene. New sources of competition, from cable, changing viewer habits, and the rise of new networks, were also culprits. In a recent phone interview, Tony Vinciquerra, Channel 4's former vice president and station manager at the time, called it "a double whammy," explaining: "The economy turned south, and cable was growing rapidly. Americans had far more choices. A person could now watch 50 (cable) channels, then 150 channels, then 200 channels. Even if the economy had stayed strong, the fundamental underpinnings of the market would have eroded."[5]

THE MARKET CONTRACTS

The signs, large and small, were everywhere. Channel 38 no longer lit up its famous "TV 38" tower each night. Viewers calling Channel 5 after 5 p.m. didn't get a receptionist, but simply a taped recording. Channel 7 eliminated monthly birthday cakes and ice cream for its employees. And Channel 4 removed a coveted laser printer in its newsroom, once used by many staffers, and placed it in the assistant news director's office. The action prompted one reporter to provide daily updates: "Day 1: Printer Held Hostage?" "Day 2 . . ."

Superficial though these things were, they symbolized the problems facing Boston's TV stations in the early 1990s. Less than two years earlier, the Boston Celtics had decided to become media players and in 1990 purchased Channel 25, the Fox Broadcasting Co. affiliate, and WEEI-AM, an all-sports station. Eighteen months later, with both stations losing money, the Celtics were looking for buyers or investors. Meanwhile, debt-ridden New England Television Corp., which owned TV Channel 7 and WHDH-AM, was still fighting off dissident stockholders and creditors.[6]

Boston had been the nation's leader in local programming. The byword was once "local"; now the operative word was "layoff." Over the past year and a half, each of the major stations suffered significant reductions in staff, through attrition, through retirement, and especially through painful layoffs. Channel 5, which had the largest staff of any Boston station, went from 328 to 255 employees; Channel 4 was downsized from 290 to 220 employees; and Channel 7 got hit the hardest, going from 290 to 175 employees. "It's a morgue around here," lamented one Channel 7 reporter, who asked not to be identified. "One by one there are people coming out of (news director) Jacques Natz's office crying. Everyone was told to leave immediately."[7]

It was an extraordinary turn of events, and no one in the media was immune. Newspapers were also in the throes of a devastating contraction, losing circulation, with advertising—the backbone for generating revenue—starting to move to the Internet. Ironically, after I had written numerous stories about the layoffs at the local TV stations, it turned out that after nine years, my own time was up at the *Patriot Ledger*. On July 26, 1991—I well remember the date—returning home from a mini vacation on Martha's Vineyard, I found a voicemail message from Terry Ryan, the paper's managing editor, requesting I call him immediately. My conversation with the other Terry was brief. He informed me, matter-of-factly, that I had been let go in the paper's third round of layoffs, and would I kindly clean out my desk and return my press pass to the paper after the weekend?

Obviously, it was quite a jolt. People were kind. Channel 5's general manager Jim Coppersmith, with whom I had often tangled, called and generously offered me office space to assist me in my job search. Emily Rooney, his news director, couldn't believe how little severance pay I had gotten. And Mark Jurkowitz, the *Boston Phoenix* media writer, wrote a story about the *Ledger*'s financial and management problems, which touched on my own demise: "Knopf's dismissal triggered shock waves both inside and outside the *Ledger*. As its highly respected TV reporter, she was a bona fide player in the Boston media market and one of the paper's marquee attractions."[8]

Some in the media refused to go down without a fight. Miles O'Brien, who had been a Channel 7 reporter/anchor for five years, spoke out publicly against his own station. In a gutsy opinion piece that ran in the *Boston Herald*, he decried his station's severe cuts of employees over an eighteen-month period, and speculated what it would mean for the news operation:

But many of us wonder how much depth and context we can now give to complex issues which require more time than a news conference at the State House. And, we wonder what will happen when we are faced with a "big story"—when a hurricane bears down on New England, when a plane falls out of the sky into a Boston neighborhood, when a blizzard paralyzes the region—will we be able to offer viewers the type of coverage they expect from the 6th largest (and possibly most competitive) television market in the country . . .

It seems clear viewers will eventually notice something different about their local news shows. Instead of hoping that won't happen, we should be asking: "Do our viewers deserve more?"[9]

A day later, Miles was no longer employed by Channel 7.

THE DEATH OF NEWSCASTS

Two of Boston's nightly newscasts were canceled altogether. *World Monitor*, produced out of Boston and carried nationally by the Discovery Channel, was part of an attempt by The First Church of Christ, Scientist to build a broadcasting and magazine empire. But in 1992, on the verge of bankruptcy, the church board closed down its broadcast programs, including *World Monitor*.

In many ways, the cancellation of Channel 2's *Ten O'Clock News* was an even more painful loss to the community. A mainstay on Boston's television news scene since 1976, the program never had the ratings of Boston's other news stations. But over the years, with a small but fiercely loyal audience—many of whom were intellectuals and opinion leaders—it had established a special niche for itself in the market. Harvard economist Robert Reich was crushed: "I can't imagine life without *The Ten O'Clock News*," he said. Christopher Lydon, the newscast's principal anchor, angrily told the *Los Angeles Times*: "It's like the *New York Times* going porno."[10]

But times were changing. WGBH was now faced with diminished financial resources stemming from the New England recession, flat viewer support, a sizable increase in PBS dues for the next year—to $700,000—and a cutback in funding from the state.[11] Fans of the show, as well as staffers who worked on the newscast, declined to go gently. Less than a week after WGBH disclosed the cutbacks of thirty employees, twenty of whom were from the Channel 2 news, the station received more than 950 phone calls and 250 letters protesting the decision. By midweek, 80 to 100 people turned out for a noon-time rally held outside the station. Signs in the crowd read "Home Is Where the License Is" and "Don't Auction Off Local Programming." One chanting demonstrator carried a poster that read "PBS, Without the P It's Just BS."

But the debate over the Channel 2 news was not only about the recession; it was also about the mission of a public television station. For given the proliferation of news sources at both the local and the national levels, the question was whether there was still a place for Channel 2's quirky *Ten O'Clock News* anymore. *Electronic Media* ran a strongly worded April 8th editorial sounding the importance of "localism" as "one of the hallmarks of broadcasting," complete with the headline "WGBH, Don't Slight Boston."[12] In the end, *Say Brother* and *La Plaza*, two minority shows, were spared, but the nightly newscast, a far more expensive enterprise, did not survive.

THE END OF THE PERSONALITY-DRIVEN MARKET

The Boston market, which had established a star system, complete with high-priced salaries, was also altered. In the past, when times were good, station officials held to the belief that stars drove the ratings and should be paid accordingly. But during the economic downturn in the 1990s, the officials became more pragmatic and felt they could get away with hiring more generic, less expensive talent.

Star anchors and expensive reporters lost much of their bargaining power. When Channel 7 anchor R. D. Sahl signed a new contract for around $350,000, it was at least $200,000 less than what Tom Ellis, his predecessor, had signed for ten years earlier. Salaries that were routinely bumped up 15 or 20 percent in the mid-1980s were now being "plateaued"—or, in some cases, reduced. Channel 4's Liz Walker stepped down in 2005, after twenty-five years on the anchor desk. Channel 5's Natalie Jacobson left her station in 2007, after nearly thirty-five years. And, Channel 4's Bob Lobel, after twenty-nine years as the town's most colorful and popular sportscaster, took a buyout in 2008.[13]

Just as President Bill Clinton, in his 1996 State of the Union Address, had declared "The era of Big Government is over," the Go-Go Golden days of Boston television stars and superstar salaries had come to a close. Industry watchers no longer boasted about Boston's lofty status as the best in the country. Instead, they feared that Boston, once a national model, had become just another media market—or worse, that it could lead the way for lower standards for the rest of the country.

The immediate crisis stemmed from Boston's advertising base, which had been decimated by the region's financial plight. "Over the last two years, the advertising base for the six commercial stations fell from $400 to $320 million by 1991," said Jim Coppersmith, WCVB's president and general manager. "Although the final figures are not yet in, we project that $80 million has simply disappeared. Without doubt this was the single most aggravating, frustrating and depressing year of my business life."[14] Another Channel 7 executive, noting that his station was seriously challenging Channel 4 for second place in the ratings, groaned: "Finally, we have the numbers but no one to sell them to."[15]

LOCAL PROGRAMMING DECLINES

With budgets slashed, employees laid off, and priorities reevaluated, the number of locally produced programs was drastically reduced:

Channel 4 junked *Evening Magazine*; reduced *People Are Talking* from a live hour to a taped half-hour talk show; and canceled *Prime Times*, a public affairs program aimed at elderly viewers. *Live on 4*, Channel 4's 5:30 p.m. newscast, was dropped in favor of *A Current Affair*, a schlocky, tabloidy syndicated show.

Channel 5 gave the pink-slip to *Good Day!*, an eighteen-year talk-show institution, while lopping off a half hour from its two-hour-long early bird newscast. The specials unit was noticeably less active, focusing instead on *Family Works*, the station's public service campaign.

Channel 7, which suffered the steepest cuts, canceled *Ready to Go*, a $2 million live daily children's show. *Our Times*, an ambitious weekly news magazine, was replaced by two syndicated game shows. *Studio 7*, a quarterly arts snow, was canceled, along with the market's first 5 p.m. newscast.

As for the independent stations, Channel 38 scrapped *A.M. Boston*, a talk show, as well as *Hersey's Hollywood*, a weekly entertainment show. Channel 56 eliminated *GreenWatch*, a pioneering environmental program. And Channel 25 shelved plans to launch a 10 p.m. newscast.

For the past twenty years, all three network affiliates had local talk shows—an important outlet for book authors, a showcase for entertainment, and a vital forum for discussing community issues. By 1992, Channel 4 was the only station with a daily talk show—*People Are Talking*—and even that show was axed in 1993.

But it wasn't only the troops—the generals became casualties as well. Jim Thistle, Channel 7's news director, seeing his own station decimated, resigned and returned to Boston University—permanently. In 1992, Barry Schulman, Channel 4's longtime program director, who played an important role in launching locally produced programs and station campaigns, such as *You Gotta Have Arts* and *For Kids' Sake*, became a downsizing victim himself. The following year, Bruce Marson, one of the truly creative minds working in local television, was let go at Channel 7, as was his creative services director Dick Weisberg.

LOCAL NEWS DECLINES

Not surprisingly, local news, the major profit center, underwent drastic changes. Two out of the three network affiliates now used solo anchors on weekends, while Channel 7 additionally went to a single anchor for its noon and 6 p.m. newscasts. Political reporters found themselves routinely covering fires. Specialty beats, such as consumer reporting, had a lower priority. More stations turned to "cheap labor" in the form of young, inexperienced freelancers. And, except for Channel 5, the other major affiliates ceased to do editorials.

Travel budgets were slashed. Local stations that once saw themselves as national and international news gatherers, were no longer as inclined to send their own reporters abroad. While two tiny TV stations in western Massachusetts sent reporters abroad during the Persian Gulf war, not one Boston TV station was represented there anymore.

Political units were downgraded. During the 1988 presidential campaign, the locals had gone wild when Governor Mike Dukakis was a candidate. Four years later, when Senator Paul Tsongas—another Massachusetts son—was a presidential candidate, Channel 7's Joe Day was the lone local TV reporter to accompany him to Iowa.

NEW STRATEGIES

Forced to improvise, the stations devised new and sometimes unorthodox strategies in marketing and sales. Some provided advertisers with more promotional opportunities as part of overall packages. Channel 38, the most profitable independent, held contests for free tickets to the World Series. With WGBH projecting a deficit for the first time in ten years, the station began offering a coupon book worth $50 in discounts at area businesses and museums for every $15 contribution.

PARTNERSHIPS WERE FORMED

As a means of cross-promotion, in October 1991, Channel 4 joined forces in the news arena with twenty cable systems in the Boston area, representing 600,000 households. The inventory consisted of NBC's *Today*, the noon and 6 p.m. newscasts, and the *7:30 Report*. The locals also launched national partnerships. WGBH (Channel 2) and ABC formed an unprecedented arrangement between a commercial network and a public station to produce a $1 million drama about AIDS and teenagers, which aired on both PBS and ABC. Channel 5, which had the fewest layoffs and still maintained the largest staff, was Boston's most aggressive station in working in the national arena. *Chronicle*, the nation's nightly news magazine, was syndicated for two years on the Arts & Entertainment Cable Network. And *Family Works*, the public service campaign, produced locally by Hearst-owned WCVB and sponsored by Heinz, aired on 107 stations. The package was expected to bring in $6 million to Hearst Broadcasting.

One of the most unlikely but creative ventures involved the 1992 decision by WGBH to open WGBH Learningsmith, a retail store in a suburban mall, in Newton's upscale Chestnut Hill section. (Alistair Cooke, the veddy proper host of *Masterpiece Theatre*, would have winced.) Located next to a Bloomingdale's home furniture store and a few doors down from Calvin Klein, the store was billed as "a general store for the curious mind." A joint business venture undertaken by the WGBH Educational Foundation and Marshall Smith, a Boston businessman who had founded the Paperback Booksmith and Videosmith chains, the store planned to stock 8,000 items, including books, computer software programs, videotapes, and learning games, to generate revenue for WGBH's local programming. Though most of the items sold had no direct tie-in to public broadcasting, the store featured an array of WGBH and PBS products, ranging from *Mister Rogers* sweatshirts to *Frontline* hole punchers, as well as books and videos related to PBS shows like *Nova* and *Masterpiece Theatre*. A year before the store opened, WGBH had hoped for $1.3 million in local corporate underwriting, but it only received $1 million.[16] After all, there was only so much these kinds of initiatives could do.

As if to symbolize the sad state of the market, teeny-tiny Channel 58 (WCVX-TV), Cape Cod's only local station, went dark altogether. The station had been struggling; nevertheless, besides old movies and syndicated reruns, it had managed to produce a nightly newscast. Now the only thing offered was "a screen full of snow and white noise."[17]

To be clear: it wasn't that the stations in the market were going out of business. The new reality was that Boston's once proud and mighty TV stations were no longer as profitable as they once were; the world had changed, and Boston was simply becoming more like other markets. From 1980 to 1987, the double-digit ad revenues had ranged from 10 to 16 percent. By contrast, Channel 4's Tony Vinciquerra acknowledged that the ad revenues for his station in 1989 were up less than 8 percent over 1988, with the other local affiliates reporting similar results.[18]

NEW KIDS ON THE BLOCK

But it wasn't only the recession that would reconfigure the Boston market. New players during the 1980s and '90s were making their presence felt—challenging the dominance of the once all-powerful "Big Three" networks and their affiliates.

CABLE AND OTHER POTENTIAL THREATS

In 1980, cable penetration was still quite small, totaling 20 percent or fewer households; by 1990, it had risen to almost two-thirds in the Boston market. Local viewers now had far more program choices. In the meantime, the ratings for the 6 and 11 p.m. news were dropping, largely because people were working later and going to bed earlier.

THE RISE OF FOX AS A "FOURTH NETWORK"

By the mid-1980s, News Corporation, Rupert Murdoch's multinational media conglomerate, decided to extend its newspaper empire into broadcasting. Forming the Fox Broadcasting Company (usually referred to as "Fox"), the company launched a "fourth network" in 1986 with the ambitious goal of competing against the Big Three (ABC, CBS, and NBC). Others had tried it, including DuMont in the 1950s and Metromedia in the 1980s, but none had succeeded. Although it initially got off to a bumpy start, Fox (seen locally on Channel 25, WFXT-TV) became a serious player by the early 1990s, with hits such as *The Simpsons*, *Married . . . with Children*, and *In Living Color*. Many of the shows were aimed at young people, the 18 to 34 demographic coveted by advertisers. Locally, Channel 25's growing power in the market was evident when the station spent $2 million to purchase the building next door and expand its facilities.[19]

LOCAL INDEPENDENTS CROWD THE AFFILIATES

In the meantime, Boston's other independent stations continued to flex their muscles. In many cities, the ABC, CBS, and NBC network affiliates were dominant, but that was less true in the Boston market, especially during the early 1990s, when Channels 25 and 38 on the UHF band were money-making powerhouses—Channel 38, by virtue of having the exclusive broadcast rights for the Boston Red Sox and Boston Bruins, while Channel 25 held exclusive rights for the Boston Celtics. "It's the best franchise in the world to have," said Dan Berkery, president and general manager of Channel 38, adding gleefully: "And who it really hurts is the three (network) affiliates."[20]

NEW NETWORKS AND PARTNERSHIPS

When federal rulings were loosened, allowing broadcast networks to own programming, two entertainment giants, Warner Bros. and Paramount, decided to create their own networks in the 1990s as a way to guarantee national distribution of their products. With most of the country's larger stations owned by networks or affiliated with them, the independents became the logical place for the young networks to extend their reach. It was also a win for the independents interested in alliances that would help them establish a distinct niche in their markets. Dubbed "weblets," by *Variety* because of their smaller audiences and reduced programming, they had names like the WB Network and the United Paramount Network. In Boston, Channel 56 (WLVI-TV) became part of the WB Network, while Channel 38 (WSBK-TV) became a UPN station.[21]

A NEWCOMER TO THE NEWS FRONT

In 1992, the Hearst Corporation (which now owned WCVB) and Continental Cablevision joined forces to create the New England Cable News (NECN)—a twenty-four-hour regional news service. This $10 million venture, the brainchild of Phil Balboni, a Hearst vice president and former Channel 5 news director, was designed to do regionally what CNN had done nationally—namely, provide an on-demand news service for New Englanders. Some wondered about its viability in an already glutted news market. Rivals worried that their new cable competitor might hurt their own ratings; and the critics, as is their way, were initially lukewarm. Despite losing millions in its first year and encountering difficulty lining up other cable companies, NECN gradually found its footing. In less than a year, it received an Associated Press award for best newscast, besting the three network affiliated news stations. And, on some occasions, it actually outdid its competitors on the breaking news front. In the years to come, NECN would become a trusted fixture on the news scene, where it continues to this day.

With the Channel 2 news gone and Channel 56 already having established an hour-long 10 o'clock newscast, the local news scene was about to become even more congested, as new and unlikely partnerships were formed by former competitors—a practice known as "repurposing." In 1993, NECN began producing a nightly news-cast to air on Channel 25. The program was produced out of NECN's Newton studios, though Fox logos were placed on microphones and equipment. Around the same time, Channel 4 began producing its own nightly newscast for Channel 38 that aired at 10 p.m.

There were several reasons for the partnerships. One involved changes in people's lifestyles. With more and more two-income families—a desirable group for advertisers—arriving home after the 6 o'clock news and going to bed before the 11, the ratings for these late-night newscasts had been dropping. In terms of viewer popula-tion, Channel 25 had been the largest Fox station without a newscast. Channel 38 wanted a news program, but did not want to invest the $3 to $4 million it would cost to start its own. And in both cases, it was an attempt for local stations to do more with less while reinforcing their station identities.

THE DEMISE OF THE LOCALLY OWNED STATION

Perhaps the saddest development, because it signaled the end of a glorious era, was the 1993 sale of locally owned Channel 7 by David Mugar to Ed Ansin, a billionaire and cofounder of Sunbeam Television, a Miami-based company, for approximately $215 million. Ansin was the owner of WSVN-TV in Miami, known for its souped-up, tabloid-style news. During its heyday, the Boston market was unique in that it had not one, but two locally owned stations with strong commitments to local programming. By 1990, however, most of of the local stations were owned by powerful media conglomerates, such as Group W (Channel 4), Hearst (Channel 5), News Corporation (Chan-nel 25), and Gannett (Channel 56). So when locally owned Channel 7 was sold to an out-of-state owner, the impetus for local programming in the market was simply not as strong as it had been. Coupled with all the other factors previously mentioned, the sale meant that Bos-ton's Golden Age was essentially over.

David Mugar—a well-intentioned man and generous philanthro-pist—had previously invested nearly twenty-five years of his life in his former station—first with a bruising thirteen-year legal battle, from 1969 to 1982, to wrest control from RKO General, the station's corrupt and irresponsible owner; then from 1982 to 1993, as the new station's board chairman and chief executive officer. His goal was a noble one—to transform a lowly, third-place station into a key player in a highly competitive major market. Alas, his dream was never fully realized, though it was not for lack of trying. By overreaching, failing to read the market, and exhibiting a lethal dose of hubris, the leadership team of Win Baker and Bill Applegate—handpicked by Mugar—brought the station to the brink of disaster. But by the mid-1980s, Mugar had learned from his mistakes and put together a highly competent and experienced new team that (mostly) knew what it was doing. Despite low ratings, Channel 7 had finally achieved respectability in the market—not an insignificant achievement. But ultimately, the station would remain haunted by its checkered past and, more recently, by its mounting financial woes. In 1985, Mugar incurred a $90 million debt when he bought out disgruntled investors. Unfortunately, unlike its two major network-affiliated rivals, which were owned by powerful media conglomerates, his locally owned station did not have the deep pockets needed to cushion the effects of the New England recession. In truth, Channel 7 was probably never as bad as those of us in the press had written, but it was also never as good as Mugar and his station executives had hoped.

The reviews on David Mugar's legacy would be mixed. Some regarded him as a dilettante, a well-meaning rich kid who never quite grew up, and for whom his TV station was just another new toy. His critics felt he lacked the leadership skills and vision necessary to make a go of an often-troubled television station. It recalled TV newsman Brit Hume's dismissal of former Massachusetts governor Bill Weld as a "bored rich guy." But from a business standpoint, Mugar's station had done well, at least in good times. Mitchell Zuckoff, then a business writer for the *Boston Globe*, had a more charitable assessment:

He (Mugar) oversaw a near-tripling of revenues, engineered a rise in profits and viewership, survived several challenges to his ownership and achieved an automation overhaul that made the station the envy of others around the nation. But he and his staff could never quite find the formula to get enough viewers to accept WHDH's local news programs over its chief competitors, WBZ-TV, Ch. 4; and WCVB-TV, Ch. 5.[22]

So what was left in the wake of New England's grievous recession and the absence of locally owned stations? On one hand, under Ansin's handpicked news director Joel Cheatwood and his flashy, tabloid-style news, Channel 7 began to thrive. Viewership would skyrocket, with the station zooming to the top of the ratings at one point. But at what cost? In terms of quality journalism, the early returns were not promising. Mused the *Globe*'s Ed Siegel: "If you're watching the Channel 7 news you're watching a station that thinks you're a no-brainer or a voyeur, with little interest in the New England area except the body count, and a good deal of interest in *People* magazine celebrity reportage."[23]

As the years went by, there was evidence that Channel 7's rivals, under pressure, were starting to follow its lead—the result being a louder, glitzier approach to the news and lower journalistic standards. In a 2001 *Boston* magazine piece, journalist David S. Bernstein charged that Channels 4 and 5 "have adapted to what they outwardly decry." To bolster his point, he quoted Jim Thistle, now the director of Boston University's broadcast journalism program. Damning Channel 7 with faint praise ("It never became the tabloid horror show that many people predicted"), he lamented the decline of the Boston market as a whole: "'We're becoming more of a headline service,' Thistle says of the local news media. Having served as news director for all three stations in the pre-Ansin era, he bemoans the prominence of puff stories—or, as he puts it, 'whatever video you can clip off the feed. Car chases in Texas, rollovers in California.'"[24]

At least after the sale, David Mugar had said good-bye to all that. Walking away with a pretty penny, he was now free to relax in one of his three homes in Boston, on Nantucket, and on Cape Cod. Around the time Ed Ansin, the new owner, took over his station, the former general manager agreed to sit down with the *Globe*'s Jack Thomas at his Cape Cod home by Popponesset Bay. Perhaps he wanted to reminisce and explain himself. Perhaps he was seeking closure. Perhaps he no longer gave a damn. At one point, he eyed his 25-foot boat tied to the pier just outside his back door. Noting it was called *7-Up*, Mugar added wistfully, "I'm going to rename it *7's Gone*."[25]

Yes, the world had changed; the magic had faded too fast. But Mugar was not the only one feeling a sense of loss. Several years later, around 1995, following my own layoff at the *Patriot Ledger,* I had finally gotten a job as the deputy press secretary for the MBTA. One day I remember greeting Kirby Perkins, a serious-minded political reporter at Channel 5—someone I used to cover when I was a TV critic, but who now did a lot more general assignment reporting. On this particular day, he had come to the Transportation Building in Boston to do a story—I think it was about train delays during a recent snowstorm. But before our formal interview, we talked and gossiped about the state of the local media scene, which is what journalists love to do.

"You know," he said quietly, "all we seem to do now is sit around the newsroom and talk about the good old days."

"Yes," I replied, "but didn't we all have a grand time?"

NOTES

ACKNOWLEDGMENTS

1 Percy Shain, "Sonya Hamlin Quitting Her TV Talk Show," *Boston Globe*, January 8, 1975.

2 In-person interview by the author with Sonya Hamlin, August 25, 2016.

INTRODUCTION

1 "Local News Coverage in a Digital Age," Pew Research Center, March 5, 2015.

2 Pew Research Center, "State of the News Media 2016," Local TV News: Factsheet (28–29), June 2016.

3 Interview with Sonya Hamlin, August 23, 2016.

4 Telephone interview with Jim Byrne, creative services director, WDCW-TV, Tribune Company, January 4, 2016.

1. MARKET FORCES SET THE STAGE

1 According to the Museum of Broadcast Communications: "Ensuing years saw removal of many long-standing rules resulting in an overall reduction in FCC oversight of station and network operations." These changes included: a) extending television licenses to five years from three in 1981; b) expanding by 1985 the number of stations an entity could own to twelve; and c) increased deregulation of television's competition, especially cable.

2 "How to Lose Your Station's FCC License," *Radio + Television Business Report*, December 13, 2013.

3 Barry Cole and Mal Oettinger, *The Reluctant Regulators: The FCC and the Broadcast Audience* (Reading, Mass.: Addison-Wesley, 1978), 134.

4 For a comprehensive examination of this case, see Sterling Red Quinlan, *The Hundred Million Dollar Lunch* (Chicago: J. Philip O'Hara, 1974).

5 Ibid., 170.

6 Robert M. Bennett with Dennis Richard, *How We Built the Greatest Television Station in America* (Nashville, Tenn.: Dunham Books, 2013), 161. See also 171–172.

7 Caroline Knapp, "Five Alive," *Boston Business*, May/June 1987, 50–100.

8 WCVB selected an old International Harvester dealership in Needham to serve as its studio facility, which the station still operates to this day.

9 Quinlan, *Hundred Million Dollar Lunch*, 115.

10 *OpenJurist*, 670 F.2d 215, *RKO General v. Federal Communications Commission*, argued September 16, 1981; decided December 4, 1981 (41).

11 Marguerite Del Giudice, "13-Year Battle Over Channel 7—Complicated as a Russian Novel," *Boston Globe*, February 28, 1982.

12 "It's all Over for RKO's WNAC-TV" (Top of the Week), *Broadcasting*, April 26, 1982, 27–28.

13 "History of Boston's Growth and Transition: 1970–1998," Boston Redevelopment Authority, Report #529, November 1999, 5.

14 John C. Hoy, "Higher Skills and the New England Economy," in *The Massachusetts Miracle: High Technology and Economic Revitalization*, David R. Lampe, ed. (Cambridge, Mass: MIT Press, 1986), 334.

15 Philip Lentz, "Dukakis Had Help with 'Massachusetts Miracle,'" *Chicago Tribune*, May 23, 1988.

16 Tony Schwartz, "Boston TV Stations Battling Over News Anchors," *New York Times*, August 30, 1982.

17 Horace Newcomb, ed., *The Museum of Broadcast Communications Encyclopedia of Television*, 2nd ed. (New York: Taylor & Francis, 2004), 152.

18 A superstation is an independent broadcast station whose signal is picked up or "uplinked" to a satellite for redistribution by local cable systems outside the station's local and regional coverage area. WTBS in Atlanta was followed by others, such as the Christian Broadcasting Network (CBN) out of Virginia, WGN in Chicago, and WWOR in New York.

19 Terry Ann Knopf, "An Anchor Adrift," *Boston Globe Magazine*, November 10, 1992.

20 R. D. Sahl, email to the author, October 20, 2015.

21 The intifadah refers to the Palestinian uprising against the Israeli occupation of the West Bank and Gaza; it began in 1987 and lasted until the Madrid Conference in 1991. However, some consider the end date to be 1993, with the signing of the Oslo Accords. All Martha Raddatz quotes in this section are from an email to me dated August 8, 2016.

22 Jim Baker, "Faint Praise Precedes Castiglione's Return," *Boston Herald*, September 9, 1984.

23 Greg Dawson, "Channel 4 Is No. 1 in May Ratings Sweeps," *Boston Herald*, May 30, 1986. "Sweep" periods help determine how much stations can charge for commercials.

24 Jack Thomas, "Ch. 56 to Enter Nightly News Derby," *Boston Globe*, December 9, 1983.

25 The station is owned by the WGBH Educational Foundation, which also owns and operates WGBX-TV (Channel 44); WGBY-TV (Channel 57) in

Springfield, Massachusetts; and public radio stations WGBH (FM) and WCRB in the Boston area and WCAI (and satellites WZAI and WNAN) on Cape Cod.

26 For more on Christopher Lydon and *The Ten O'Clock News*, see Terry Ann Knopf, "Getting with It," *Boston*, March 1988.

27 Ibid.

28 Ibid.

29 It wasn't until 2016 that a television network dared to explore the life and work of the controversial photographer when HBO presented the documentary *Mapplethorpe: Look at the Pictures*. In his April 3, 2016, review, *New York Times* TV critic James Poniewozik called it "an insightful work of biographical criticism."

2. WBZ-TV: CHANNEL 4 LAYS THE GROUNDWORK

1 Elizabeth Sullivan, *Boston Globe*, June 6, 1948.

2 YouTube, 35th Anniversary Show, WBZ-TV, June 9, 1983. Part 1. www.youtube.com/watch?v=l4fbEC4CWgY.

3 Donna Halper, "WBZ Timeline," June 9, 1998.

4 Ibid.

5 Westinghouse was also one of the founding owners of the Radio Corporation of America in 1919. In 1926, RCA launched the National Broadcasting Company, a group of twenty-four radio stations, including WBZ in Boston, which made up the first radio network in the United States.

6 Les Brown, *The New York Times Encyclopedia of Television* (New York: New York Times Books, 1977), 182.

7 Jack Thomas, "Channel 5 Offers a News Alternative; *Chronicle* Aims to Give Boston Information with Substance," *Boston Globe*, January 24, 1982.

8 Monica Collins, "5's *Chronicle*: TV Milestone," *Boston Herald*, January 25, 1982.

9 Terry Ann Knopf, "Mourning Becomes Evening," *Boston*, April 1989.

10 Ibid.

11 Sonya Hamlin, email to author, July 19, 2016.

12 "Two Climb 585 Feet All for Fair Harvard," *Boston Herald*, May 12, 1948.

13 Tony Schwartz, "Boston's TV Stations Battling Over News Anchors," *New York Times*, August 30, 1982.

14 Much of this section is drawn from an earlier article of mine called "No Tears for Tom," *Boston*, April 1987. Over the course of his forty-year career, Tom Ellis worked at four different Boston stations, including all three of the major network affiliates.

15 Telephone interview with Tom Ellis, May 25, 2016. Bob Bennett did not respond to an email requesting comment about the famous tape he sent to New York.

16 Garry Armstrong, email to author, June 8, 2016.

17 For her many years of public service in fighting for greater diversity, Shaw was given the Open Door Award at a ceremony held at historic Old South Church. See Jan Ransom, "Reporter Honored for Barrier-breaking Career," *Boston Globe*, May 9, 2016.

18 Eleanor Roberts, "Ch. 4 Didn't Pick Up Carter's Option," *Boston Herald-Traveler*, July 22, 1968. See also Anthony LaCamera, "All's NOT Quiet on the Local Front," *Boston Record American*, July 2, 1968.

19 Terry Ann Knopf, "A New Face on the 11 O'clock News; Liz Walker Is Boston's First Black Anchorperson on Weekdays," *Boston Globe*, February 1, 1981.

20 Ibid.

21 This section is adapted from my previous article "Private Matter, Public Affair," which originally appeared in *Boston*, January 1989.

22 Terry Ann Knopf, "From Talk Show to Peep Show: *People Are Talking* Swings to Titillation in Ratings Scramble," *Boston Globe*, August 16, 1981.

23 Catherine Foster, "The Arts Have a Friend in This Television Station," *Christian Science Monitor*, November 6, 1984.

3. WCVB-TV: CHANNEL 5 BLASTOFF!

1 Robert M. Bennett, with Dennis Richard, *How We Built the Greatest Television Station in America* (Nashville, Tenn.: Dunham Books, 2013), 186.

2 Ibid., 246.

3 In 1982, when WCVB was sold to Metromedia, Bennett left the station to become president of Metromedia Broadcasting (now Fox Television), the largest division of Metromedia, Inc.

4 Bennett, *How We Built the Greatest Television Station*, 214.

5 Tony Schwartz, "Some Say This Is America's Best TV Station," *New York Times*, February 15, 1981.

6 Robert A. McLean, "'Morning Show' Says 'Good Night,'" *Boston Globe*, June 22, 1974. For more on the the the *Good Morning!/Good Day!* success story, go to WCVB-TV *Good Day!* Vintage Television, Retrospective, 1989, Part 1 of 2, www.youtube.com/watch?v=J6WM-ToO9Jw.

7 Bob Bennett, telephone interview, August 17, 2015.

8 Robert A. Mclean, "Bite Your Tongue, Cover Girl!," *Boston Globe*, April 14, 1977.

9 A year later, Martha Mitchell died at the Memorial Sloane-Kettering Cancer

Center. Her death was attributed to multiple myeloma, a rare type of malignancy that attacks bone marrow. She was fifty-seven.

10 Richard Schickel, *Intimate Strangers: The Culture of Celebrity* (Garden City, N.Y.: Doubleday & Company, Inc., 1985).

11 Howard Altman, "Celebrity Culture: Are Americans Too Focused on Celebrities?," *CQ Researcher* 15, no. 11 (2005): 247.

12 Kurt Anderson, "Celebrity Death Watch," *New York*, April 3, 2006.

13 Howard Altman, "Celebrity Culture: Are Americans Too Focused on Celebrities?," *CQ Researcher* 15, no. 11 (2005): 247.

14 Our biggest "get"? Muhammad Ali. Not only was he a World Heavyweight Champion (twice over, with a third to come), but he was also colorful, quotable, controversial, and had become a cultural icon, especially to the counterculture generation opposed to the Vietnam War. It was the only time that I could remember when hordes of employees around the WCVB building, including hard-nosed reporters, lined the hallways to get a glimpse of a celebrity walking into the station.

15 Pat Mitchell went on to become the president and CEO of Public Broadcasting Service (PBS) in 2000, the first woman to hold this position. In 2006, she became the president and CEO of the Paley Center for Media (formerly the Museum of Television and Radio) in New York City—a position, as of this writing, she still holds.

16 Terry Ann Knopf, "Plugola: What the Talk Shows Don't Talk About," *Columbia Journalism Review* 15, no. 5 (1977): 44. Incidentally, nearly forty years later, this unsavory practice continues, even at the national level. In 2014 on ABC's *The View*, Cameron Mathison, once a hunky star on *All My Children*, came on and demonstrated how on-screen kissing was better with the use of a breath freshener. One trick, he confided, was to put Listerine under the pillow when the camera rolled. But the viewers were never told he actor was actually shilling for the mouthwash company.

17 In fairness, beginning with coanchors Chet Curtis and Natalie Jacobson, Channel 5 had an unusually large number of staffers, on and off the air, who were married to one another, including news director Emily Rooney and reporter Kirby Perkins; producer Linda Polach and noon anchor reporter Jim Boyd; Arnie Reisman, *Chronicle* writer/producer, and Paula Lyons, the station's consumer reporter; and Deborah Sinay, who held numerous sales positions, including vice president/national sales manager, and Charles Kravatz, whose positions in news and public affairs included assistant news director and senior executive producer of news programming. (And, for the record, Susan Wornick, the station's noon anchor and consumer reporter,

once ventured outside the "family" when she married Channel 4 sports anchor Bob Lobel. The two later divorced.)

18   This kind of annoying, sexist behavior still surfaces, and on one recent occasion, even involved a certain president of the United States. In 2006, during a G8 meeting of world leaders gathered in St. Petersburg, Russia, George W. Bush raised eyebrows when he gave an impromptu back rub to German chancellor Angela Merkel, who flung her arms into the air and seemed to grimace. Several websites later dubbed Bush the "groper in chief."

19   Bennett, *How We Built the Greatest Television Station*, 194.

20   Bruce McCabe, "Take Three for Jim Thistle," *Boston Globe*, April 22, 1988.

21   Unless otherwise noted, much of this section on Jim Thistle comes from two of my previous pieces: "Strictly a Beer and Peanuts Guy," *Patriot Ledger*, May 20, 1982; and "Local Hero," *Boston*, June 1988.

22   Caroline Knapp, "Five Alive," *Boston Business*, May/June 1987, 50–100.

23   Phone interview with Clark Booth, December 6, 2015.

24   For a variety of reasons, which included a strained relationship with Peter Jennings, Emily Rooney was let go by the network after seven months. For more, see Ed Siegel, "Rooney's Career with ABC: Nasty, Brutish and Short," *Boston Globe*, January 7, 1994. Rooney eventually returned to Boston and had a successful eighteen-year run as host of WGBH-TV's *Greater Boston*, stepping down in 2015 to concentrate on her radio talk show on WGBH-FM.

25   Christopher Baxter, "Jim Thistle, 66; Brought Old-style Journalism to TV News," *Boston Globe* (obit.), July 30, 2008.

26   Monica Collins, "5's *Chronicle*: TV Milestone," *Boston Herald American*, January 25, 1982.

27   Former vice president Walter Mondale eventually received the nomination, but was defeated by the incumbent president Ronald Reagan in 1984.

28   Ed Siegel, "So Far, a Weak Ch. 5 Campaign," *Boston Globe*, March 4, 1985.

29   Dean Johnson, "Singers Rock Against Racism," *Boston Herald*, July 26, 1985.

30   Paul LaCamera, email, October 12, 2015.

31   Bennett, *How We Built the Greatest Television Station*, 229.

32   John J. O'Connor, "Henry Fonda and Myrna Loy," *New York Times*, December 30, 1981.

33   Schwartz, "Some Say This Is America's Best TV Station."

34   Terry Ann Knopf, "Group W Television: Local Heroes," *Channels: The Business of Communications* 6, no. 6 (1986): 58–59. Les Brown, formerly of the *New York Times*, was the magazine's founder and editor in chief.

35   Knapp, "Five Alive."

36   Francine Achbar, email, September 15, 2015.

37   Ibid.

4. WHEV-TV: CHANNEL 7 DECLARES WAR

1   Jack Thomas, "The Change at Channel 7; . . . And, a Look at New England Television, Winner of License," *Boston Globe*, May 9, 1982.

2   Jack Thomas, "A Preoccupation with Prettiness," *Boston Globe*, August 4, 1976.

3   Five days later, the *Boston Globe* rubbed salt in his wound, reporting that Guptill had failed to file his state income tax returns for several years, and was a defendant in at least seven lawsuits relating to his failure to pay debts. Two years later, the station received more negative press when it was revealed that Larry Sales, an anchor, reporter, and host of its "Urban Affairs," did not have a journalism degree from the University of Missouri, as he had claimed on his resume. In breaking the story on October 10, 1981, the *Globe*'s headline was "A Newsman's Lie Haunts Channel 7." Sales eventually left the station.

4   Thomas Francis, "Satan or Savior? Competitors Beware: Bill Applegate, the Master of 'Flash and Trash' News, Has Risen again, This Time in Cleveland," *Cleveland Scene*, March 1, 2001.

5   Terry Ann Knopf, "Ch. 7's Bill Applegate, 'You Bet It's War,'" part 3 of Boston's News War, *Patriot Ledger*, August 26, 1982.

6   Jack Thomas, "At Ch. 7 It's Win or Else," *Boston Globe*, August 27, 1982.

7   WNEV-TV, "New Day Dawning" station promo (1982), Vintage Television, www.youtube.com/watch?v=EG75v4-2P7k.

8   A word of caution about salaries. Reporters often have great difficulty in pinning down the salaries of on-air people. Such information is closely guarded by station officials and agents, both for competitive reasons and for matters of privacy. As such, the figures cited in this chapter should be regarded as reasonable estimates, though not always precisely accurate.

9   Terry Ann Knopf, "Tom Ellis Quits Channel 5," *Patriot Ledger*, June 11, 1982.

10 Bob Bennett, telephone interview, August 17, 2015.

11 Terry Ann Knopf, "Tired of the 'Star System,' Ch. 5 News Director Quits," *Patriot Ledger*, June 22, 1982.

12 Jack Thomas, "Ch. 7 Expansion Drive Sets Off Salary War," *Boston Globe*, August 28, 1982.

13 Jack Thomas, "Curtis, Jacobson in 5-Year Pact with Ch. 5," *Boston Globe*, July 9, 1982.

14 Tony Schwartz, "Boston TV Stations Battling Over News Anchors," *New York Times*, August 30, 1982.

15 Jack Thomas, "The Million-Dollar Anchor Team," *Boston Globe*, July 10, 1982.

16 Jack Thomas, "News Teams Race for the Ratings; Channel 7 Gambles Millions in a Bid to Get Out of Last Place," *Boston Globe*, September 12, 1982.

17 Thomas, "At Ch. 7 It's Win or Else."

18 Terry Ann Knopf, "Ch. 7 Tries to Squelch Confidential Memo," *Patriot Ledger*, June 22, 1982.

19 Thomas, "At Ch. 7 It's Win or Else."

20 Ibid.

21 Terry Ann Knopf, "Ch. 7's News War Is Getting Messy," *Patriot Ledger*, November 16, 1982.

22 Terry Ann Knopf, "TV War: Dispatch from the Trenches," *Patriot Ledger*, June 30, 1982.

23 Terry Ann Knopf, "Ch. 5's Phil Balboni: 'No one will catch us—ever,'" *Patriot Ledger*, Part 2 of Boston's News War, August 25, 1982.

24 Terry Ann Knopf, "In the Race for Ratings Jeff Rosser Is Waiting for the Starting Gun to Fire," *Patriot Ledger*, Part 1 of Boston's News War, August 24, 1982.

25 Barbara Matusow, *The Evening Stars: The Making of the Network News Anchor* (Boston: Houghton Mifflin Company, 1983), 112.

26 Critics' quotations are from Monica Collins, "Report Card, Tom and Robin," *Herald American*, September 14, 1982; Jack Thomas, "Toot! Whistle! It's the New Ch. 7 Newscast," *Boston Globe*, September 14, 1982; and Terry Ann Knopf, "'The Tom and Robin Show': A Hit and Miss Opening Night," *Patriot Ledger*, September 14, 1982. One of the problems with the new news team was they were hyped ad nauseam. See station promos and excerpts from their first revamped newscast in 1982, WNEV-TV, Vintage Television, www .youtube.com/watch?v=IHi9ODokiAc.

27 Indeed, during his lengthy career, Tom later took acting lessons at Brandeis University, appeared in some TV commercials and soap operas, and had bit parts in films, such as *Marathon Man* and in the John Cusack–James Spader film *True Colors*, in which he played an FBI agent.

28 Letter to the editor, "From now on, she'll tune in to 4 or 5" (headline), *Boston Globe*, September 13, 1982.

29 Terry Ann Knopf, "Is Local News Going to the Dogs?" *Patriot Ledger*, October 13, 1982.

30 Jack Craig, "Is Zip Zany or a Zero?," *Boston Globe*, March 27, 1983.

31 Loretta McLaughlin, "The When and Why of Withholding Care," *Boston Globe*, March 1, 1983.

32 Throughout his career, Carlton Sherwood had a penchant for conservative causes. During the 1984 presidential campaign, he was the writer-director of an anti–John Kerry documentary called *Stolen*. He also authored the book *Inquisition*, a passionate defense of Reverend Sun Myung Moon, who had served time on a series of tax offenses.

33 Geralyn A. White, "A Day That Was Doomed Before It Dawned: A Case Study

of Opportunities and Constraints: Boston's WNEV-TV Channel 7 News May 22, 1982–November 1, 1983" (honor's thesis, Harvard University, 1984), 118.

34 Ibid.

35 Ed Siegel, "Ch. 4's Yanoff Takes a Top Job at Ch. 7," *Boston Globe*, June 3, 1983.

36 Terry Ann Knopf, "Channel 7 Goes Shopping for Success," *Patriot Ledger*, May 23, 1985.

37 Frank Shorr, telephone interview, February 25, 2016.

38 Phyllis Eliasberg, telephone interview, April 6, 2016.

39 Linda Ellerbee, *And So It Goes: Adventures in Television* (New York: G. P. Putnam's Sons, 1986), 12.

40 Fox Butterfield, "Boston CBS Station Posts Needed Gains," *New York Times*, May 23, 1984.

41 Terry Ann Knopf, "The New England News Exchange: An Appraisal," *Patriot Ledger*, April 30, 1984.

42 Butterfield, "Boston CBS Station Posts Needed Gains."

43 Ironically, Jim Thistle enjoyed one last hurrah when he was enticed to become Channel 7's vice president of news in 1988. However, he never enjoyed the same success he had at Channel 5. Disillusioned with the direction of news, he left three years later and returned to teaching at Boston University, where he remained until his death in 2006, from throat cancer. At the time of his death, he was sixty-six. Jeff Rosser went on to become the general manager of a series of local TV stations and since 1999 has been an executive at Raycom, a broadcast chain, where he presently oversees ten stations.

44 Ed Siegel, "Channel 7 on the Upswing," *Boston Globe*, March 12, 1988.

45 Mary Fox Garner, *The Hidden Souls of Worlds: Keys to Transformation Through the Power of Words* (New York: SelectBooks, Inc., 2004), 166.

5. THE LIFE OF A TV CRITIC

1 Matthew Arnold, a British poet and cultural critic, had two collections of criticism published in 1865 and 1888. In "The Function of Criticism at the Present Time," his most famous essay from the first series, he defines criticism, delineates its functions, and explains the essentials of a good critic.

2 With the contraction of print outlets over the last two decades and a much quieter local television scene, in Boston only the *Globe* and *Herald* presently have TV beats.

3 Terry Ann Knopf, "The Bad Boy of Boston Television," *Boston*, July 1986.

4 Nancy Merrill, "Turning the Tables: Nancy Merrill Reviews a Critic's Performance," *Patriot Ledger*, May 4, 1984.

5 Norma Nathan, "Chet Bashes Critic at Birthday Bash," *Boston Herald*, April 14, 1987.

6   Monica Collins, "It's a Girl for Natalie, Chet and Channel 5," *Boston Herald American*, May 20, 1981.

7   Margalit Fox, "Chet Curtis, Half of Married News Team Whose Divorce Made News, Dies at 74," *New York Times*, January 23, 2014.

8   Terry Ann Knopf, "Hey, Hey! Geraldo Rivera's Back on Center Stage," *Patriot Ledger*, April 16, 1987.

9   Terry Ann Knopf, "Harvard Hosts *General Hospital*," *Boston Globe*, June 28, 1981.

10   Terry Ann Knopf, "Grossman vs. GE: Did NBC Owner Try to Sway the News?" *Electronic Media*, November 11, 1991.

11   Terry Ann Knopf, "A Recharged, Reflective, Mike Wallace," *Patriot Ledger*, May 20, 1985.

12   As an example, see Tom Shales, "Gunga Dan," *Washington Post*, April 7, 1980. In this brutal but hilarious essay, he satirized a very theatrical Dan Rather who, as part of a *60 Minutes* report, managed to sneak into Afghanistan, disguised as an Afghan resistance fighter, complete with a little beard growth, a funny hat, and some togs.

13   Terry Ann Knopf, "Space Shuttle Disaster: Once Again, TV Functions as the Great Unifier," *Patriot Ledger*, January 29, 1986.

6. "BANNED IN BOSTON"

1   Neil Miller, *Banned in Boston: The Watch and Ward Society's Crusade Against Books, Burlesque, and the Social Evil* (Boston: Beacon Press, 2010), 17.

2   Douglas Martin, "'R. J. Sinnott, 76, Last Wielder of 'Banned in Boston' Cudgel," *New York Times,* May 3, 2003.

3   James Carroll, review of *The Boston Irish: A Political History*, by Thomas H. O'Connor, *New York Times*, July 16, 1995.

4   Eric Moscowitz, "Olympic Bid Has Boston Asking: 'Huh? What Inferiority Complex?,'" *Boston Globe*, January 17, 2015.

5   Alan Lupo, *Liberty's Chosen Home: The Politics of Violence in Boston* (Boston: Little, Brown and Company, 1977), x.

6   Carroll, review of *The Boston Irish*.

7   Cited in Ronald P. Formisano, *Boston Against Busing: Race, Class, and Ethnicity in the 1960s and 1970s* (Chapel Hill, N.C.: University of North Carolina Press, 1991), 42.

8   Bruce, Gellerman, "'It Was Like a War Zone': Busing in Boston," WBUR-FM, September 5, 2014. (First of two parts.)

9   Lupo, *Liberty's Chosen Home*, 72.

10   Bill Plaschke, "In Shunning L.A., USOC Turns Down a Gold-Medal Performer," *Los Angeles Times*, January 8, 2015. Ironically, in the face of strong

opposition from Boston's residents and city officials, the United States Olympic Committee later withdrew its nomination of Boston as its proposed city.

11 Christiane Amanpour, Keynote Speech at the Edward R. Murrow Awards Ceremony, Minneapolis, Minn., September 13, 2000.

12 David Brisson, "Rippon Faces Deadline on Choice Between Boston and Britain," *Boston Herald*, April 29, 1984.

13 Terry Ann Knopf, "Angela Rippon; an Arts Reporter with 'True Brit,'" *Patriot Ledger*, January 24, 1984.

14 Jack Thomas, "Ch. 7 Acquires a British Accent," *Boston Globe*, January 30, 1984.

15 Ed Siegel, "Rippon Leaving Ch. 7, Returning to England," *Boston Globe*, January 6, 1985.

16 Thomas, "Ch. 7 Acquires a British Accent."

17 Knopf, "Angela Rippon."

18 Jim Baker, "Why I'm Starting Over," *Boston Herald*, January 24, 1984.

19 Jim Baker, "Britain's Former 'Queen Bee' Buzzes Here for the First Time," *Boston Herald*, January 31, 1984.

20 WFSB-TV in Hartford didn't run the program, but only because it had previously scheduled a syndicated show for that time period. Meanwhile, at least viewers in the New Bedford, Massachusetts, area could see the program on Channel 6 (WLNE-TV). And, in the end, Channel 38 (WSBK-TV), an independent Boston station, stepped in and agreed to air the rejected special a week after CBS aired the show nationally.

21 Bruce McCabe, "Ch. 7 Won't Run *Inside the Sexes*," *Boston Globe*, November 17, 1988.

22 Terry Ann Knopf, "Bone Spurs and Brainless Bans," *Patriot Ledger*, November 22, 1988. ("Bone spurs" referred to the local media's obsession at the time with Boston Celtics' superstar Larry Bird's foot problems.)

23 The Centers for Disease Control and Prevention, "HIV and AIDS—United States, 1981–2000," *Morbidity and Mortality Weekly Report* (MMWR), June 1, 2001.

24 Quotations in this section, unless otherwise noted, come from Terry Ann Knopf, "TV Doctors, Bosses Split on Condom Ads," *Patriot Ledger*, January 26, 1987. Billing itself as "a news journal for the broadcasting industry," see also *Broadcasting*, January 26, 1987, 41–42.

25 David Nyhan, "TV Sells Sex, But Not Safe Sex," *Boston Globe*, January 25, 1987.

26 Terry Ann Knopf, "TV Industry Out of Touch with Public Over Condom Ads," *Patriot Ledger*, February 26, 1987.

27 Kay Longcope, "Nuns Speak Out on Love, Sex in Forthcoming Book," *Boston Globe*, March 17, 1985.

28 Quotations in this section, unless otherwise noted, come from Terry Ann Knopf, "Lesbian Nuns, Channel 4 and the 11th Commandment," *Patriot Ledger*, April 9, 1985.

29 Greg Dawson, "When Controversy Becomes Hype," *Boston Herald*, April 9, 1985.

30 Terry Ann Knopf, "Lesbian Nuns' Editors Banned Again," *Patriot Ledger*, April 11, 1985.

31 Dudley Clendinen, "Book on Lesbian Nuns Upsets Boston, Delights Publisher," *New York Times*, April 12, 1985.

32 Ibid.

33 Much of this section originally appeared in Terry Ann Knopf, "Where were Boston's TV Stations during the Church Sex Abuse Scandal?" *Columbia Journalism Review*, February 26, 2016.

34 Dan Rea, telephone interview, December 16, 2015.

35 Terry Ann Knopf, "Ch. 2 Paints a Fawning Portrait of Cardinal Law," *Patriot Ledger*, September 17, 1985.

36 Lisa Grace Lednicer, "Mass. Lawmakers Hail Pope Francis's Message," *Boston Globe*, March 31, 2014.

37 Jack Thomas, "Scandal Darkens a Bright Career," *Boston Globe*, April 14, 2002.

38 David Boeri, telephone interview, December 14, 2015.

39 David France, *Our Fathers: The Secret Life of the Catholic Church in an Age of Scandal* (New York: Broadway Books, 2004). See especially the chapter "The Globe and the Catholic Church."

40 Geoghan was later defrocked, convicted of sexual abuse, and given a nine- to ten-year prison sentence in 2002 to be served at the maximum-security Souza-Baranowski Correctional Center in Shirley, Massachusetts. But on August 23, 2003, less than a year later, while in protective custody, Geoghan was bound, gagged, strangled, and stomped to death by a fellow inmate. His killer was serving time for having murdered a man he believed to be homosexual.

41 Fox Butterfield and Pam Belluck, "Scandals in the Church: The Money," *New York Times*, April 24, 2002.

42 Steve Marantz, "Law Raps Ex-priest coverage," *Boston Globe*, May 24, 1992.

43 Monica McGoldrick, "Irish Families in America," in *Ethnicity and Family Therapy*, eds. M. McGoldrick, J. K. Pearce, and J. Giordino, 1st ed. (New York: The Guilford Press, 1982), 311.

44 Ibid., 313.

45 Elisabeth Noelle-Neumann, *The Spiral of Silence: Public Opinion—Our Social Skin*, 2nd ed. (Chicago: The University of Chicago Press, 1993).

46 Ibid., 173.

47 Joe Bergantino, "Where Boston's TV Stations Were During the Church Sex Abuse Scandal," *Huffington Post*, March 8, 2016.

48 Ibid.

49 Joe Bergantino, telephone interview, November 3, 2015.

50 Rea, telephone interview.

51 Boeri, telephone interview.

52 Clark Booth, telephone interview, December 7, 2015.

53 Pamela Ferdin and Paul Duggan, "In Boston, Driven by Disillusionment," *Washington Post*, October 30, 2002.

54 Boeri, telephone interview.

7. ISMS & SCHISMS: RACE, GENDER, AND SEXUAL ORIENTATION

1 Jason Mittell, *Television and American Culture* (New York: Oxford University Press, 2010), 2.

2 Alessandra Stanley, "Characters Inspired by You-Know-Who: *Madame Secretary, State of Affairs*, and Other Series Channel Hillary Rodham Clinton," *New York Times*, September 3, 2014.

3 Terry Ann Knopf, "The 'Good' Women Still Drink Sherry," *New York Times*, May 7, 1972.

4 In the 1980s and 1990s, when the country returned to its more normal state of not-so-benign neglect, the major networks largely lost interest in African American characters and racial themes. As a result, such shows declined in favor of others like *Seinfeld* and *Friends*, which had all-white casts.

5 Terry Ann Knopf, "At Channel 5, More Than the Hats Are White," *Patriot Ledger*, December 16, 1982. The next two quotes by Jim Boyd and Pam Cross that follow are from the same column.

6 Owing to funding problems, the massive fourteen-part series was aired in two stages. The first six episodes (1–6) aired in 1987; the second (7–14), *Eyes on the Prize II*, aired in 1990, beginning with the assassination of Dr. Martin Luther King Jr. in 1968, and ending with Harold Washington's election as Chicago's first African American mayor in 1983.

7 Terry Ann Knopf, "*Frontline* Report on Boston Street Cops Called Racist," *Patriot Ledger*, March 27, 1987. The quotes that follow from Michael Kirk and Alan Foster are from the same column.

8   Quotations in this section, unless otherwise noted, come from Terry Ann Knopf, "Black Journalists Criticize 'Frontline,' WGBH Hiring," *Patriot Ledger*, May 14, 1987.

9   Quotations in this section, unless otherwise noted, come from Terry Ann Knopf, "'Common Ground' Preview a Night of Bitter Nostalgia," *Patriot Ledger*, March 20, 1990.

10 Terry Ann Knopf, "The Liberation of Edith Bunker—Sort Of," *Miami Herald*, January 22, 1978.

11 Although many thought the amendment was headed for approval, Phyllis Schlafly and other opponents successfully mobilized conservative women in opposition, arguing that the ERA would be a drawback to housewives. By 1977, the amendment had gotten thirty-five of the necessary thirty-eight state ratifications. But despite a congressional extension until 1982, it never reached the required number.

12 Ellen Goodman, "Karen Klein in Her Own Right," *Boston Globe*, July 18, 1970.

13 Sonya Hamlin, email to author, July 19, 2016.

14 Marlene Sanders and Marcia Rock, *Waiting for Prime Time: The Women of Television News* (Urbana and Chicago: University of Illinois Press, 1988), 6–10.

15 David Shedden, "Early TV Anchors," Poynter Institute, April 4, 2006.

16 Judy Flander, "Women in Network News," *Washington Journalism Review* (March 1985): 39–43.

17 "Why There Are Still No Female Dan Rathers," *TV Guide*, August 6–12, 1983.

18 However, Boston can't lay claim to having been the first local market to have a woman on the weeknight anchor desk (as well as host her own television show). That honor belongs to the colorful Dorothy Fuldheim, who, in 1959, at the age of fifty-four, began anchoring the news at WEWS-TV in Cleveland. Some locals best remember her for the time in 1970 when she threw Yippie Jerry Rubin off her show. "He was vulgar," she explained. For more, see Patricia M. Mote's 1997 biography, *Dorothy Fuldheim: The FIRST First Lady of Television News* (Quixote Publications).

19 Terry Ann Knopf, "Shelby at 50," *Boston*, April 1986.

20 Bruce McCabe, "Women in TV News Game Moving Forward, But . . . ," *Boston Globe*, January 4, 1976.

21 Ibid.

22 Knopf, "Shelby at 50."

23 Ibid.

24 For more, see Christine Craft, *Not Just Another Pretty Face: Too Old, Too Ugly, and Not Deferential to Men* (Roseville, CA: Prima Lifestyle Publishing, 1988). Even today, the situation for on-camera women hasn't improved as much

as one might like to think. Click on your local or network news to see for yourself. Furthermore, I'll give you two words: "Candy Crowley." An award-winning, well-liked, and well-respected CNN political correspondent and anchor of *State of the Union*, Crowley unceremoniously left CNN in 2014, at the age of sixty-six and after twenty-seven years at the network. CNN Worldwide president Jeff Zucker took pains to insist the decision was hers. But some insiders claimed she simply had been put out to pasture because he wanted younger and prettier faces on camera to compete with his rival Roger Ailes over at the Fox News Channel.

25 Terry Ann Knopf, "Ladies in Waiting," *Boston*, September 1989. Women fared somewhat better in the 1990s. Emily Rooney became Channel 5's news director in 1990—the first woman in Boston to hold that position. Three years later, she became the executive producer of ABC's *World News Tonight*. In 1993, when Debra Zeyen became Channel 4's general manager, she also became the first to hold that position in the Boston market.

26 Sanders and Rock, *Waiting for Prime Time*. For a more recent examination of network newswomen, see Sheila Weller, *The News Sorority: Diane Sawyer, Katie Couric, Christiane Amanpour—and the (Ongoing, Imperfect, Complicated) Triumph of Women in TV News* (New York: Penguin Press, 2014).

27 The details of this episode came during an in-person meeting with Linda Harris (now known as Lyn May) and several subsequent phone conversations I had with her, which took place between 2015 and 2016. She left Channel 4 in 1984, moving to Washington, D.C., where she later married Lee May, a Washington-based correspondent for the *Los Angeles Times*.

28 Brian Stelter, "Gay on TV: It's All in the Family," *New York Times*, May 8, 2012.

29 Terry Ann Knopf, "Is *Soap* a Dirty Show?," *Miami Herald*, September 8, 1977.

30 Dennis Altman, " Legitimation through Disaster: AIDS and the Gay Movement," in *AIDS: The Burdens of History*, eds. Elizabeth Fee and Daniel M. Fox (Berkeley: University of California Press, 1988), 313.

31 Centers for Disease Control and Prevention, "HIV and AIDS—United States, 1981–2000," Table 1, June 1, 2001.

32 The reason for Dr. Caldwell's departure was apparently more pragmatic than dramatic. Mark Harmon and the show's producers were at odds over the actor's contract. Thus, a decision was made to have the character leave St. Eligius the following season—to help other AIDS sufferers. See Steve Daley, "*St. Elsewhere* Contracts a Problem with AIDS," *Chicago Tribune*, January 31, 1986.

33 Jack Thomas, "Learning to Cover AIDS: Spending Times with Patients Seen as Key," *Boston Globe*, April 15, 1987.

34 Terry Ann Knopf, "Four Ch. 4 Cameramen Shun AIDS Assignment," *Patriot*

Ledger, September 17, 1985. The quotes from Stan Hopkins and Kathleen Graham were taken from this story as well.

35 Brian McGrory, "Doctors, AIDS Activists Say Furor Over Physician Not Justified," *Boston Globe*, June 28, 1991.

36 Terry Ann Knopf, "Stu Soroka: 'A Great Flake and a Gentle Guy,'" *Patriot Ledger*, April 26, 1990.

37 Ibid.

38 Ibid.

39 Quotes in this section, unless otherwise noted, come from Terry Ann Knopf, "Goodbye to a Fellow Critic: When AIDS Hits Close to Home," *Patriot Ledger*, December 13, 1990. The paper where Ron Doyle had worked is now called the *MetroWest Daily News*.

40 In February 1997, Ellen DeGeneres disclosed she was gay on *The Oprah Winfrey Show*. That April, her character on the ABC sitcom *Ellen* came out of the closet to her therapist, played by Oprah Winfrey.

41 Terry Ann Knopf, "Boston Anchor Says He's Gay," *Electronic Media*, March 18, 1993.

42 Ibid.

8. DUKE RUNS FOR PRESIDENT IN 1988:
THE LOCALS GO NATIONAL

1 In "Non-Stop News," the *New Yorker*'s Ken Auletta on January 5, 2010, wrote: "During the 2008 elections, Obama was the object of near-veneration, possessed of a persona and a campaign that were irresistibly compelling to all but his rivals and the right-wing press. *Time*, for example, saw fit to put Obama on its cover six times in eleven months."

2 When Trump became the Republican nominee for president, running against the Democrat Hillary Clinton, the media's ardor cooled amidst his error-prone campaign and questions about his temperament.

3 This chapter is adapted from Terry Ann Knopf, "Duke Fever," *Boston*, November 1987.

4 For a nostalgic look back at the 1988 presidential campaign by Boston TV reporters, see Terry Ann Knopf, "Campaign Daze," *Boston*, November 1988.

5 John Aloysius Farrell, "Mass., Iowa Diverge on Debate," *Boston Globe*, August 2, 1987.

6 Eleanor Randolph, "Dogging 'the Duke' in Boston," *Washington Post*, August 9, 1987.

7 Wayne King, "Study Puts New Hampshire on the Map, and in a Big Way," *New York Times*, August 10, 1987.

8   Bruce Mohl, "Reporters Become Part of the News," *Boston Globe*, February 6, 1987.

9   Randolph, "Dogging 'the Duke' in Boston."

10   Martin Schram, *The Great American Video Game: Presidential Politics in the Television Age* (New York: William Morrow and Company, Inc., 1987), 187.

11   Ibid., 185.

12   Hart had withdrawn in disgrace in May 1987 amid the *Miami Herald*'s revelations about his relationship with sometime model/actress Donna Rice. On December 15, he reentered the race, but only received about 4 percent in the New Hampshire primary. In March 1988, he dropped out of the presidential race for good.

13   The Neil Kinnock speech was not Biden's only problem. It turned out the candidate had also lifted significant portions of speeches from Robert Kennedy and Hubert Humphrey. Other allegations of past law school plagiarism and exaggerating his academic record also surfaced. In the face of the revelations, Biden withdrew from the race on September 23, 1987.

EPILOGUE: FADE TO BLACK

1   Sally Bedell Smith, *In All His Glory: The Life of William S. Paley* (New York: Simon and Schuster, 1990), 606.

2   Jennifer M. Gardner, economist, Division of Labor Force Statistics, Bureau of Labor Statistics, *Monthly Labor Review*, June 1994, 3.

3   Rich Karlgaard, "The Not So Great Recession," *Forbes*, March 11, 2010.

4   Charles Stein, "Recession: This Time New England Loses," *Boston Globe*, August 19, 1990.

5   Tony Vinciquerra, telephone interview, April 4, 2016.

6   Some of the material in this section is taken from Terry Ann Knopf, "Tough Times in Boston; Recession Knocks Wind Out of Market's Sails," *Electronic Media*, January 13, 1992.

7   Terry Ann Knopf, "New Layoffs Rock Boston Affiliate," *Electronic Media*, September 23 1991.

8   Mark Jurkowitz, "Slip-Sliding Away: Recession and Mismanagement Foil the *Ledger*'s Dreams of Glory," *Boston Phoenix*, August 9, 1991.

9   Miles O'Brien, "TV Cuts Will Hurt Product," *Boston Herald*, October 1, 1991. O'Brien later worked as a science and aviation correspondent and anchor at CNN and, more recently, has been a science correspondent and producer for *The PBS NewsHour*.

10   Reich and Lydon quotes are from Elizabeth Mehren, "No News Is Bad News for WGBH," *Los Angeles Times*, April 29, 1991.

11   Terry Ann Knopf, "WGBH Studies Local Cuts as Its Mission Is Debated," *Electronic Media*, April 8, 1991.

12   Editorial, "WGBH, Don't Slight Boston," *Electronic Media*, April 8, 1991.

13   Johnny Diaz, "As TV News Affiliates Struggle to Stay Relevant, the Era of Celebrity Anchors Such as Chet Curtis Comes to a Close," *Boston Globe*, July 10, 2011.

14   Terry Ann Knopf, "Tough Times in Boston; Recession Knocks Wind Out of Market's Sails," *Electronic Media*, January 13, 1992.

15   Ibid.

16   Marshall Smith, who oversaw the growth of Learningsmith to a dozen stores, sold a majority stake in it to the Boston venture-capital firm Halpern, Denny & Co. in 1994. The refinanced company, based in Burlington, Massachusetts, continued to expand, peaking at eighty-seven stores (all but one in shopping malls) in forty states. But in the wake of some poor business decisions, the company filed for bankruptcy in 1999.

17   Susan Bickelhaupt, "Cape Cod TV Station Goes Down the Tubes," *Boston Globe*, July 4, 1991.

18   Frederic M. Biddle, "TV Advertising Rates Showing Signs of a Slowdown," *Boston Globe*, January 7, 1990.

19   For more on the rise of Fox, see Daniel Kimmel, *The Fourth Network: How Fox Broke the Rules and Reinvented Television* (Chicago: Ivan R. Dee, 2004).

20   Biddle, "TV Advertising Rates."

21   However, as predicted by some experts, each struggled to turn a profit; by 2006, the two had joined forces to become the CW Network, a combination of CBS and Warner.

22   Mitchell Zuckoff, "Mugar on Mugar: Ch. 7 Owner Sizes Up Sale; Looks Ahead," *Boston Globe*, June 3, 1993.

23   Ed Siegel, "Six O'Clock Highs and Lows; Ch. 7 Takes Tabloid Path in Race to Win Local News Game," *Boston Globe*, November 4, 1993.

24   David Bernstein, "Breaking News," *Boston*, November 2001.

25   Jack Thomas, "Mugar on Television: Out But Not Down: Channel 7's Former Owner Looks Back on 11 Turbulent Years," *Boston Globe*, November 4, 1993.

INDEX